TWENTIETH CENTURY VIEWS

The aim of this series is to present the best in
contemporary critical opinion on major authors,
providing a twentieth century perspective on
their changing status in an era of profound
revaluation.

Maynard Mack, *Series Editor*
Yale University

DREISER

DREISER

A COLLECTION OF CRITICAL ESSAYS

Edited by

John Lydenberg

Prentice-Hall, Inc. *Englewood Cliffs, N.J.*

Quotations from the following works of Theodore Dreiser are used by kind permission of World Publishing Company and of Harold Dies, Agent for the Dreiser Estate:

The 'Genius'. © 1915 by John Lane Company; © 1923 by Horace Liveright, Inc.; © renewed 1943 by Theodore Dreiser.

The Financier. © 1912 by Harper & Brothers; © 1927, 1940 by Theodore Dreiser.

Jennie Gerhardt. © 1911 by Harper & Brothers; © 1923 by Horace Liveright, Inc.; © 1926 by Theodore Dreiser; © renewed 1938 by Theodore Dreiser.

An American Tragedy. © 1925 by Horace Liveright, Inc.; © 1926 by Theodore Dreiser; © renewed 1953 by Helen Dreiser.

Hey, Rub-a-Dub-Dub. © 1920 by Boni & Liveright, Inc.; © 1926 by Theodore Dreiser; © renewed 1947 by Helen Dreiser.

Newspaper Days, or A Book About Myself. © 1922 by Boni & Liveright, Inc.; © renewed 1949 by Helen Dreiser.

Quotations from the following works of Theodore Dreiser are used by kind permission of Harold J. Dies, Trustee of the Dreiser Trust:

The Stoic. © 1947 by Helen Dreiser.

A Traveller at Forty. © 1913 by The Century Company; © 1930 by Theodore Dreiser.

PRENTICE-HALL INTERNATIONAL, INC. (*London*)
PRENTICE-HALL OF AUSTRALIA, PTY. LTD. (*Sydney*)
PRENTICE-HALL OF CANADA, LTD. (*Toronto*)
PRENTICE-HALL OF INDIA PRIVATE LIMITED (*New Delhi*)
PRENTICE-HALL OF JAPAN, INC. (*Tokyo*)

Contents

vii

In memory of
Molly
—a better radical

Introduction

by John Lydenberg

Distance does lend perspective: the old debates about whether Dreiser was an immoral man and whether his works were fit to read seem antiquated, somewhat amusing, and wholly irrelevant today. But where literature is concerned distance doesn't necessarily bring agreement. A storm center of swirling controversy in his day, Dreiser still remains controversial, with admirers as faithful as ever and detractors as disdainful as any of his former moralistic critics.

Views about Dreiser have seldom been balanced or judicious. The most significant essays have not been critical analyses; the most lively disagreements have not been over matters of interpretation. The issue has almost always been more basic, the debates, matters not of definition, but of artistic life or death. Those who have disliked Dreiser have not been cool critics but hot enemies seeking to drive him from the field entirely. Aiming mortal blows at him, they determined the nature of the battle: his defenders had to give violence for violence. Instead of fencing like gentlemen to score academic points, the adversaries slashed at each others' vitals with sabres or bludgeoned with maces. Other critics have deemed themselves too lofty for the fray, have dismissed Dreiser because he was not Henry James, and have ignored him as not even worthy of dignified critical comment.

Certainly Dreiser did not set out to be an artist, and one could well argue that he never saw himself primarily as one. He was for eight years a journalist, successful and undistinguished: a newspaper man, an editor, a writer of success stories for popular magazines. Then, after a few dilatory attempts at short stories, he wrote his first novel, almost by chance, at the urging of a friend. When *Sister Carrie* failed to catch on he went through a period of depression but soon returned to hack-writing and then to increasing success and prominence as an editor. Apparently during this next eight-year period he was not suffering from artistic ambitions that were being stifled.

As artist, Dreiser was a natural, a primitive. He was not concerned with giving his readers what Mencken liked to call beautiful

1

letters, although his taste was such that he often wrote in the
sentimental vein of the day, and his attempts to be "literary"
resulted in excruciatingly ugly, turgid prose. But when he told
his story straight out, the bad fine writing disappeared and he
conveyed that sense of simple, unadorned reality which outraged
the genteel and rallied the rebels to his defense. He wrote what he
had to write:

> On thinking back over the books I have written, I can only say:
> Ladies and gentlemen, this has been my vision of life. . . . You may
> not like my vision, ladies and gentlemen, but it is the only one I have
> seen and felt, therefore it is the only one I can give you.

Dreiser has been traditionally, and quite properly, categorized
as a literary naturalist. He described a jungle world of unceasing,
meaningless struggle in which the strong survived and the weak
were crushed. The ideals and the ideas of morality that existed
bore no relation to the rewards that society meted out.

> Life was persistently demonstrating to me that self-interest and only
> self-interest ruled—that strength dominated weakness. . . . The will
> to power was in all individuals above the grade of amoeba, and even
> there. All of us were mouthing one set of ideas and acting according
> to a set of instincts entirely opposed to our so-called ideas.

His books look like naturalistic novels too: they are bulky tomes
filled with details. If he did not keep notebooks à la Zola, he did
often research his material thoroughly and larded some of his
novels with great blobs of raw journalism.

But that is the surface of Dreiser, and is essentially misleading.
Although his novels are important for their depiction of the crude
realities of American life, their true strength comes from qualities
not usually associated with naturalism. They are filled with Dreiser's pity and compassion, saturated with his brooding sense of
what he liked to call "the mystery and terror and wonder of life,"
and continually asking Why, Why, Why? As an artist he was always
a seeker, not merely a journalist turned novelist. In many ways
the essential Dreiser is like the American transcendentalist—a
kinship Dreiser recognized late in life when he edited a volume
of selections from Thoreau. His novels were but projections of
himself; they grew out of him. He could almost have talked of
them as Whitman did of his *Leaves of Grass* when he spoke of "me
and my book." When we touch Dreiser's books we feel we are
touching Dreiser the man, not reading an objective account of
people out there, nor experiencing a fictional world of imagined
characters.

That is not to say that Dreiser's characters cannot be fitted into the conventional categories of naturalistic "heroes." We usually say that the naturalistic protagonist is either a victim, the little man like Henry Fleming in *The Red Badge of Courage,* caught in the trap of life or of war (since to the naturalist life is war, and war life), or a conqueror, a superman, like Jack London's Wolf Larsen, driving the herd-men before him and ruthlessly using them for his amoral ends. Dreiser's leading characters can easily be so categorized. Sister Carrie starts as a wisp in the wind, blown help- lessly about the cold streets of Chicago, carried off by Hurstwood to New York, where she is insensibly transformed into a sort of superwoman who climbs over Hurstwood, as he, the once confident strong man, slides down and down to the Bowery and suicide. " 'What's the use,' " he says as he turns on the gas. The eponymous heroine of Dreiser's second novel, Jennie Gerhardt, is sweet and kindly and is the victim of male chauvinism and of society's double standards, always the concubine and never the bride; lurking, veiled, in the back of the church at her last lover's funeral, faithful to the bitter end. The weakest of Dreiser's protagonist-victims is Clyde Griffith in *An American Tragedy,* described by his lawyers as "a mental and moral coward," the typical little man who is the victim of all the forces of society and his own societally-determined emptiness.

At the other extreme we have Frank Cowperwood, of *The Financier* and *The Titan,* the strong man who sees ethics and morality as mere words, as either disguises for the egotistic self- aggrandizement of the strong or as defensive rationalizations for the failures of the weak.

> He saw no morals anywhere—nothing but moods, emotions, needs, greeds. People talked and talked, but they acted according to their necessities and desires.

> So far as he could see, force governed this world—hard, cold force and quickness of brain. If one had force, plenty of it, quickness of wit and subtlety, there was no need for anything else. Some people might be pretending to be guided by other principles—ethical and religious for instance; they might actually be so guided—he could not tell. If they were, they were following false or silly standards. In those directions lay failure. To get what you could and hold it fast . . . that was the thing to do. . . .

But Cowperwood is no monster like Wolf Larsen, no villain to be hissed. If we do not always approve of him, Dreiser yet makes us see him as more admirable than the little goodygoody reformers who would pull him down from the heights to which he has fought his way. Dreiser does not make a villain of him; "I like big, raw, crude, hungry men who are eager for gain—for self-glorification," he wrote at about the same time in *A Traveler at Forty*. If Clyde is the American failure, Cowperwood is the American success; and that's the way it is—*c'est la vie, c'est la guerre*.

In *The "Genius,"* Eugene Witla combines the two characteristics more explicitly than did Carrie and Hurstwood. Where the other characters are like Dreiser because they are impregnated with his feelings about life, Witla is actually patterned very closely on Dreiser in his specific traits and his behavior. He is the struggling artist in a materialistic society and a would-be realist; he craves power and success; he makes his wife suffer by his constant infidelities as he searches hopelessly to fulfill his inchoate desires. Dreiser leaves us confused and annoyed at the vacillations of the "hero" of this the weakest of his major novels, largely because here he achieved absolutely no distance from his fictional character and, as a consequence, his own confusions are not decently cloaked. Unlike Zola, or Zola's American epigone Frank Norris, Dreiser was not writing to any naturalistic formula; he wrote about what he knew and felt deeply, and Carrie and Hurstwood and Cowperwood and Eugene Witla were simply Dreiser, Dreiser's two irreconcilable sides, Dreiser's fears and desires.

Scott Fitzgerald, whose style and stories are as un-Dreiserian as anything could be, once said that he considered Dreiser and Mencken to be America's two greatest writers. Though we might tend to take this statement, in its extravagance, as just another expression of Fitzgerald's hero-worshipping enthusiasm, it goes much deeper and represents a relation more profoundly true. At different social levels and in different ways, the two had much in common. They were both "outsiders" who yearned to be "in." They were both quintessentially American in this yearning, caught up in the American dream and its nightmare distortions. They were both "spoiled priests." And each wrote his same basic story over and over again.

In "The Crack-Up" Fitzgerald said that he wanted quiet to discover why he "had become identified with the objects of [his] horror or compassion." Why, he asked himself, had he accepted the values of the rich and tried to be one of them, when he believed that "the very rich . . . are different from you and me" and was horrified at their selfishness and their carelessness? As Fitzgerald formulates his question he implies that he had first regarded the rich with detachment from the outside, that he had recognized their shallowness and cruelty and had disapproved of them before he had been seduced by them—that he had been the priest before he was spoiled.

Whatever the actual sequence of Fitzgerald's feelings, it seems clear that with Dreiser the identification came first and the horror and compassion second. Dreiser *was* his characters from the outset, their dreams and their desires were his, their spoiled version of the American dream, inarticulate and largely unrecognized as such, was his from the very first. The "double vision" that Mizener attributes to Fitzgerald was, for Dreiser, a relatively slow development. Pity he always had. He pitied Carrie and Hurstwood for what happened to them in a world they never made or controlled— a world he did not understand. With Jennie and Eugene Witla he showed more comprehension of the social forces that bore down upon them. It was not really until *An American Tragedy* that we feel him looking with horror upon the American "ideals" which proved so fatal to those who embraced them. And his subsequent writings, largely non-fiction, consisted largely of denunciations of the horribly-soured American dream.

Certainly pity, compassion, was the dominating motive behind Dreiser's writing. His autobiographical volumes are full of his feeling of fellowship for the defeated and forlorn. For example, in *Dawn,* he writes:

> . . . I can never look on crowded tenements or small, shabby cottages in cheap, mean streets, or poorly-clothed children, men, or women, with grimy hands and faces and a weary, troubled or labored look, without reverting into thought to this particular period of my life, and wishing, without quite knowing how, to point out a way by which life might be better organized, wishing that it would not permit the untrained or the inadequate to stew so persistently and helplessly in their own misery—as they still do, though not forever, we may hope.

Far from being the objective "naturalist" and the inhuman barbarian whom Stuart Sherman sees, Dreiser is rather the complete sentimentalist whom that other great sentimentalist, Sherwood Anderson, describes in his preface to *Horses and Men* (quoted in my essay). Donald Friede, one of Dreiser's publishers, tells of accompanying him to see the dramatization of *An American Tragedy*. Through it Dreiser sat immobile, absolutely silent, until at the end he turned with tears in his eyes to Friede, saying "The poor boy! The poor bastard! What a shame!" What unbelievable identification, and naïveté; and how touching! Clyde was no object, no specimen in a test-tube experiment; he was real, he was what Dreiser might have been but for the grace of God, a "moral coward" indeed, merely a poor boy whom one could but cry over, as one cried over all the cruel world's heartbreaks.

But Clyde was not a defeated victim of American industrialism, condemned to a life of misery in the slums. He was an American boy on the make, a social climber, a dreamer of the American dream. Like Dreiser, he wanted the "grace and mobility," to use Fitzgerald's phrase, that he imagined came with riches and success. His Sondra Finchley was Dreiser's crude, wholly unbelievable version of Daisy Buchanan, the girl in white of Jay Gatsby's corrupting dream. Dreiser had once been Clyde, and much of his strength lies in his ability to make us feel that we too have been Clyde, in his yearnings and his early follies. By then, Dreiser could look upon that with which he had been identified with both compassion and horror. The Dreiser who had dreamed the American dream had become its insistent and bitter critic.

Outsider he had always been, and critic he now was, but his alienation remained different from that of most of his fellow writers. He could not leave America, make a separate peace, and renounce all responsibility like Hemingway. He could not portray his Americans with the cold, analytic cruelty that characterized Dos Passos' treatment. Unlike Willa Cather, he had no past traditions to view nostalgically and to use as a contrast to a sordid present. He was not a satirist like Sinclair Lewis, and he could never create an Elmer Gantry. He did not, could not, hate. Instead:

Dear, dear, darling Yankee land—"my country tis"—when I think of you and all your ills and all your dreams and all your courage and your faith—I could cry over you, wringing my hands.

In an essay praising Dreiser, John Berryman wrote, "What distinguishes Dreiser from his contemporaries is a kind of stupidty, and a kind of unself-consciousness." A simple stupidity which led him to pile detail on detail, wide-eyed, painstakingly, blunderingly, to make his primitivist novels. He didn't understand; he wondered and worried. "For myself," he said in *A Traveler at Forty*, "I accept now no creeds. I do not know what truth is, what beauty is, what love is, what hope is. I do not believe any one absolutely and I do not doubt any one absolutely. I think people are both evil and well-intentioned." And from this floundering came the disturbingly powerful novels, reflecting the strangely powerful and confused man, and presenting truly the confused, groping, driving America that he loved and deplored.

II

A word about the selections that follow. There are none from any of the book-length studies of Dreiser, although much excellent material is to be found in those volumes. Having to choose, I decided to use only essays complete in themselves rather than to carve chunks out of larger wholes (and then immediately violated that principle by including parts of general works on American literature by Fiedler and Lynn). The other notable omission is anything in the way of reminiscences or anecdotes about Dreiser the man. I hope that the flavor of his personality comes through in the comments to be found in many of the critical essays.

The two opening pieces can be seen as a sort of continuation of this Introduction; they should help bring into even sharper focus what we can call "the problem of Dreiser." Alfred Kazin looks back to the first reactions to *Sister Carrie,* documenting the shock, dismay and discomfort it caused some of its few readers. He then proceeds to sketch the varying responses to Dreiser's later works, interweaving his view of Dreiser the writer with those of Dreiser's interpreters. Kazin's essay is as sensitive and balanced and eloquent as anything of its length I have come across. The piece that follows is my own—written about the same time as the preceding article and complementing it in its emphasis on Dreiser the man rather than on Dreiser the novelist. Written specifically for a collection of essays on "American radicals," it may seem a touch too argumentative for a sober background analysis, but it illuminates aspects of Dreiser that we glimpse only dimly in the Kazin article.

Part II deals with what we might call the Ur-Dreiser or the folk Dreiser—the Dreiser of the 1890s, when as newspaper man and hack journalist he blundered his way into writing a novel and becoming, almost despite himself, a literary figure. From quite different viewpoints, Kenneth Lynn and Leslie Fiedler show how fully Dreiser was a part of the popular culture of his time, how uncritically he accepted the Horatio Alger ethos, how impossible it was for him to stand apart and view with any detachment the reality he and his family had experienced. The selection from Lynn is part of a much longer essay in his book, *The Dream of Success.* He argues that Dreiser never really gave up the success dream, that it dominated his life and his works—a lasting domination neatly symbolized by his desire to be buried in Los Angeles' Forest Lawn. Though Lynn makes his case persuasively, he has to do it by denying to Dreiser the complexity that most of us recognize now, and by ignoring that part of the man that looked with horror on his dream. Fiedler stresses another aspect of Dreiser's immersion in his culture: his acceptance of the sentimental vision and his use of the sentimental mode and style in his novels. If this interpretation is even more partial than Lynn's, it also has its element of truth and it is made as we would expect with Fiedler's usual panache. Malcolm Cowley shows us Dreiser as Sister Carrie's brother in an essay that is essentially objective and much more wide-ranging than the other two. He shows us the transition of Dreiser from newspaper man to novelist, and he recounts the familiar but important details of the origin of *Sister Carrie* and the tribulations of its first, reluctant publication by Doubleday. Later research has revealed facts that somewhat modify this version of the Dreiser-Norris-Doubleday contretemps, but the basic story remains unchanged.

The remaining articles are arranged more or less chronologically. Stuart Sherman's "The Barbaric Naturalism of Mr. Dreiser" (1915) is the best known of the early attacks on Dreiser—representing well the attitudes of the critical and academic establishment of the day. Avoiding the simple moralizing of most of those who could not stomach the novelist, he gives a reasonably accurate, if thoroughly unsympathetic description of Dreiser's naturalistic tendencies, holding that by stripping his characters of moral instincts the author reduces them to mere animal behavior. "In this work of suppression, Mr. Dreiser simplifies American life almost beyond recognition," argues Sherman, himself simplifying Dreiser almost beyond recognition. (It may be worth noting that ten years later both the times and the critic had changed enough so that Sherman found himself praising *An American Tragedy*.)

H. L. Mencken, a long-time acquaintance and an on-and-off friend of Dreiser's, banged the drums loudly and insistently for the novelist for over a decade, until the general acclaim that *An American Tragedy* received forced this congenital dissenter to shift from defense to attack. Here he takes out after two of his favorite bugaboos—Professor Sherman and John S. Sumner of the New York Society for the Suppression of Vice—in an essay that is characteristically rambunctious, flamboyant, and intemperate. By contrast, Randolph Bourne gives a sensitive and subtle appreciation that does much to explain why young American writers were bound to find Dreiser attractive in spite of his shortcomings.

Lionel Trilling's magisterial dismissal of Dreiser (1946) brings us into another era—with different concerns, and, of course, with more sophisticated analyses. Here Dreiser is weighed and found wanting, not in the scales of genteel, Christian humanism, but in the balance of political liberalism. He is rejected because of the limitations of his mind, because his vision of America does not provide adequate sustenance for the intellectual analyses that would help in the needed post-war task of reforming American society. Like Stuart Sherman and H. L. Mencken, Trilling tends to use Dreiser as a symbol, a weapon in his own cause, and, inevitably, once again, Dreiser's *novels* get lost in the moral shuffle.

Gerald Willen and Charles Walcutt reject the old debates and the old stereotypes of naturalism and endeavor to look carefully at just what Dreiser was actually doing in his novels. Willen shows how inadequate was Stuart Sherman's contention that Dreiser consistently deprived his characters of their basic humanity. Dreiser's moral view was certainly not that of the average critic or reader of the day, but his rejection of contemporaneous moral preachments was in no sense a rejection of morality *per se*; indeed, for all his confusions, he was in Willen's view a serious moralist. The essay by Walcutt is an early version of what became a much longer chapter in his pioneer and indispensable book, *American Literary Naturalism: The Divided Stream*. In showing how Dreiser, far from representing the antithesis of American transcendentalism, was clearly related to that idealistic tradition, Walcutt makes it easy to see how the mysticism and religious sentiment of the two posthumous novels were not the aberration that many careless readers at first took them to be. His long essay is particularly useful in this collection because it alone deals in detail with *The Stoic* and *The Bulwark,* and it alone surveys Dreiser's entire career as novelist.

The essays in the last group were written in the 1960s. The first two, in praise of *An American Tragedy,* might seem to portend the close of the debate over Dreiser's merits, issuing as they do from such disparate critics. To find Dreiser being praised by Robert Penn Warren—Southern Agrarian, a first-generation New Critic, author of lushly rhetorical romantic novels, a poet as well as a gentleman—was astounding, to say the least. It would have been equally surprising if Irving Howe—an outsider like Dreiser, an independent, dissenting socialist—had disparaged the novelist. The two differ in their approach and in their emphasis: Howe stresses society's role in formulating Clyde's goals ("He is that part of ourselves in which we take no pride. . . ."), while Warren, after careful analysis of the artistic merits of the novel, discusses "Clyde's grim, sleazy story" as an illustration of the problem of identity in American society. But the differences are largely differences of emphasis, and these two critics, whom one might expect to be so far apart, come together in their estimate of *An American Tragedy* as presenting what is truly an American tragedy in a most convincing and moving novel.

Only one essay in this collection—that by Ellen Moers on *Sister Carrie*—represents the serious attempts of more academic scholars to break totally from the polemical mold and to subject Dreiser's writing to close, scholarly inspection. There are indeed, in the late fifties and then increasingly during the sixties, a good number of such studies which I would have liked to include. I could claim that space prevents me from reprinting more of those solemn essays. But obviously I made a choice: I chose to emphasize the polemical writings. It seems to me that the character of Dreiser's work is such that the cool appraisals contribute less to an understanding of the novels than do the passionate attacks and defenses. Thus I close the volume with Charles Thomas Samuel's "Mr. Trilling, Mr. Warren and *An American Tragedy*" in such a way as to bring us full circle, back to the position if not the tone or manner of the early, disdainful rejections of Dreiser as beneath serious critical consideration.

But still, she's come a long way, Carrie.

PART ONE

The Stature of Theodore Dreiser

by Alfred Kazin

> "The impression is simply one of truth, and therein lies at
> once the strength and the horror of it."
>
> —The Newark *Sunday News* on
> *Sister Carrie,* September 1, 1901.

At a time when the one quality which so many American
writers have in common is their utter harmlessness, Dreiser makes
painful reading. The others you can take up without being involved
in the least. They are "literature"—beautiful, stylish literature.
You are left free to think not of the book you are reading but of
the author, and not even of the whole man behind the author, but
just of his cleverness, his sensibility, his style. Dreiser gets under
your skin and you can't wait to get him out again: he stupefies
with reality:

> Carrie looked about her, very much disturbed and quite sure that
> she did not want to work here. Aside from making her uncomfortable
> by sidelong glances, no one paid her the least attention. She waited
> until the whole department was aware of her presence. Then some
> word was sent around, and a foreman, in an apron and shirt sleeves,
> the latter rolled up to his shoulders, approached.
> "Do you want to see me?" he asked.
> "Do you need any help?" said Carrie, already learning directness
> of address.
> "Do you know how to stitch caps?" he returned.
> "No, sir," she replied.
> "Have you had any experience at this kind of work?" he inquired.
> She answered that she had not.
> "Well," said the foreman, scratching his ear meditatively, "we do
> need a stitcher. We like experienced help, though. We've hardly got

time to break people in." He paused and looked away out of the
window. "We might, though, put you at finishing," he concluded
reflectively.

"How much do you pay a week?" ventured Carrie, emboldened by
a certain softness in the man's manner and his simplicity of address.

"Three and a half," he answered.

"Oh," she was about to exclaim, but she checked herself and allowed her thoughts to die without expression.

"We're not exactly in need of anybody," he went on vaguely, looking her over as one would a package.

The city had laid miles and miles of streets and sewers through
regions where, perhaps, one solitary house stood out alone—a pioneer
of the populous ways to be. There were regions open to the sweeping
winds and rain, which were as yet lighted throughout the night with
long, blinking lines of gas-lamps, fluttering in the wind. Narrow
board walks extended out, passing here a house, and there a store, at
far intervals, eventually ending on the open prairie.

"He said that if you married me you would only get ten thousand
a year. That if you didn't and still lived with me you would get nothing at all. If you would leave me, or if I would leave you, you would
get all of a million and a half. Don't you think you had better leave
me now?"

These are isolated passages—the first two from *Sister Carrie,* the
third from *Jennie Gerhardt*—and normally it would be as unkind
to pick passages from Dreiser as it would be to quote for themselves
those frustrated mental exchanges that Henry James's characters
hold with each other. For Dreiser works in such detail that you
never really feel the force of any until you see the whole structure,
while James is preoccupied with an inner meditation that his own
characters always seem to be interrupting. But even in these bits
from Dreiser there is an overwhelming impression that puzzles and
troubles us because we cannot trace it to its source. "One doesn't
see how it's made," a French critic once complained about some
book he was reviewing. That is the trouble we always have with
Dreiser. Carrie measuring herself against the immensity of Chicago,
that wonderful night scene in which we see a generation just off
the farms and out of the small towns confronting the modern city
for the first time; the scene in which Hurstwood comes on Carrie
sitting in the dark; Jennie Gerhardt's growing solitude even after
the birth of her child; Clyde Griffiths and Roberta Alden walking
around the haunted lakes when he is searching for one where he
can kill her—one doesn't see the man writing this. We are too
absorbed. Something is happening that tastes of fear, of the bottom

loneliness of human existence, that just barely breaks into speech from the depths of our own souls; the planet itself seems to creak under our feet, and there are long lines of people bitterly walking to work in the morning dark, thinking only of how they can break through the iron circle of their frustration. Every line hurts. It hurts because you never get free enough of anything to ask what a character or a situation "really" means; it hurts because Dreiser is not trying to prove anything by it or to change what he sees; it hurts even when you are trying to tell yourself that all this happened in another time, that we are cleverer about life than Dreiser was. It hurts because it is all too much like reality to be "art."

It is because we have all identified Dreiser's work with reality that, for more than half a century now, he has been for us not a writer like other writers, but a whole chapter of American life. From the very beginning, as one can see in reading over the reviews of *Sister Carrie,* Dreiser was accepted as a whole new class, a tendency, a disturbing movement in American life, an eruption from below. The very words he used, the dreaminess of his prose, the stilted but grim matter-of-fact of his method, which betrayed all the envy and wonder with which he looked at the great world outside—all this seemed to say that it was not art he worked with but *knowledge,* some new and secret knowledge. It was this that the reviewers instantly felt, that shocked the Doubledays so deeply, that explains the extraordinary bitterness toward Dreiser from the first—and that excited Frank Norris, the publisher's reader (Dreiser looked amazingly like the new, "primitive" types that Norris was getting into his own fiction). Dreiser was the man from outside, the man from below, who wrote with the terrible literalness of a child. It is this that is so clearly expressed in Frank Doubleday's efforts to kill the book, in the fact that most literary and general magazines in the country did not review the book at all, that even some newspapers reviewed the book a year late, and that the tone of these early reviews is plainly that of people trying to accustom themselves to an unpleasant shock.

Sister Carrie did not have a bad press; it had a frightened press, with many of the reviewers plainly impressed, but startled by the concentrated truthfulness of the book. The St. Louis *Mirror* complained that "the author writes with a startling directness. At times this directness seems to be the frankness of a vast unsophistication. *** The scenes of the book are laid always among a sort of people that is numerous but seldom treated in a serious novel." The general reaction was that of the Newark *Sunday News,* almost a year after the book had been published. "Told with an unsparing realism and detail, it has all the interest of fact. . . . The possibility of it all is horrible: an appalling arraignment of human society. And there is here no word of preachment; there are scarcely any philosophic reflections or deductions expressed. The impression is simply one of truth, and therein lies at once the strength and the horror of it."

This was the new note of the book, the unrelieved seriousness of it—but a seriousness so native, so unself-conscious, that Dreiser undoubtedly saw nothing odd about his vaguely "poetic" and questioning chapter titles, which were his efforts to frame his own knowledge, to fit it into a traditional system of thought, though he could not question any of his knowledge itself. Writing *Sister Carrie,* David Brion Davis comments, "was something like translating the Golden Plates." For Carrie was Dreiser's own sister, and he wrote without any desire to shock, without any knowledge that he could. Compare this with so "naturalistic" a book as Hardy's *Tess of the d'Urbervilles,* where the style is itself constantly commenting on the characters, and where the very old-fashioned turn of the prose, in all its complex urbanity, is an effort to interpret the story, to accommodate it to the author's own tradition of thought. Dreiser *could* not comment; so deeply had he identified himself with the story that there was no place left in it for him to comment *from.* And such efforts as he made to comment, in the oddly invertebrate chapter titles, were like gasps in the face of a reality from which he could not turn away. The book was exactly like a dream that Dreiser had lived through and which, in fact, after the failure of *Sister Carrie,* he was to live again, up to the very brink of Hurstwood's suicide.

It was this knowledge, this exclusive knowledge, this *kann nicht anders,* this absence of alternatives, that led people to resent Dreiser, and at the same time stunned the young writers of the period into instant recognition of his symbolic value to them. We never know how much has been missing from our lives until a true writer comes along. Everything which had been waiting for them in the gap between the generations, everything which Henry James said would belong to an "American Balzac"—that world of industrial capitalism which, James confessed, had been a "closed book" to him from his youth—everything free of "literature" and so free to become literature, now became identified with this "clumsy" and "stupid" ex-newspaperman whose book moved the new writers all the more deeply because they could not see where Dreiser's genius came from. To the young writers of the early twentieth century, Dreiser became, in Mencken's phrase, the Hindenburg of the novel—the great beast who pushed American life forward for them, who went on, blindly, unchangeably, trampling down the lies of gentility and Victorianism, of Puritanism and academicism. Dreiser was the primitive, the man from the abyss, the stranger who had grown up outside the Anglo-Saxon middle-class Protestant morality and so had no need to accept its sanctions. In Sherwood Anderson's phrase, he could be honored with "an apology for crudity"; and in fact the legend that *Sister Carrie* had been suppressed by the publisher's wife was now so dear to the hearts of the rising generation that Mrs. Doubleday became a classic character, the Carrie Nation of the American liberal epos, her ax forever lifted against "the truth of American life." So even writers like Van Wyck Brooks, who had not shared in the bitterness of Dreiser's early years, and who as socialists disapproved of his despair, now defended him as a matter of course—he cleared the way; in the phrase that was to be repeated with increasing meaninglessness through the years, he "liberated the American novel."

Dreiser now embodied the whole struggle of the new American literature. The "elderly virgins of the newspapers," as Mencken called them, never ceased to point out his deficiencies; the conservative academicians and New Humanists, the old fogeys and the young fogeys—all found in Dreiser everything new, brutal and alien they feared in American life. Gertrude Atherton was to say during the first World War that Dreiser represented the "Alpine School of Literature"—"Not a real American could be found among them with a magnifying glass"; Mary Austin was to notice that "our Baltic and Slavic stock will have another way than the English of experiencing love, and possibly a more limited way. . . . All of Theodore Dreiser's people love like the peasants in a novel by Bojer or Knut Hamsun. His women have a cowlike complaisance such as can be found only in people who have lived for generations close to the soil"; Stuart Sherman, in his famous article of 1915 on "The Barbaric Naturalism of Theodore Dreiser," made it clear that Dreiser, "coming from that 'ethnic' element of our mixed population," was thus unable to understand the higher beauty of the American spirit.

So Dreiser stood in no-man's-land, pushed ahead like a dumb ox by one camp, attacked by the other. Everything about him made him a polemical figure; his scandals, miseries, and confusions were as well-known as his books. The "liberals," the "modernists," defended books like *The "Genius"* because "it told the truth"—and how delighted they must have been when John S. Sumner tried to get the book banned in 1915 and anybody who *was* anybody (including Ezra Pound, John Reed and David Belasco) rushed to its defense. To the English novelists of the period (and *Sister Carrie* owed its sudden fame to the edition Heinemann brought out in

London) he was like a powerhouse they envied amid the Georgian doldrums of literary London. How much of that fighting period comes back to you now when you discover Arnold Bennett on his feverish trips to America identifying all the raw, rich, teeming opportunities of American life with Dreiser, or listen to Ford Madox Ford—"Damn it all, it *is* fun to see that poor old language, that vehicle for conveying moderated thoughts, having the guts kicked out of it, like a deflated football, over all the fields of the boundless Middle West." While Mencken, in Dreiser's name, slew William Lyon Phelps in his thousands, the young English discovered that Dreiser was the friend of art. Each side in the controversy used Dreiser, and each, in its own way, was embarrassed. How many times did the young Turks have to swallow Dreiser's bad books, to explain away his faults, and how clear it is from reading Paul Elmer More (who was a deeper critic than his opponents and would have been almost a great one if he had not always tried to arm himself against American life) that he was always more moved by Dreiser's cosmic doubts than he could confess. More settled the problem, as he settled every writer he feared, by studying the man's "philosophy"—where he could show up Dreiser to his heart's content, and, in a prose that could not have been more removed from the actualities of the subject, prove that he had disposed forever of this intellectual upstart.

This pattern remained to the end—Dreiser was the great personifier. When he went to Russia, even the title of the book he wrote had to begin with Dreiser rather than with Russia; when Sinclair Lewis praised Dreiser in his Nobel Prize speech, he did so with all the enthusiasm of a Congressman trying for the farm vote; when Dreiser delivered himself of some remarks about Jews, the *Nation* was not so much indignant as bewildered that this son of the common people could express such illiberal sentiments; when he spoke against England at the beginning of the Second World War, there was a similar outcry that Dreiser was letting the masses down. It is typical of Dreiser's symbolic importance that a writer now so isolated as James T. Farrell has been able to find support for his own work only in Dreiser's example; that the word *plebeian* has always been used either to blacken Dreiser or to favor him; that Eisenstein suffered so long to make a film of *An American Tragedy* that would be the ultimate exposure of American capitalism. When Dreiser joined the Communists, his act was greeted as everything but what it really was—the lonely and confused effort of an individual to identify himself with a group that had taken him up in his decline; when he died in 1945, in the heyday of American-Soviet friendship, one left-wing poet announced that Dreiser's faults

had always been those of America anyway, that he was simply
America writ large—"Much as we wish he had been surer, wiser,
we cannot change the fact. The man was great in a way Americans
uniquely understand who know the uneven contours of their land,
its storms, its droughts, its huge and turbulent Mississippi, where
his youth was spent." Even Dreiser's sad posthumous novels, *The
Bulwark,* and *The Stoic,* each of which centers around a dying old
man, were written about with forced enthusiasm, as if the people
attacking them were afraid of being called reactionary, while those
who honestly liked them reported that they were *surprisingly* good.
And how F. O. Matthiessen suffered all through the last year of
his life to do justice to Dreiser as if that would fulfill an *obligation*
to the cause of "progressivism" in America.

But soon after the war all this changed—Dreiser was now simply
an embarrassment. The reaction against him was only partly literary, for much of it was founded on an understandable horror of
the fraudulent "radicals" who had been exploiting Dreiser before
his death. And thanks not a little to the cozy prosperity of a permanent war economy, America, it seemed, no longer required the
spirit of protest with which Dreiser had been identified. The writers
were now in the universities, and they all wrote about writing. No
longer hoary sons of toil, a whole intelligentsia, post-Communist,
post-Marxist, which could not look at Alger Hiss in the dock without shuddering at how near they had come to his fate, now tended
to find their new ideology in the good old middle-class virtues. A
new genteel tradition had come in. Writing in America had suddenly become very conscious that literature is made with words,
and that these words should look nice on the page. It became a
period when fine writing was everything, when every anonymous
smoothie on *Time* could write cleaner prose about God's alliance
with America than poor old Dreiser could find for anything, when
even the *Senior Scholastic,* a magazine intended for high-school
students, complained of Dreiser that "some of the writing would
shock an English class." It is of this period, in which we live, that
Saul Bellow has noted in his tribute to Dreiser: "I think that the
insistence on neatness and correctness is one of the signs of a modern nervousness and irritability. When has clumsiness in composition been felt as so annoying, so enraging? The 'good' writing of
the *New Yorker* is such that one experiences a furious anxiety, in
reading it, about errors and lapses from taste; finally what emerges
is a terrible hunger for conformity and uniformity. The smoothness
of the surface and its high polish must not be marred. One has a
similar anxiety in reading a novelist like Hemingway and comes
to feel that in the end Hemingway wants to be praised for the

offenses he does not commit. He is dependable; he never names certain emotions or ideas, and he takes pride in that—it is a form of honor. In it, really, there is submissiveness, acceptance of restriction."

The most important expression of the reaction against Dreiser is Lionel Trilling's "Reality in America." This essay expresses for a great many people in America just now their impatience with the insurgency that dominated our famously realistic fiction up to the war, and not since Paul Elmer More's essay of 1920 has anyone with so much critical insight made out so brilliant a case against Dreiser; not since William Dean Howells supported Stephen Crane's *Maggie* and not *Sister Carrie* has anyone contrasted so sharply those notorious faults of style and slovenly habits of thought which our liberal criticism has always treated as "essentially social and political virtues" with the wonderful play of mind and fertility of resource one finds in Henry James. Never has the case against the persistent identification of Dreiser with "reality" in America—coarse, heavy, external reality—been put with so much intellectual passion. For Mr. Trilling is writing against the decay of a liberal movement ruined largely by its flirtation with totalitarianism, by its disregard of human complexity and its fear of intellect. No one who has followed the extent to which our liberal critics have always acknowledged that Dreiser *is* a bad thinker—and have excused it on the grounds that the poor man at least "told the truth about American life"—can help but share Mr. Trilling's impatience with what has recently passed in this country for liberal "imagination."

But may it not be suggested that Henry James as a cultural hero serves us as badly as Dreiser once did? What happens whenever we convert a writer into a symbol is that we lose the writer himself in all his indefeasible singularity, his particular inimitable genius. A literature that modeled itself on Dreiser would be unbearable; a literature that saw all its virtues of literature in Henry James would be preposterous. If one thing is clear about our addiction to Henry James just now, it is that most of our new writing has nothing in common with James whatever. For James's essential quality is his intellectual appetite—"all life belongs to you"— his unending inner meditation, and not the air of detachment which so misleads us whenever we encounter it on the surface of the society James wrote about—the only society he knew, and one he despaired of precisely because it was never what it seemed. Just now, however, a certain genteel uninvolvement is dear to us, while Dreiser's bread lines and street-car strikes, his suffering inarticulate characters, his Chicago, his "commonness"—are that bad dream from which we have all awakened. As Dreiser's faults were once acclaimed as the virtues of the common man, so now we are ashamed of him because he brings up everything we should like to leave behind us.

There is no "common man"—though behind the stereotype (how *this* executioner waits!) stand those who may yet prepare all too common a fate for us all. Literary people, as a class, can get so far away from the experience of other classes that they tend to see them only symbolically. Dreiser as "common man" once served a purpose; now he serves another. The basic mistake of all the liberal critics was to think that he could ever see this world as something to be ameliorated. They misjudged the source of Dreiser's strength. . . . For . . . these writers and painters were "naturalists" only in the stark sense that the world had suddenly come down to them divested of its supernatural sanctions. They were actually obsessed with the transcendental possibilities of this "real" world; like Whitman, they gloried in the beauty of the iron city. In their contemplative acceptance of this world, in their indifference to social reform, in their awe before life itself, they were actually not in the tradition of political "liberalism" but in that deeper American strain of metaphysical wonder which leads from the early pietists through Whitman to the first painters of the modern city.

This gift of contemplativeness, of wonder, of reverence, even, is at the center of Dreiser's world—who can forget the image of the rocking chair in *Sister Carrie,* where from *this* cradle endlessly rocking man stares forever at a world he is not too weak but too bemused to change? And it is this lack of smartness, this puzzled lovingness for the substance of all our mystery, that explains why we do not know what to *do* with Dreiser today. For Dreiser is in a very old, a very difficult, a very lonely American tradition. It is no longer "transcendentalist," but always it seeks to transcend. This does not mean that Dreiser's philosophy is valuable in itself, or that his excursions into philosophy and science—fields for which he was certainly not well equipped—have to be excused. It does mean that the vision is always in Dreiser's work, and makes it possible. Just as the strength of his work is that he got into it those large rhythms of wonder, of curiosity, of amazement before the power of the universe that give such largeness to his characters and such unconscious majesty to life itself, so the weakness and instability of his work is that he could become almost too passive before the great thing he saw out there, always larger than man himself. The truth is, as Eliseo Vivas says . . . that Dreiser is "not only an American novelist but a universal novelist, in the very literal sense of the word. The mystery of the universe, the puzzle of destiny, haunts him; and he, more than any other of his contemporaries, has responded to the need to relate the haunting sense of puzzlement and mystery to the human drama. No other American novelist of his generation has so persistently endeavored to look at men under the aspect of eternity. It is no . . . paradox, therefore, that . . . while Dreiser tries to demonstrate that man's efforts are vain and empty, by responding to the need to face the problem of destiny, he draws our attention to dimensions of human existence, awareness of which is not encouraged by current philosophical fashions. . . ." [1] To understand how this gets into Dreiser's work one must look not back of it but into it for that sense of "reality" which he thirsted for—that whole reality, up to the very shores of light, that made him cry out in *Jennie Gerhardt:* "We turn our faces away from the creation of life as if that were the last thing that man should dare to interest himself in, openly."

This is what makes Dreiser so painful—in his "atheism," his cosmology; this is what dismays us in our sensible culture, just as it bothered a generation that could never understand Dreiser's special bitterness against orthodox religion, against the churches; this is what drove Dreiser to look for God in the laboratories, to write essays on "My Creator." He may have been a "naturalist," but he was certainly not a materialist. What sticks in our throats is that Dreiser is outside the agreed boundaries of our concern, that he does not accept our "society" as the whole of reality, that he may crave after its fleshpots, but does not believe that getting along is the ultimate reach of man's effort. For we live in a time when traditionalists and "progressives" and ex-progressives alike are agreed that the man not to be trusted is the man who does not fit in, who has no "position," who dares to be distracted—when this great going machine, this prig's paradise in which we live just now, is the best of all possible worlds.

Dreiser committed the one sin that a writer can commit in our society—he would not accept this society itself as wholly real. And it is here, I think, that we can get perspective on his famous awkwardness. For what counts most with a writer is that his reach should be felt as well as his grasp, that words should be his means, not his ends. It is this that Malcolm Cowley noticed when he wrote that "there are moments when Dreiser's awkwardness in handling words contributes to the force of his novels, since he seems to be groping in them for something on a deeper level than language."

---

[1] "Dreiser, an Inconsistent Mechanist," by Eliseo Vivas, in Alfred Kazin and Charles Shapiro, eds., *The Stature of Theodore Dreiser: A Critical Survey of the Man and His Work* (Bloomington: The University of Indiana Press, 1955).

This is what finally disturbs us about Dreiser in a period when fine writing is like a mirror that gives back our superficiality. Dreiser hurts because he is always looking to the source; to that which broke off into the mysterious halves of man's existence; to that which is behind language and sustains it; to that which is not ourselves but gives life to our words.

Theodore Dreiser: Ishmael in the Jungle

by John Lydenberg

I

"I was an Ishmael, a wanderer." [1] So Dreiser spoke of himself during his homeless newspaper days in the 1890s. Did he think of himself as an outcast, too? As the son of Hagar, the slave girl, instead of Sarah, the proper wife? Whether he did or no, his birth on the wrong side of the Terre Haute tracks marked him as drastically as did Ishmael's birth in the wrong tent. America does not cast out the sons of its servant girls to wander in the desert, but in the 1870s it did not really accept them as priests in its Back Bay or Fifth Avenue temples. If not an outcast, Dreiser was at least an outsider.

At one time the outsider seemed about to push his way in. Only a few years after he had stood on the banks of the East River so lonely and disheartened that he planned to jump in, he was a $10,000-a-year editor of the Butterick publications. Flashily dressed, confident behind his shiny desk, he fashioned articles that would please the new-rich ladies who sought culture and chic in the slick pages of the *Delineator*. Dreiser had the force, the ability, and the drive to make his way in, and he could have stayed in and huckstered his way ever onward and upward like a good American.

But stronger than the allure of success was something in this outsider which made him reject respectability, or even sheer unrespectable power. Dreiser was by instinct a loner, an *"isolato,"* to use Melville's term, like so many of our great writers. As an outsider he wanted to get in, to glitter among the strong, the rich, the admired. But he could never *be* one of them; he could never wholemindedly accept their ways or their views. So having proved that he could force his way across the tracks, he withdrew, not to his natal

"Theodore Dreiser: Ishmael in the Jungle" by John Lydenberg. From Harvey Goldberg, ed., *American Radicals* (New York: Monthly Review Press, 1957), pp. 37–52. Copyright © 1957 by Monthly Review Incorporated. Reprinted by permission of Monthly Review Press—and of the author.

[1] Quoted in F. O. Matthiessen, *Theodore Dreiser* (New York, 1951), p. 34.

place on the wrong side, but to the tracks themselves, where he could stand alone, exposed, and observe both the sides that he knew so well from experience and sympathy.

The term "rugged individualist" is peculiarly appropriate for Dreiser not merely because of the ironic implications of applying it to him, but because it is literally so apt. His pictures show him rough, solid, and hard despite sagging flesh, big-boned and forbidding. Anecdotes reveal him alone and aloof at parties, shy and a trifle wistful, but withdrawn chiefly because he chose to remain outside, wondering and watching. Society could not soften him; nor could either hostile critics or friendly guides polish him. He was immobile and unmalleable. He was what he was—not pretty or pleasing, not a good writer by most standards, not even very intelligent, but integral, a whole man.

In *My Life with Dreiser,* Helen Richardson shows how little even the love of one he loved could tame or mold him. She lived with him most of the time from about 1920 until he died, marrying him in 1942 after the death of his long-estranged wife. She had to learn to take him as he was and to endure his desertions, his moods, and his tempers, for he could not be changed, only escaped, and she would not escape at the price of losing him. His friend, admirer, and defender, H. L. Mencken, tells of the "gigantic steadfastness" with which Dreiser ignored all his attempts "to entice him in this direction or that, fatuously presuming to instruct him in what would improve him and profit him." [2] Mencken's flinty barbs could not even scratch Dreiser's adamant. Muckrakers, reformers, radicals of all sorts tried to draw him into their camps where each was so sure that Dreiser belonged. But they were no more successful than Mencken: Dreiser would write as he pleased. Of course the genteel critics and all the respectable defenders of the purity of the American Girl and the happiness of the American Way flung taunts, arrows, and stink bombs at him continuously from *Sister Carrie* in 1900 until his death. He was as impervious to the Methodists as to Mencken.

The latter described Dreiser as the Hindenburg of the American novel. Today a bulldozer might provide a more appropriate image. Caring nothing for shouts or shots, unable to see or to save the flowers or the tender saplings, he drove his bulldozer over the whole terrain, shattering the old buildings and pushing aside the rubble until the ground was cleared and the foundations laid bare. He demolished not out of hatred but out of a feeling that the structures, with their conventional fronts or painted with familiar

[2] Edmund Wilson, editor, *The Shock of Recognition* (Garden City, N.Y., 1947), p. 1160.

slogans, served to hide the realities of life, and these he had to uncover at any cost.

Instead of steel or ice in his heart, there was bewilderment and wonder and pity. This was the quality that Sherwood Anderson chose to emphasize in the foreword of *Horses and Men,* which he dedicated to Dreiser:

> Long ago when he was editor of the *Delineator,* Dreiser went one day, with a woman friend, to visit an orphan asylum. The woman once told me the story of that afternoon in the big, ugly grey building with Dreiser, looking heavy and lumpy and told, sitting on a platform, folding and refolding his pocket-handkerchief and watching the children all in their little uniforms, trooping in.
>
> "The tears ran down his cheeks and he shook his head," the woman said, and that is a real picture of Theodore Dreiser. He is old in spirit and he does not know what to do with life, so he tells about it as he sees it, simply and honestly. The tears run down his cheeks and he folds and refolds the pocket-handkerchief and shakes his head.

II

Dreiser's position in American literature is very special. He was the first important writer to come from a non-Anglo-Saxon, lower-class background. It was not simply a matter of coming from relatively poor or humble folk—that was indeed more usual than unusual among American writers: witness, for example, Thoreau, Whitman, Twain, Howells, and Crane. Nor was it a matter merely of feeling isolated; we have only to think of others like Poe, Hawthorne, Melville. The difference was that all of these "belonged" in a most essential respect. They came from the old settlers; they were of the great white Protestant middle class that dominated nineteenth-century America and its literature, and that determined what was orthodox and genteel. Whatever their personal or psychological problems, however they might intellectually or emotionally reject the standards of their society, they were insiders. They scarcely knew of the existence of that strange new society that was growing unrecognized beneath the crust of the old America.

Both Dreiser's parents were German immigrants, his father a fiercely puritanical Catholic and his mother a Mennonite whose original piety had become overlaid with a pagan mysticism. Dreiser was one of eleven children. His family's attempt to rise in the American way had ended with an accident to his father shortly before Theodore's birth. Thereafter, the father's work was intermittent and never such as to support the family. The younger children stole coal from the Terre Haute railroad yards in the winters, and the older sisters took up with men who could offer them temporary financial security if not matrimony. When Theodore was eight, the mother took him and the three younger children off—not to seek anyone's fortune, but as Dreiser would say, in a vagrom search for a less uncomfortable life, somewhere.

In Vincennes, Indiana, they lived with a friend over the fire station until they discovered that the rest of the quarters were being used as a bawdy house. In Sullivan, Indiana, they moved into a barren box of a house adjacent to the railroad yards; there the mother took in washing and rented out a scarcely-spare room. Then one day the glamorous older brother Paul—already famous as songwriter Paul Dresser—turned up and suggested they move to Evansville where he had a pleasant cottage for them. This he rented from his mistress—a local madam and the original of "My Gal Sal"—until the affair broke up and the Dreisers had to move on again. After a year in Chicago they went to Warsaw, in northern Indiana, where for the first time, at thirteen, Theodore was permitted to go with Protestants to a public school instead of to a Catholic school, and where also he heard the local sports crack wise about the difference between his sisters and the nice middle-class girls they would later marry.

Dreiser was brought up properly to believe in the standard American moralities. Good and evil could be distinguished readily according to the rules taught in schools, Sunday and weekday; the rewards for following the good and scorning the evil were clear, and the punishments for doing otherwise were certain.

In glaring contrast to the morality he was taught was the life he observed and lived. His kind, patient, beloved mother said nothing and held the family together as best she could: when a virginal daughter handed her ten dollars proffered by a local lawyer, she took it and bought food without a word to condemn the coming loss of "virtue." "Proper" morals came from those young Dreiser had no love for. They came through his broken father, who would turn up at their latest home, sick, hungry, jobless, but not too cowed to shout imprecations at his daughters for their immoral ways and to warn them of the vast punishments they were heaping up for themselves. They came through his respectable acquaintances in Warsaw who looked up to their own protected sisters and down upon the sisters they casually ruined across the tracks. Paul rose in the artistic demimonde, brother Rome dropped down through gambling and drink. Rome may have been "bad" but Paul certainly was not "good." What mattered, so far as Theodore could see, was not their morality or immorality; the significant difference was that Paul, like his mother, was always kind and generous, Rome boastful, unfeeling, and selfish. On the porch of the Sullivan rooming house old men rocked away their lonely last years; did their fate have any relation to their virtues?

The world he was taught about had a nice clear-cut meaning; his experience showed him a world which denied that meaning and seemed to have no other. What, possibly, could the defeat of these helpless old men be said to mean? Where did one see the working out of the principle that virtue was rewarded and only vice punished? People did what they had to do, what they could do. They survived. What grounds could there be for praise or blame? Certainly none were to be found in any of the official moralities. In the last analysis all that remained was "goodness of heart," the quality Dreiser attributed to Jennie Gerhardt and knew in his mother.

He did not formulate his thoughts this way at the time. He was simply bewildered, dreamy, unhappy, but thrilled and excited by the life of the big city to which he returned, on his own, in 1887. He drifted through odd frustrating jobs for a few years and then into reporting in 1892. Newspaper work was the training ground for many authors from the '90s on, and the breeding ground par excellence of cynicism. At no time was life in America more raw; never did the disparities between precepts and practices gape more widely and openly; and no experience was as effective as the journalist's in preventing a man from comfortably ignoring the raw disparities. It was only too easy to conclude with one of Dreiser's first editors that "Life is a god-damned stinking, treacherous game, and nine hundred and ninety-nine men out of every thousand are bastards." [3]

The adoption of that attitude would have provided one solution for Dreiser—and had he accepted it, we would never have heard of him. Happily he couldn't, for he was too much a child of his time, the young man from the country, fascinated at the shiny fruit dangled before him, bright-eyed at the wonders of the city, enthralled by the men and women in their fine clothes and handsome carriages, the grand gay hotels, the wonderful insolence of the powerful. For all he was an outsider, he was also the typical American with the conventional goals: "My eyes were constantly fixed on people in positions far above my own. Those who interested me most were bankers, millionaires, artists, executive leaders, the real rulers of the world." "No common man am I," he said then of himself as he dreamed of a Horatio Alger rise from rags to riches.[4]

[3] Dreiser, *A Book About Myself* (New York, 1922), p. 59.
[4] *Ibid.*, pp. 33, 34.

But he had neither the cynicism nor the blindness needed for one who would successfully follow that dream. The ultimate effect of his newspaper experience, superimposed upon that of his youth, was to make him not a cynic but a skeptic, a questioner, a seeker. Like Lincoln Steffens, he saw a world made up of the strong and the weak instead of the good and the bad. The strong were successful, and success brought its rewards, but these were scarcely the rewards of virtue, however much the conventionally pious would like to think it so. Nor were the rewards the Devil's brand, as some reformers would have it; the sentimentalist's equation of strong with bad and weak with good was simply the converse of the orthodox view and no less inapplicable to the real American jungle. One could only say that people were what they were, that victory in the battles was sweet but impermanent, that defeat was more common, and that it was a pity the world had to be so:

> For myself, I accept now no creeds. I do not know what truth is, what beauty is, what love is, what hope is. I do not believe any one absolutely and I do not doubt any one absolutely. I think people are both evil and well-intentioned.[5]

III

This, then, was the Dreiser who at the age of twenty-eight sat down to write his first novel. The life he had experienced was neither gracious nor moral. He had succeeded as a free-lance writer in the great New York city that had so frightened and appalled him at first. He had learned that the fight was as ruthlessly ungloved in the publishing world as in that of the new industrialists whose life stories he had been writing. And he had made his way up in that world so that in 1899 he was sufficiently well known for the first edition of *Who's Who in America* to include his name, listing him as "Journalist-Author."

"Author" was, as a matter of fact, a misnomer. Though in his early newspaper days the example of some of his colleagues had led him to attempt a few plays and short stories, he had done so only halfheartedly and he quickly gave up. He was as exceptional among American authors in his lack of literary training and ambitions as in his family background. The other novelists who had started out as newspapermen had, with few exceptions, seen their journalism as preparation for "serious" writing. They recognized a literary tradition and sought to be "writers" within that tradition.

[5] Dreiser, *A Traveler at Forty* (New York, 1913), p. 4.

Dreiser had a call, as do all great artists, but it was not a call to "write." What he had to do was simply *describe* the America he had experienced, tell how he felt about the life he had known, point out the bewildering, contradictory, unadmitted truths. No other important American author showed such a lack of concern for the craft of writing. Paradoxically, this was for him a source of strength as well as a weakness. Scorning the tricks of fine writing, he never succeeded in developing grace or beauty or even facility, but by the same token he never succumbed to the temptation to follow one or more of the roads to popularity. When *Sister Carrie* failed, instead of trying to find a manner that would satisfy readers, critics, and publishers, he simply abandoned fiction and responded again to the siren call of success. But at the *Delineator* desk his own personal call soon came back again, louder, irresistible; and he gave up editing to be an author, cost what it might. Like Thoreau, whom he later came to admire greatly, he marched to a drummer that no one else heard; like Emerson and Thoreau, he found that he must follow his own genius, wherever it led, that to be a man and a writer he must be a nonconformist however much the world might whip him with its displeasure.

In *A Book About Myself,* Dreiser tells how his budding desires to write short stories had been nipped by his reading of the magazines.

> I set to examining the current magazines. . . . I was never more confounded than by the discrepancy existing between my own observations and those displayed here, the beauty and peace and charm to be found in everything, the almost complete absence of any reference to the coarse and the vulgar and the cruel and the terrible. . . . But as I viewed the strenuous world about me, all that I read seemed not to have so very much to do with it. Perhaps, as I now thought, life as I saw it, the darker phases, was never to be written about. Maybe such things were not the true province of fiction anyhow. I read and read, but all I could gather was that I had no such tales to tell, and, however much I tried, I could not think of any. The kind of thing I was witnessing no one would want as fiction.[6]

Yet he had tried a few short stories while vacationing with Arthur Henry, an old newspaper friend from Toledo. Then in the fall of 1899, only half in earnest, he responded to Henry's insistence that he should try a novel. According to his account, he put the words "Sister Carrie" atop a blank page of paper, with no idea of what he was going to say, and then went on to write the first half of the novel with no planning and little difficulty.

---

[6] *A Book About Myself,* pp. 490–91.

He was able to do that because he was simply recording his own experiences and emotions instead of trying to tell a tale that would belong to the "true province of fiction." Indeed, one could say that in *Sister Carrie* Dreiser was not writing a novel at all; he was simply transcribing a part of his version of the American experience. Although taken scene by scene or character by character almost everything in it could have been found in preceding novels, taken as a whole it was unique as a social novel. Its uniqueness lay in the fact that Drouet, Carrie, and Hurstwood were facets of their author; whereas in other novels the drummer, the poor girl from the country who fell to the wiles of the city slicker, the flashy front-man who absconded with the cash and paid with his soul or his life, these were either stock figures or at their best characters observed from above with varying degrees of condescension or sentimentality. If Dreiser could not write popular magazine fiction because he was outside the official American culture and the conventional literary circles, he could write something different and true and lasting because he was inside the jungle of the new urban, industrial society.

Henry James and Edith Wharton wrote about their American aristocrats from intimate acquaintance. Howells and a multitude of now-unread minor novelists described with authority the life of the old middle class. Twain, and after him Howe, Frederic, Garland, gave authentic accounts of the rural societies they had grown up in. All of them sensed the changes in postbellum America, and most of them tried in one way or another to show these changes in their books. But none of them could deal directly, from first hand experience, with what was most distinctive about the new society. Novelists had, of course, already written about the ignorant, destitute immigrants from southern and eastern Europe, about tenements and saloons and sweatshops, about jobless workers, radicals, labor organizers, prostitutes, industrialists, political bosses; and between *Sister Carrie* and *Jennie Gerhardt* a spate of muckraking novels exposed in ever more odorous detail the great American Augean stables. Most of these were righteous, indignant novels describing the evils in lurid details, and implicitly or explicitly urging the good people to do something, to throw out rascals or rescue the perishing or care for the falling. And most—possibly all —were written by the old insiders who could only see from the outside this world across the tracks.

Howells's streetcar strike is viewed from an easy chair, not from the carbarns and the strikers' saloons as is Dreiser's. Crane, the rebel against his respectable Protestant background, observes Maggie the girl of the slums and the streets sardonically, ironically, and so unsentimentally as to shock his friends; but Carrie is Dreiser's sister. It is significant that Howells liked *Maggie*, ignored *Sister Carrie*. McTeague's disintegration is depicted with a fine use of symbolic actions selected by Norris with care (and remembrance of Zola); Hurstwood's decline is that of the old men Dreiser had known, and it is given added poignancy by the fear never far from the surface of Dreiser's heart that he might one day join the Hurstwoods in breadlines and flophouses. One might claim a similarity between Dreiser and Robert Herrick, in the fact that Cowperwood —the subject of a trilogy, *The Financier* (1912), *The Titan* (1914), *The Stoic* (1947)—was modeled closely after a real tycoon, Yerkes, as Herrick's American citizen, Van Harrington, the hero of *The Memoirs of an American Citizen* (1905), was based on the careers of the great meat packers. But the difference is more significant: Professor Herrick could never have been his Van Harrington, whereas, in at least a part of him, Dreiser was Cowperwood, sharing his drive for power and his love of ostentation and luxury, his inability to accept official views of right and wrong, and his disdain for the *unco guid* who hid their weaknesses behind a cloak of reformist morality. Clyde Griffiths in *An American Tragedy* (1925) was but another part of Dreiser—his background and his longings; and as Clyde stole money to buy his teasing Hortense a coat, so Dreiser himself had once "borrowed" twenty-five dollars from his employer that he might be more nattily attired. Of all his novels we can say, paraphrasing Whitman, Dreiser was the man, he was there, he suffered.

Dreiser was as alone and as integral in his art, if such we can call it, as in his life. Where other novelists adopted a literary theory and tried to make their fiction fit it, or introduced a particular subject matter because they thought it should be dealt with, Dreiser wrote only about what he knew, as he knew it. Traditionless himself, he was unable or unwilling to adopt the traditions, literary or social, of the genteel arbiters of the thought of his day. And so, all unwittingly, simply because he looked at the world about him with untrained, uncultured eyes and insisted on being himself, he brought a revolution to American literature.

As he accepted no literary formulas, so he adopted no political or social formulas—at least as far as his fiction was concerned. T. S. Eliot's observation about Henry James that "he had a mind so fine that no idea could violate it" is possibly even more applicable to Dreiser, at least if for "fine" we substitute "honest" or "stubborn." At first glance this assertion may seem absurd, for Dreiser was continually being seduced by plausible theories. Indeed he fancied himself a Thinker and went around arguing the Big Questions with anyone he thought had a new idea. He even published several volumes in which he essayed to formulate the philosophical or social theories that currently attracted him, dreary writings that merely express in pseudo-intellectual terms his inability to "understand."

Understanding of this sort was not his forte. Lionel Trilling in a righteous Columbiad has cited Dreiser's intellectual failings as symbolic of the degeneration of the liberal imagination. Such an attitude is almost as perverse as the simple moralism of Stuart Sherman, literary critic of the 1920s, which supporters of Dreiser regularly use to show the myopia of his contemporaries. For one thing, Dreiser was no more of a "liberal" than Thoreau. More important, the power of his novels lies precisely in the fact that they were not illustrations of any political ideas or social theories. When he introduces his jejune philosophizing into his novels, we hurry ashamedly over the turgid, pretentious passages, ignoring them as intrusions. His strength lies not in his thought but in his observation of the social milieu, his feeling for the way people lived and dreamed and despaired. His account of the American experience of his time, of the lure of wealth and power and the fear of poverty and defeat, of tawdry dwellings and gaudy hotels, of the weak and the strong, the seeker and the sought, is unsurpassed because in his novels his mind did remain inviolate and he saw his American scene not as revealing any dialectical process, or endorsing any moral or political theory, but simply as being Life, wonderful, terrible, very mysterious.

IV

Until he had finished all his major novels, Dreiser resisted the appeals of the Left as firmly as he did the admonitions of Comstockery. In 1916, Floyd Dell exhorted him in the old *Masses*: "Life at its best and most heroic is rebellion. All artists, big and little, are in their degree rebels. You yourself are a rebel. . . . Why do you not write the American novel of rebellion?" [7] But Dreiser stubbornly insisted that he was an observer and an artist. Alongside his sympathy for the downtrodden lay his empathy for those who strove greatly and successfully for power. Much as he would have liked to see a better world, he did not see how it could be brought into being, nor could he imagine what it would be like—except, vaguely, that it should contain less suffering and more goodhearted-

[7] Quoted in Bernard Smith, *Forces in American Criticism* (New York, 1939), p. 298, from *The Masses*, vol. 8 no. 10 (August 1916): 30.

ness. When tempted to explain his views he would sometimes castigate American ideals and institutions and hypocrisies as the
source of social injustices, implying that changes should be made.
More often he would assert that the world's ills were ineradicable
because some men were born strong and some weak, and suffering
lay in the nature of things. In *A Traveller at Forty* (1913), he
wrote:

> There are those who still think that life is something which can
> be put into a mold and adjusted to a theory, but I am not one of
> them. I cannot view life or human nature save as an expression of
> contraries—in fact, I think that is what life is. . . . I cannot see
> how there can be great men without little ones; wealth without
> poverty. . . .
> I did not make my mind. I did not make my art. I cannot choose
> my taste except by predestined instinct. . . . I indict nature here
> and now, as I always do and always shall do, as being aimless, point
> less, unfair, unjust. I see in the whole thing no scheme but an ac
> cidental one—no justice save accidental justice.[8]

He insisted that he cared more for the spectacle of contending
forces than for any permanent good that might come out of them.
"I like labor leaders," he wrote in the same book. "I like big, raw,
crude, hungry men who are eager for gain—for self-glorification." [9]
Over a decade later, when he was working in Los Angeles on the
tragedy of Clyde Griffiths's America, he gave a reporter an interview which showed him little changed:

> I want to be back where there is struggle. . . . I like to wander
> around the quarters of New York where the toilers are. . . . That's
> health. I don't care about idlers or tourists, or the humdrum, or artis
> tic pretenders that flock out here, or the rich who tell you—and that
> is all they have to tell—how they did it. They would have interested
> me when they were struggling. . . .
> It is wrong and can't be righted. When you know that, the unal
> terableness isn't going to cause you any tears. I don't worry about it.
> One could lose his mind if he took it to heart.
> I don't care a damn about the masses. It is the individual that
> concerns me.

Despite the element of pose in that public statement, it suggests
the essential character of Dreiser's social views as they informed his
fiction. He was concerned above all with the individual. He enjoyed struggle and admired the victors. But he did not think for a
minute that the mighty were right. If he pretends sometimes to

[8] *A Traveller at Forty,* p. 34.
[9] *Ibid.,* p. 178.

amorality, he here shows his real feelings by characterizing the outcome of the struggle as "wrong." Only when he denies that it causes him any tears is he really disingenuous. No tears in the *American Tragedy*?

The popular success of *An American Tragedy* (no other novel of Dreiser's came close to being a best seller) brought him increased attention from reformers of all sorts. The Soviet Union invited him to visit the country as a guest, promising, on his insistence, that he would be free to see what he wanted and say what he thought. He was interested in Russia because of "its change, its ideals, its dreams," skeptical about it because he was an individualist. On leaving, he publicly criticized many aspects of the new society, concluding that "more individualism and less communism would be to the great advantage of this mighty country." [10] But at home he defended the Soviets against what he considered complacent or dogmatic American criticisms. Communists were outsiders as he had been, and he would stand up for them against the smug insiders. There were also important things to say in favor of Russia: for all her poverty, she had no unemployed and no breadlines as did the rich United States even during the boom of the 1920s.

With the coming of the depression, Dreiser found himself drawn more and more into political controversies, until finally they came to occupy almost his entire attention. The reasons for the shift were many: his passive sympathy for the poor turned into an active insistence that something had to be done to stop the rapidly increasing misery; the social consciousness and political involvement of writers of the '30s was so pervasive and so pressing that few could remain aloof; after *An American Tragedy* Dreiser was for the first time relatively free from financial worries and the pressure to publish; and apparently he felt a growing need to escape from his loneliness.

It would be easy to say that the Communists got their ring through his nose and led him along their twisting line from 1930 until his death in 1945. Nor would it be entirely inaccurate. For he did follow along their line. Yet, like the led bull, he was not the tame creature of his leaders; he conceded to them none of his integrity or spirit of independence. By the early '30s, Dreiser had become a signer and a joiner. He would give his name to any good cause; he soon learned to speak in public, something he had always dreaded and avoided; and reporters could now get from him impassioned, partisan, newsworthy statements where formerly they had simply been told that life was unknowable and social forces

[10] Quoted in Robert Elias, *Theodore Dreiser: Apostle of Nature* (New York, 1949), p. 298.

uncontrollable. If it was Communist guidance that he most often seemed to take, that was partly because the Communists, typically, were most assiduous in wooing him, and partly because he saw them both as maligned victims of all the American reactionaries, and as clear-sighted, open-minded (so it really seemed to Dreiser and to many others then) analysts of the middle-class hypocrisies and illusions. But he was not a party man; he was still his old self, and on occasion he resigned from an organization that he decided was really Communist-dominated and following paths he did not wish to take.

But while he was fighting alongside the Communists for the Scottsboro boys, the Spanish Loyalists, nonintervention during the days of the Nazi-Soviet Pact, and a second front almost immediately thereafter, he was at the same time pursuing another, apparently divergent, course. The mysticism that had always lurked behind his materialism came increasingly to the fore. Having rejected the conventional absolutes of American orthodoxy, he sought restlessly for an absolute of his own. The outcome of this search appears in his posthumous books, on which he had worked intermittently between *An American Tragedy* in 1925 and his death. *The Stoic,* last volume of the Cowperwood trilogy, ends with the heroine's rather soggy conversion to Yoga. *The Bulwark* much more convincingly depicts a Quaker's doubts and his ultimate reconciliation to religion as he comes to recognize the beneficence of the life force working through all things.

On Good Friday of 1945, Dreiser took Communion in a Congregational church. In the fall he joined the Communist Party, issuing a statement written for him by his Communist friends, but insisting that he still remained his own master and would continue to speak his own mind.

Failure of nerve? Betrayal of radicalism? Possibly both, in a sense. But neither action was entirely inconsistent with his earlier attitudes, and neither was a denial of his integrity. Despite his constant excoriation of religionists and moralists, he had always had a strong religious, mystical strain. He had always wanted to discover final answers to the whys of existence. He had always longed to find some all-embracing meaning to his life of wandering and the struggles and heartbreaks of his fellows. If, toward the end, he found some peace in the mysticisms of Eastern religion, or the mystery of the sharing of Christ's body and blood, or the symbolism of world brotherhood in Communism, this did not mean that he had fallen into acceptance of his father's puritan moralism or Russia's totalitarianism.

And in the last analysis these two acts did not matter, just as his writings since 1925 do not matter much now. This Ishmael had, in his old age, tried on the mantle of Isaac, but what we will remember and cherish is the bitter fruit of his days as Ishmael the outcast, wandering alone in the desert, telling the truths that the orthodox and well-born saw not or dared not tell.

V

Dreiser's books seem to have been hewed out of stone. Uncouth and often ugly, so bold that they were hard to read, they were ignored or derided when Dreiser was erecting them on the foundations he had laid bare. But they last. The paint flakes off the fashionable wooden structures built on sand, and the boards rot and fall off. Who now reads David Graham Phillips or Robert Herrick or our American Winston Churchill? Garland, Frank Norris, even Howells as social realist, have faded. And it is not at all unlikely that Dos Pasos and Steinbeck will shortly recede as Sinclair Lewis is already doing.

Dreiser was a radical in the great, and much dishonored, American tradition because he insisted on being himself. He resisted the admonitions and cajoleries of the critics; he saw through all the creeds of the orthodox and accepted none from the reformers. Because he had the courage, the stubbornness, the lack of literary sensitivity to write as he did, Dreiser built far better than he or his contemporaries knew. No novelist today would think of using his fiction as a model. But none will write social novels with such lasting power unless he has Dreiser's essential qualities of integrity and independence, wonder and pity.

Dreiser and the Success Dream

by Kenneth Lynn

Theodore Dreiser asserted, with a blunt directness which no other American writer at the turn of the century could match, that pecuniary and sexual success were the values of American society, that they were his values, too, and that they were therefore worthy of his total attention as a literary artist. The indebtedness to Dreiser expressed by later American writers is a formal acknowledgment of the fact that his was the most significant exploration made by any novelist in his generation of the themes of money and sex, the two themes which have become so very much the major concern of our modern literature.

Theodore Dreiser was driven all through his childhood and adolescence by the urgent desire to escape. The "peculiarly nebulous, emotional, unorganized and traditionless character" of his family life offered him very little to cling to. His father, John Paul Dreiser, had been the vigorous, prosperous owner of a woolen mill until a stunning series of disasters shortly before Theodore's birth broke him down completely. The uninsured mill was destroyed by fire; while rebuilding it, a beam fell on him, injuring his head and shoulders; some deeds and other valuable papers were stolen from his house; his three eldest boys died in rapid succession. In later years a wealthy mill owner told Dreiser that all his father had lacked in order to re-establish himself as a successful woolen manufacturer was "the courage to go ahead and organize another plant of his own," while as late as his eighty-first year his father was offered a salary of twenty thousand dollars a year to become an expert adviser for a large woolen company. But John Paul could not bring himself to capitalize on any of these opportunities; after the accidents which reduced him to poverty he was a beaten, terrified man. Dreiser remembered him only as "a morose and dour figure, forlorn and despondent, tramping about the house, his hands behind his back and occasionally talking to himself." A fanatical Catholic, Dreiser's father seemingly had only one remaining ambition—to subject his children to as severe a religious discipline as possible. Dreiser's mother, on the other hand, was a warmhearted, profoundly sympathetic woman, a great comfort to all the family, but equally ineffectual as a provider. An incorrigible optimist, her eye was "always on the future, where lay wonder and delight, if not fame and power," but she could never make ends meet in the present.

When Dreiser was eight or nine, his father's inability to locate even a part-time job, and the failure of the latest of his mother's perennial boardinghouse schemes, split the family, and Dreiser, in company with his mother and two of the other children, began a long hegira through a succession of Indiana towns. One summer and autumn in Sullivan, Indiana, a drab mining town, they were so poor that Dreiser had no shoes to wear. Winters always meant being cold and hungry, so that "for years, even so late as my thirty-fifth or fortieth year, the approach of winter invariably filled me with an indefinable and highly oppressive dread."

Out of the tangled mess of his broken family life, his rootlessness, his poverty, came the dream of escape, and the image of escape was the flight to the city. Several of Dreiser's older brothers and sisters had already fled, one brother to the West, another to New York, two sisters to Chicago. Their visits home and the stories they told fed Dreiser's imagination; in between their visits there was the daily sustenance of the pulp magazines—*Brave and Bold, Pluck and Luck,* and *Work and Win*—with their stories of poor small-town boys like himself who found happiness and affluence in the city. What Fred Fearnot could do, so could he. How much the success myth came to mean to Dreiser can perhaps be best sensed in his simple admission that "over half the glory" of life in these boyhood years was the visible arrival and departure of the trains—the highway of escape.

Although impractical herself, his mother constantly urged on Dreiser "the need of energy, study of a practical character, ambition, self-denial," if he were properly to prepare himself for "the battle of life." Like her, however, Dreiser was an optimist and a daydreamer. Alger's formula for rising from rags to riches was pluck and luck, but the youthful Dreiser was interested only in the latter half. "I was for mooning about and dreaming of how delightful it would be to do this and that, have this and that—without effort—by luck or birth, as it were." At the suggestion of his seventh-grade teacher, he read *Self-Help* by Samuel Smiles, which made him "see that there were many things to do and many, many ways of finding how to do them. Some people drifted into things, and most successfully; others thought them out." Thought and drift, pluck and luck: henceforth Dreiser believed with the mythology that the recipe for success had two essential ingredients, but for many years he would not relinquish the notion that there was a superior efficacy in luck.

In the summer of his sixteenth birthday, Dreiser left home and went, "like a boy hero out of a Horatio Alger, Jr., novel, to Chicago to seek his fortune." The city seemed to him "a land of promise, a fabled realm of milk and honey. . . . Here, as nowhere else, youth might make its way." The luxury of the magnificent city almost seemed to speak to him: "All that life or hope is or can be or do, this I am, and it is here before you! Take of it! Live, live, satisfy your heart!" As the formula for success had two parts, so the images of what success could mean, as they passed before his dazzled eyes, sifted down into two categories. "Burning with desire," he dreamed of "the mansions that should belong to me! . . . The beauties who should note and receive me." Pluck and luck meant success, and success meant wealth and women. These conclusions, arrived at in mid-adolescence, stained Dreiser's mind forever.

Although the opportunities for success were everywhere, Chicago brought to Dreiser a long chain of defeats. For a time he could not land a job at all; when he did succeed in getting one—cleaning a railway stable—he was fired after a half day. Hired next by a hardware store to clean stoves, he lasted exactly two hours before being told he was too weak for the job and dismissed. His connection with a household-furnishings company was abruptly terminated when he was caught stealing twenty-five dollars to buy himself a winter coat.

His relations with girls were equally unsatisfactory. When he measured his poor clothes, his lack of *savoir-faire,* and his homeliness against his own standard of the successful man, he found it impossible to believe that any girl could be interested in him. When occasions for sexual conquest arose, his insecurities rendered him completely and humiliatingly inadequate. In masturbation, as in his dreams of wealth, he found solace from the failures of the real world.

After four years in Chicago, Dreiser was still "without trade or profession, a sort of nondescript dreamer without the power to earn a decent living and yet with all the tastes . . . of one destined to an independent fortune." Then came the turning point, the crucial moment which the success myth had taught him every career contained. "The newspapers—the newspapers—somehow, by their intimacy with everything that was going on in the world, seemed to be the swiftest approach to all this of which I was dreaming." He hung around the city rooms in the hope that something might turn up, and finally he was taken on as a regular feature writer by the *Chicago Globe,* a "by no means distinguished paper."

In the seething caldron of the newspaper world, Dreiser shucked off the last vestiges of the moralistic qualms which, the heritage of his father's rigid Catholic discipline, had heretofore caused him to feel guilty as he ran after money and women. Most of his journalistic colleagues, Dreiser discovered, "looked upon life as a fierce, grim struggle in which no quarter was either given or taken, and in which all men laid traps, lied, squandered, erred through illusion." With their conclusions he now heartily agreed. He doubted in these newspaper years that any human being ever coveted success more completely than he did. "My body was blazing with sex, as well as with a desire for material and social supremacy—to have wealth, to be in society. . . ." The problem was how to get what he was after, no matter the means.

Moving to St. Louis, he angled for and got the post of drama reviewer on the *Globe-Democrat,* thus gaining access to the theatrical world, which, with its suavity and its glitter, exhilarated Dreiser beyond anything he had ever known. He affected Bohemian clothes and a dramatic air, and fantasied that he was just on the verge of a liaison with some beautiful actress. Wondering if becoming a littérateur might open the door to easy cash and easy women, he was immensely pleased and excited when someone told him he ought to write a play. One of his newspaper colleagues had written a novel about Paris which Dreiser was allowed to read in manuscript. It impressed him tremendously. The author had never been to Paris, but his novel's "frank pictures of raw, greedy, sensual human nature, and its open pictures of self-indulgence and vice" sounded wonderfully authentic to Dreiser. Definitely, "art" was the open sesame to success. "This world was a splendid place for talent, I thought. It bestowed success and honor upon those who could succeed. Plays or books, or both, were the direct entrance to every joy which the heart could desire." Dreiser had even been prepared "to accept socialism," if it would only bring him "a great home, fine clothes, pretty women, the respect and companionship of famous men," but now he was positive he had found a better way to achieve his desires.

Dreiser was also prompted in the direction of becoming a novelist by his fear of failure at newspaper work. "I was always driven," he said, "by haunting fear of losing this or any position I had ever had, of not being able to find another (a left-over fear, perhaps, due to the impression that poverty had made on me in my extreme youth)." Newspaper assignments sent him to the theater, but they also sent him to the slums. Such glimpses of life "in all its helpless degradation and poverty" caused him to break into a cold sweat when it occurred to him that the lot of the poor, "their hungers, thirsts, half-formed dreams of pleasure, their glittering insanities and broken resignations at the end," might be his lot, too. Owning a small-town paper seemed to offer security, so he quit St. Louis with the notion of looking for one. When nothing came of his search, Dreiser wandered East, picking up free-lance jobs on papers here and there. Out of a regular job and almost out of money, he was haunted—it is one of his key words—more than ever. "The most haunting and disturbing thought always was that hourly, I was growing older. . . . Some had strength or capacity or looks or fortune, or all, at their command, and then all the world was theirs . . . but I, poor waif . . . must go fumbling about looking in upon life from the outside." Although Arthur Brisbane soon hired him as a reporter on the glamorous *New York World,* Dreiser's fears of failure were fanned even higher by his awareness that in the brutally competitive big league of Manhattan journalism he was barely keeping his head above water. "I was haunted by the thought that I was a misfit, that I might really have to give up and return to the West, where in some pathetic humdrum task I should live out a barren and pointless life." Receiving only marginal assignments on the *World,* Dreiser knew he had to do something —to stand still was death. There were several men employed on the paper who in their spare time wrote fiction.[1] Their example helped Dreiser make his decision. "I began to think that I must not give up but must instead turn to letters, the art of short-story writing. . . ." In the spring of 1895 he took the plunge and re-signed from the *World.*

His initial short stories earned him only rejection slips. When his funds had diminished to the point where the return to the West was imminent, Dreiser suggested to the sheet-music publishers with whom his brother Paul was associated [2] that they publish three or four new songs each month and surround them with the trappings of a magazine—articles, pictures, and criticism. They agreed, and Dreiser found himself "Editor and Arranger" of *Ev'ry Month. The Woman's Magazine of Literature and Popular Music.* An indiffer-

---

[1] One of the men was David Graham Phillips.

[2] Paul Dreiser, or Paul Dresser, as he called himself, was the author of many popular songs of the day, including "On the Banks of the Wabash" and "My Gal Sal."

ent reporter, he was much better suited to the calmer, if occasionally froufrou, role of editor of a magazine for women.

He wrote many editorials (dramatically signed "The Prophet") for *Ev'ry Month,* commenting on everything from the phenomenon of mental telepathy to the social emancipation of women. These editorials served Dreiser as a kind of literary notebook, most of the topics of his fiction first appearing here in the guise of comments on contemporary events. An editorial in September, 1896, which began by commenting on the impending Bryan-McKinley election, quickly turned aside from politics to a reflection on how valuable reading was for the opportunity it gave to learn of the triumphant lives of great men. Contemplating such careers from the comfortable vantage of his editorial chair, Dreiser no longer found the struggle of life so overwhelming as it had seemed on the *World.* Nature was powerful, but man was even more so: "In the presence of such a creature pity has no mission. . . . Nothing can withstand him, for he is working in harmony with great laws which place splendid powers in his hand and assist him to rise." To the successful young editor of *Ev'ry Month,* the universe was really and truly the splendid place the success myth had always said it was.

The following month Dreiser began his column, in what would become his most characteristic vein as a novelist, by describing the lure of the metropolis. "To go to the city," he wrote, "is the changeless desire of the mind. . . . It is a magnet which no one understands." This reflection brought him to consider a tragic result of the city's magnetic appeal—the thousands of people who had been drawn to New York by its glamour, only to find themselves trapped in a world of long hours and low pay. But Dreiser's conclusion was that this pathetic condition was necessary and inevitable. "Oppression can be avoided, that is true," he conceded, "but the vine must have roots, else how are its leaves to grow high into the world of sunlight and air? Some must enact the role of leaves, others the role of roots, and as no one has the making of his brain in embryo he must take the result as it comes." Here, in this metaphor of roots and leaves, Dreiser first set forth his life-long opposition to political and economic reform.

In February, 1897, Dreiser discussed the financial panic which was currently ruining many businessmen in New York, then switched to a lengthy analysis of the number of starving and freezing cases in the city that winter. Dreiser found these cases horrible to think about, but once more he concluded that such things must be:

> It is only the unfit who fail—who suffer and die. . . . They are unfit, because, unlike the fit ones, they lack these peculiarities which

aid one to survive. They are too shy to complain openly, too thin-skinned to endure pity, too fearful of public opinion to seek refuge in a workhouse, and too timid and weak-bodied to risk seizing what is not their own.

Then followed one prophetic sentence: "In this world generally failure opens wide the gates to mortal onslaught, and the invariable result is death."

After two years with *Ev'ry Month,* Dreiser had become sufficiently confident of his abilities to crack the magazine market to go back into free-lancing, where there was just as much money as in editing, and more chance to build a writing reputation. Between 1897 and 1899 he sold enough articles to warrant being included in the first edition of *Who's Who.* His most important work in this period was done for Orison Swett Marden, who had launched in the same year that Dreiser quit *Ev'ry Month* a new magazine bearing the bluntly descriptive name of *Success.* Marden had had a spectacularly successful career as the manager and then the owner of a chain of hotels, but fires and overconfident investments had wiped him out in the mid-nineties. He instantly started out for the top again by writing a book of inspirational essays. *Pushing to the Front, or, Success under Difficulties* had a fabulous sale; together with its sequels, Marden's book sold three million copies by the end of the century. *Pushing to the Front* relied for its power upon concrete descriptions of the mental and moral qualities most necessary to success, as evinced in the lives of iron-willed great men. By this "uplifting, energizing, suggestive force" Marden hoped to "encourage, inspire, and stimulate boys and girls who long to be somebody and do something in the world, but feel that they have no chance in life."

With the money from his book sales, Marden started *Success.* The Marden magazine formula called for writers who would interview the great business, political and artistic leaders of America for the stories of their careers. Dreiser, already on record as to the value of reading about the lives of the great and the strong, was perfectly suited for Marden's scheme. Beginning with the third issue of the magazine, which published his interview with Edison, Dreiser went on to become Marden's key writer. In the first two years of *Success,* an article by Dreiser appeared almost on the average of once a month. Interested in the newly liberated American woman, Dreiser did a series for Marden on women in the arts; but his principal work consisted of interviews with business tycoons, inventors, actors, and writers, including Philip Armour, William Dean Howells, Marshall Field and Anthony Hope. Dreiser, with his fascinated belief in luck, asked Carnegie if he did not consider that his early promotion to superintendent of the western division of the Pennsylvania Railroad had been "a matter of chance." (Carnegie replied adamantly, "Never.") Through Thomas A. Edison, Dreiser first came across an aspect of the success myth which had never before occurred to him, but which would eventually constitute one of the great problems in his novels—what happens to a person after he succeeds? Edison told Dreiser that he had come to hate the thought of the inventions he had completed, the products he had finished. He liked the process of working, but when the invention was "all done and is a success, I can't bear the sight of it. I haven't used a telephone in ten years, and I would go out of my way any day to miss an incandescent light. . . . I continue to find my greatest pleasure, and so my reward, in the work that precedes what the world calls success." In both *Sister Carrie* and the Cowperwood series Dreiser would have occasion to remember Edison's words.

Marden thought Dreiser's interviews so superior that he paid him the supreme compliment of pirating them for the inspirational books he continued to turn out. No acknowledgments, either by credit line or in cash, ever recorded the fact that *Talks with Great Workers* and *How They Succeeded: Life Stories of Successful Men Told by Themselves,* both of which appeared under Marden's name, were in large part written by a man who was totally unaware that they had even been published. Ironically, these books appeared and sold well at precisely the time when Dreiser, sick and broke, and despondent over the suppression of *Sister Carrie,* was sinking into poverty and the contemplation of suicide.

Dreiser and the Sentimental Novel

by Leslie A. Fiedler

It is only Dreiser who proves capable of reviving that theme [seduction] for serious literature, for he takes it seriously: finding in the impregnation and abandonment of helpless women no mere occasions for melodrama (as in Twain) or for exercises in irony and contrasting style (as in Crane). Dreiser is qualified first of all by his essentially sentimental response to the plight of the oppressed, by what he himself calls—attributing the feeling to one of his characters—an "uncritical upswelling of grief for the weak and the helpless." There is in him none of the detachment and cynicism of Crane, none of the utter blackness and pessimism of Twain; he is as "positive" through his tears as any female scribbler. Even his famous determinism is essentially sentimental at root, amounting effectively to little more than the sob of exculpation: "Nobody's fault! Nobody's fault!" Much is made by his friendlier critics of the fact that just before the beginning of his writing career Dreiser discovered Balzac; much more should be made of the fact that long before that encounter, his imagination had already been formed by Ouida and Laura Jean Libby. If, on the one hand, the daughters of the non-Anglo-Saxon American poor find in him a voice, on the other, the stickier writers for women through him achieve literary respectability.

It is no accident that for several years he was able to edit successfully the Butterick magazines, purveyors of fashion, fiction, and useful articles ("What to Do When Diphtheria Comes") to lower-middlebrow women; nor was his writing for such an audience an unfortunate interruption in his career, a prostitution of his talent. Nobody, as many writers have learned to their grief through both success and failure, can deceive such an audience for very long; one hint of condescension gives the game away. If Dreiser managed to

please such a group of readers, it was because at the *deepest level,*
he shared their values; and the friends who worked so hard to save
him from the deleterious effect of such "hack work," and finally
persuaded him to abandon it—understood nothing. When Dreiser
in " 'The Genius' " describes the young artist, Eugene Witla (his
barely disguised self-portrait), as beginning with a love of the
painting of that insufferable anti-artist Bouguereau this is not just
a revelation of the author's insufficient culture; it is also a revelation
of his fundamental taste. For better or worse, Dreiser is bound in
weakness and in strength to the values of the sentimental lower
middle class.

When he wrote on rejection slips sent to contributors to *The
Delineator,* "We like realism, but it must be tinged with sufficient
idealism to make it all a truly uplifting character. . . . The fine
side of things—the idealistic—is the answer for us . . . " he was not
merely playing with a straight face the part for which he had been
hired. To his good friend H. L. Mencken, to whom surely he
could speak frankly, he wrote in quite the same vein that he would
like for another of his magazines (this one presumably freer from
outside control), *The Bohemian,* no "tainted fiction," but stories
that testified to their authors' "knowledge of life *as it is,* broad,
simple, good-natured." If there is a fundamental flaw in Dreiser, it
resides neither in his stylistic clumsiness, which for strength's sake
is easily forgiven, nor in his tritely elegant literary vocabulary, the
kitsch interior-decorating with which he cannot forbear touching
up his scenes, but in the fact that his novels are in fact "uplifting"
—which is to say, sentimental rather than tragic.

How, then, did Dreiser come to be, as one of his publishers was
later to put it, "the one man to have first created an audience for
daring books," the defendant in obscenity trials which came to
seem to his contemporaries forums at which the cause of a new,
frank literature could be advocated? It is hard now to see the sense
in which Dreiser's books, whatever their other merits, are daring
at all. Certainly, they do not describe the sexual act or its more
passionate preliminaries with a frankness or pornographic intensity
comparable to George Lippard's. Dreiser came of the kind of people who copulate in the dark and live out their lives without ever
seeing their sexual partners nude; and he was brought up on the
kind of book which made it impossible for him to write convincingly about the act of love; his subject was, like theirs, when erotic
at all, the traditional "consequences of seduction."

His notion of a passionate interchange between lovers involves
such "poetic" apostrophes as, "Oh, Flower Face! Oh, Silver Feet!
Oh, Myrtle Bloom!" The erotic, that is to say, demanded for him

a veneer of the poetic; and his concept of poetry is perhaps best indicated by the metrical chapter titles in *Sister Carrie:* "And This is Not Elf Land: What Gold Will Not Buy," "The Way of the Beaten: A Harp in the Wind." It is all a little like what his brother, Paul Dresser (also the champion of the fallen woman in "My Gal Sal"), was doing in the popular song. There is power in Dreiser, to be sure; no one gives better the sense of the dazzled entry of the small-town girl into the big city; no one renders better the seedy milieu of the status-hungry on their way up or down; but no American writer is more the victim of the sentimental wound, less capable of dealing with passion. When he resists the impulse to poeticize, Dreiser does love scenes like this: "Carrie rose up as if to step away, he holding her hand. Now he slipped his arm about her and she struggled, but in vain. He held her quite close. Instantly there flared up in his body the all-compelling desire. His affection took an ardent form. . . . She found him lifting her head and looking into her eyes. What magnetism there was she could never know. His many sins, however, were for the moment all forgotten." It is banality raised to the power of evasion, an implicit denial of the reality of passion.

He could never portray, for all his own later hectic career as a lover, any woman except the traditional seduced working girl of sentimental melodrama. Yet because the deceived woman, the seduced virgin are for Dreiser the images through which he understands America and himself, he stumbles into scandal. The man who makes good and the girl who goes bad, these stereotypes of the folk (occasionally reversed, for variety, to the girl who rises and the man who falls) are the sole symbols that move him to write, and it is with the fallen girl that he begins his career. He is in fact the avenging brother that earlier writers only imagine; and Sister Carrie, like Jennie Gerhardt after her, is a household image, one of those sisters of his own, who were always getting into trouble: running off with married men or embezzlers, coming home pregnant. The phrase which came unbidden into his mind was not a simple girl's name, as in the typical woman's book, but "*Sister* Carrie," and in the novel itself he tries to justify the first word in various ways. Meeting her married sister in Chicago at the beginning of the book, Caroline Meeber is hailed by that full title, "half affectionately" bestowed on her, Dreiser tells us, by her family; and by the end of the story, when she is translated into a kind of unchurched nun, celibate, lonely, and dedicated to charity, it seems even more appropriate. Surely, the quasi-religious pun is intended; and yet, first of all, Carrie is not the sister of her fictional family or even a Little Sister of the Poor, but one of Dreiser's own sisters, redeemed

from the shabby failures of her actual life. If not a brother's vengeance, *Sister Carrie* is his amends.

Why, then, did it irk and shock so many readers? How, to begin
with, could so conventional an account of a small-town girl, seduced first by the flashy drummer, Drouet, then talked into a biga-
mous marriage with the repentant embezzler, Hurstwood, so horrify
the wife of Dreiser's publisher? Legend at least tells us that she was
so dismayed that she persuaded her husband not to promote the
book which he had already contracted to print. There is no apparent moral ambiguity in Dreiser's presentation. Both Hurstwood's robbery and Carrie's love affairs are called evil, and Hurstwood is quite satisfactorily punished, degraded to the level of a
skid-row panhandler, left about to commit suicide in a flophouse.
Before that, he has been harried from failure to failure, his pride
and virility broken until he crawls in the slush, begs a few dollars
from the woman he has wronged. Not even Montraville or Holling-
worth had been so degraded for their offenses! Even Carrie, though
she has the kind of success denied her seducer, and achieves the
material comforts of which she once scarcely knew how to dream,
cannot find happiness in her career as an actress or in herself. To
make the point clear, Dreiser lingers almost tearfully over Carrie's
melancholy figure at the end, pauses to apostrophize her: "Oh,
Carrie, Carrie! . . . know, then, that for you is neither surfeit or
content. In your rocking chair, by your window dreaming, shall
you long alone. In your rocking chair, by your window, shall you
dream such happiness as you may never feel." It is the lyrics of a
popular song again— "Old Rocking Chair's Got Me," *obligato*.
What more did Mr. and Mrs. Doubleday want? Blood? The death
of the girl who had fallen? Crane had already provided that in a
book which no one would print, which sold even fewer than the
650 copies of *Sister Carrie* that went out of the one thousand
printed. Dreiser, with an instinct for self-dramatization, liked to
speak of the "suppression" of his first book, but in fact it did as
well as Melville's *Pierre*.

It is true that Dreiser lapsed at this point into ten years of silence,
which is to say, a decade of editing, and writing articles and short
stories, but no novels; yet this seems to have been less a lock-out
on the part of the publishers (actually he was given an advance
during this period on a book which he never finished) than some
deep, psychological slow-down within him. Carrie had represented
more than an expurgated version of his unfortunate sister (when he
emended life it was always in favor of that "sufficient idealism"
which he had urged on his contributors); she had been, in a way,
a disguised portrait of himself: a Portrait of the Artist as a Girl

Gone Wrong. "Thus in life there is ever . . . the mind that reasons, and the mind that feels," Dreiser had written in *Sister Carrie*, thinking of himself. "Of the one come the men of action . . . of the other, poets and dreamers—artists all. As harps in the wind, the latter respond to every breath of fancy, voicing in their moods all the ebb and flow of the ideal. Man has not yet comprehended the dreamer any more than he has the ideal. For him the laws and morals of the world are unduly severe. Ever hearkening to the sound of beauty, striving for the flash of its distant wings, he watches to follow. . . . So watched Carrie, so followed. . . ." In this respect, too, she is a sister to her author, also a "harp in the wind"; and it is perhaps precisely the bovarysm revealed in such a passage, the *Weltschmerz* and self-pity, the half-secret caviling at moral restraints which put off the popular reader.

In *Jennie Gerhardt,* Dreiser did not again make the mistake of portraying the anti-bourgeois sentimental artist in the girl who goes bad. This time he draws a portrait of his mother as reflected in the experience of his sisters, his poor suffering mother, whom he could never forget holding up to him as a child her shabby shoes and saying, "See poor mother's shoes? See the hole there?" He was the mama's boy par excellence, dreaming always of that figure "potent and alive," who had—despite the ogre papa—made their home seem "like Fairyland." In the novel, the mother-sister figure is identified not only with Jennie, but with all of "the distraught and helpless poor," while the figure of the father is fractured into the religious tyrant Mr. Gerhardt; Senator Brander, Jennie's first lover, who wants to marry her but dies too soon; and Lester Kane, son of a rich family, who deserts Jennie when he is threatened with disinheritance. None of the three, however, though each makes Jennie suffer in some way, can finally qualify as a villain, not even old Gerhardt. They are finally all melted down in the universal solvent of Dreiser's pity for victims—revealed as not the rejecting fathers they first seemed, but weak sons, pleading forgiveness from the eternally offended Jennie-Mother. It is only the abstract "system" which is the really Bad Father; and if the seduction novel in Dreiser's hands takes on social meanings once more, those meanings are not translatable into any conventional theory of the class struggle. In his books, humanity as a whole struggles against the inhuman nature of things as they are. Seducer and victim are equally betrayed, equally to be pitied: Lester Kane is condemned by his own weakness to die apart from his love, and Jennie for all her strength can only look through the iron grille of the cemetery at his coffin being lowered into the earth.

The fictional world of Dreiser is the *absolutely* sentimental world, in which morality itself has finally been dissolved in pity; and in such a world, Charlotte Temple is quite appropriately reborn. No theme but seduction can contain the meanings Dreiser is trying to express, no catastrophe but deflowering start his heroines on their way toward total alienation. But any allusion to deflowering had become in Dreiser's time taboo; and even the once-standard description of an unmarried mother's affection for her illegitimate child, a sympathetic rendering of her refusal to consider it unclean, had come to seem in bourgeois circles a flaunting of decency itself. To the anti-bourgeois camp in the literary world of the early twentieth century, Dreiser's orthodox sentimental plea for sympathy rather than scorn for the fallen woman seemed, therefore, a revolutionary manifesto, an emancipation proclamation! And in the context of the developing struggle, in the courts and in the magazines, he did, indeed, become the spokesman for the forces combating genteel censorship, winning in the end a freedom in the handling of sex which he himself was incapable of exploiting.

Meanwhile, his theme had become more and more explicitly the denial of personal moral responsibility, the assertion that the individual who was to be pitied could not be blamed. After a while, he was scarcely distinguishable from his friend Clarence Darrow, making a tearful, mechanistic courtroom plea for a criminal facing the sentence of death. It is appropriate, therefore, that the novel in which Dreiser gives full-dress treatment to the contention that nothing is anybody's fault should take place largely in the courtroom, quote extensive sections of an actual court record. In *An American Tragedy,* which was published in 1925, a poor boy on the make in society (his prototype in real life came from a fairly comfortable family) lets drown (his prototype deliberately plotted and executed the crime) a factory girl whom he has got pregnant, and who stands in the way of his marriage to a rich debutante. Even in the columns of the newspapers, Dreiser can only find new instances of what early reading and experience have made for him an obsessive theme. Whatever he thinks he is trying to prove, he must prove it by setting in motion the Seducer and the Seduced, the passionate or vain young man indulging his desire for power and the baffled girl, lonely and eager to be fed well, dressed well, inducted into the mysteries of beauty. What makes *An American Tragedy* particularly American is the fact that Clarissa falls prey not to Lovelace but to Horatio Alger!

For his services in reviving a myth as old as the bourgeois novel itself, Dreiser was identified as a "naturalist," a term of contempt to the genteel, and a rallying cry for those who were engaged in the struggle against gentility. Given that name, however, he became confused with other writers who like him exploited the urban scene, like him rendered accurately the impoverished speech of the culturally dispossessed, and like him documented their fables with closely observed data out of contemporary life. Unlike many of the others with whom he was linked, however, Dreiser evokes— when he is not calling up Horatio Alger—the spirit of Richardson and Mrs. Rowson, Brockden Brown and George Lippard. There is so great a difference between the sentimental "naturalist" like Dreiser (dedicated to pitying the ravished poor), the historical-romantic "naturalist" like Crane (seeking in the details of slum life the exotic once found in medieval England or the South Seas), and the gothic "naturalist" like Faulkner (raising the real horrors of social conflict and decay to a power of grotesqueness once projected only in the supernatural) that the classification "naturalist" confuses more than it enlightens.

The battle which Dreiser fought inadvertently at first he engaged in quite consciously after a while; by those who hailed him as a great emancipator, he was persuaded that it had been his aim all along to release Americans in life and art for the pursuit of passion; and especially in "The 'Genius' " he abandoned his more essential seduction theme to plead the cause of Don Juan. It is partly Dreiser's own fault, therefore, if he has come to seem part of the Lawrentian sexual revolution of the '20's, otherwise carried forward by that homegrown D. H. Lawrence, Sherwood Anderson; though perhaps most of the responsibility lies with such champions of his work as Dorothy Dudley. In her study of Dreiser's impact on America, Miss Dudley reports the following astonishing conversation between Dreiser and herself on the subject of his mother. " 'Was she really so alive, so "pagan" as you call her? Was your father enough for her then, or did she find others? 'She did if she wanted to, I'm certain of that. She had a way of doing what she wanted to do without disturbing the rest of us. But I was too young, I don't know about that.' 'Well, maybe she did. Maybe your father was not your father. How do you know?' " This fondest fantasy of the erotic sentimentalism of the '20's—illegitimacy or putting one over on Father—Dreiser disavows. His mother's "paganism" he would apparently like to keep spiritual, abstract, and he shies at adultery, which is not, in any case, a main subject of his essentially American books. The new mystique of passion Dreiser never really embraced—not retroactively for his mother anyhow; but the older mystique of virginity he had left behind. And this defection perhaps cut him off from the kind of middlebrow popularity which, granted his gifts and limitations, he should have enjoyed.

Sister Carrie's Brother

by Malcolm Cowley

When he finished *Sister Carrie*, his first novel, Theodore Dreiser was a big, shambling youngster of twenty-nine with an advancing nose, a retreating chin, and a nature full of discordancies. He
was dreamy but practical, rash but timid, persistent in his aims but
given to fits of elation or dejection. His manners must have been
frightful, in spite of the hours he had spent in his boyhood poring
over *Hill's Manual of Etiquette*. He was full of understanding and
sympathy for the weakness of others, including drunkards, wastrels,
and criminals, but often he failed to show generosity toward those
he regarded as rivals, with the result that his career was full of
sudden friendships and estrangements.

He was an appealing young man in many ways and yet, on the
basis of what he afterwards wrote about himself, he could hardly
be called an admirable character. He was possessed by cheap ambitions; his early picture of the good life was to own what he called
"a lovely home," with cast-iron deer on the lawn; to drive behind
"a pair of prancing bays," and to spend his evenings in "a truly
swell saloon," with actors, song writers, and Tammany politicians,
amid "the laughter, the jesting, the expectorating, and back-slap-
ping geniality." His taste was worse than untrained; it was actively
bad except in fiction, and when he was offered the choice between
two words, two paintings, two songs, or two pieces of furniture, he
took the one that looked or sounded more expensive. In his "af-
fectional relations," as he called them, he was a "varietist," to use
his expensive word for a woman-chaser; and he makes it clear that
he treated some women abominably after he caught them. If the
character of Eugene Witla in *The "Genius"* is a self-portrait, as it
seems to be, then his neighbors must have said rightly that his first
wife was a saint to put up with him.

Yet Dreiser painted the portrait knowing that it would be rec-

"Sister Carrie's Brother." From *A Many-Windowed House: Collected Essays
on American Writers and American Writing*. By Malcolm Cowley. Edited with
an Introduction by Henry Dan Piper (Carbondale, Ill.: Southern Illinois University Press, 1970), pp. 153–65. Copyright © 1970 by Southern Illinois University Press. Reprinted by permission of the publisher.

ognized; and in other books he described his transgressions in the first person. Once in his life he stole money; he needed a new over-coat and held out twenty-five dollars from his weekly collections for a Chicago furniture house. That petty crime must have been the hardest to confess to his reader, but he told the story in all its details, including his terror and shame when the theft was dis-covered. In writing of himself or his background he had a massive honesty that was less a moral than a physiological quality. It was his whole organism, not his conscious mind or his moral code, that made him incapable of any but minor falsehoods. Several times he tried writing false stories for money, but the words wouldn't come; and later in his career he found it physically impossible to finish some of the novels he had started, if their plots took a turn that seemed alien to his experience. He wasn't satisfied with easy an-swers. "Chronically nebulous, doubting, uncertain," he says of him-self, "I stared and stared at everything, only wondering, not solv-ing." It would take him thirty years to find—in his own life—the right ending for his last novel, *The Bulwark.*

There were always persons who believed in him and came to his help at critical points in his career. There was his mother first of all, a woman who could read a little, but couldn't sign her name until Dorsch, as she called him, and his youngest sister learned to write in the second grade of a German-language parochial school; they taught her to form the letters. But the mother understood her Dorsch sympathetically; and later when he confided to her that he wanted to be a writer more than anything else in the world, she made her painful little sacrifices so that he could read and study. Then there was the teacher at the Warsaw, Indiana, high school who was so impressed by this earnest and fumbling student that later she rescued him from his underpaid work at the warehouse in Chicago where he was showing symptoms of tuberculosis; she arranged to have him admitted to the University of Indiana and paid most of his expenses for his one college year out of her slender purse.

There was a copyreader on the Chicago *Globe,* a quietly raging cynic who took a fancy to Dreiser, insisted that he be hired, and taught him to write signed stories. There were various newspaper editors, including Joseph B. McCullagh of the St. Louis *Globe-Democrat,* who trained him and pushed him ahead. There was Arthur Henry, formerly of the Toledo *Blade,* who encouraged him to write *Sister Carrie*: the writing faltered and stopped for two months when Henry went away, then started again when Henry returned, read the early chapters and said, yes, it was going fine. There was most of all his brother Paul, who helped him in his recurrent fits of depression; he would go searching for Theodore, find him hiding in a cheap lodging house, force money on him, and invent a job that he could fill. Then, in later years, there were all the publishers (including Horace Liveright) who offered him large sums in the form of advances against royalties on novels that in most cases were never written; who gave him the money as a business venture, partly, but also as a token of respect for the work he had done.

Largely as a result of the interventions that saved him time and again, Dreiser came to have a mystical faith in his star. What he said of Eugene Witla might have been applied to himself: "All his life he had fancied that he was leading a more or less fated life, principally more. He had thought that his art was a gift, that he had in a way been sent to revolutionize art in America, or carry it one step forward." It was, however, only during his periods of elation that Dreiser regarded himself as a favored ambassador of fate. When he became dejected, "he fancied," as Dreiser said of Witla and presumably of himself, that "he might be the sport or toy of untoward and malicious powers, such as those which surrounded and accomplished Macbeth's tragic end, and which might be intending to make an illustration of him." Hurstwood, in *Sister Carrie,* was such an "illustration"; his story was based on Dreiser's fancies of sinking into the depths. Cowperwood, the financier of a later trilogy, was Dreiser riding the storm and battling among the Titans.

Believing himself to be a marked man, he displayed a curious self-confidence. James Oppenheim wrote a poem about the time when he and Dreiser watched an amazing sunset over the Hudson. "Could you describe that, Dreiser?" he asked. "Yes, that or anything," was the answer. Dreiser could describe anything, from the stupid to the sublime, because in a sense he could describe nothing; he never learned to look for the exact phrase. One sometimes feels that he would have been a great philosopher if he had acquired the art of thinking systematically, instead of merely brooding over ideas, and a great writer if he had ever learned to write. Or might one call him a great inarticulate writer? There are moments when Dreiser's awkwardness in handling words contributes to the force of his novels, since he seems to be groping in them for something on a deeper level than language; there are crises when he stutters in trite phrases that are like incoherent cries.

His memoirs make it clear that what he respected in himself was the intensity of his emotions and his sense of what he calls, in another trite phrase, "the mystery and terror and wonder of life."

He often heard voices. One of them—it was the voice of Chicago—spoke to him in his youth, and later he transcribed its words into a sort of elemental poetry. "I am the pulsing urge of the universe," it said to him. "All that life or hope is or can be or do, this I am, and it is here before you! Take of it! Live, live, satisfy your heart!"

A phrase often applied to Dreiser by others is "standing alone" or "marching alone." "It was Dreiser standing alone who won the battle against the censors," I heard a publisher say. In his Nobel Prize address, Sinclair Lewis told the Swedish Academy that Dreiser "more than any other man, marching alone, usually unappreciated, often hated, has cleared the trail from Victorian and Howellsian timidity and gentility in American fiction to honesty and boldness and passion of life." Although Dreiser deserved the tribute, its phrasing was inaccurate. He marched forward and at last won the battle, but he was seldom alone, except in the fits of dejection when he hid away from the world. Even then there was always someone who sought him out, gave him money or encouragement, and insisted that he go back to writing. Indeed, these helpers appeared so often at critical moments that one is tempted, like Dreiser himself, to regard them as emissaries of the powers that watched over him.

There were, however, less supernatural reasons for the support he received, and they also help to explain the abuse and hatred that made it necessary. In those days a new social class was appearing in the larger American cities. It consisted of young, ambitious, yearning, rootless men, chiefly from the Middle West, who were indifferent to the past and felt that their aspirations had never been portrayed in American literature. They knew that Dreiser was one of them, in his faults as well as his virtues, and they sensed that he would be loyal to his class. It was class loyalty that they expected of him, not personal gratitude. If he wrote great novels, they would not deal with foreigners and aristocrats, or with bygone days, and they would not be written politely for women and preachers. Instead the books would describe persons like those who helped him, like his brothers and sisters, his teachers, his newspaper friends, and his publishers, who would be appearing for the first time in serious fiction. It was the new men who recognized his integrity and chose him—elected him, one might say—to be their literary representative.

The post was dangerous. Later, when he fought their battles, Dreiser would be exposed to attacks from all those who disliked the vulgarity and what seemed to be the dubious moral standards of the new class from which he came. Instead of "marching alone," he

would stand in a double relationship to American society: he would
be the spokesman for one group and the scapegoat of others.

II

In the summer of 1900 Dreiser joined forces with Frank Norris
for a battle against the genteel tradition in American letters. Norris
was then thirty years old, was newly married, and was working
hard to finish his biggest novel, *The Octopus*. Meanwhile he was
supporting himself by reading manuscripts for the new publishing
house of Doubleday, Page and Company, which had issued his *Mc-
Teague* the year before. One of the manuscripts he carried home
was that of a first novel called *Sister Carrie*. "I have found a masterpiece," he said to his first caller in the office one morning. "The
man's name is Theodore Dreiser."

"I know him," the caller interrupted.

"Then tell him what I think of it. It's a wonder. I'm writing him
to call."

A few weeks earlier Dreiser had found a masterpiece too. He had
read *McTeague* and had been excited to learn that another novelist
was trying to present an unretouched picture of American life.
When he went to see Norris in the Doubleday office, he found that
they were almost of an age—Norris was one year older—and that
they shared the same literary convictions. There was, however, an
essential difference between them. Norris had reached the convictions by an intellectual process, largely as a result of reading Zola
and deciding that Zola's methods could be applied to American
material. Dreiser insists that he hadn't read Zola when he wrote
his first novel. He had become a Naturalist almost without premed-
itation, as a result of everything his life had been or had lacked.
Unlike Norris he couldn't choose among different theories or move
from the drably pitiful to the boisterous to the sentimental. He
wrote what he did because he had to write only that or keep silent.

It was his friend Arthur Henry who first persuaded him to write
fiction. They used to work at the same table, encouraging each
other, and they each finished five or six stories. Dreiser's stories were
accepted, not by genteel magazines like the *Century* and *Scribner's,*
but by the new ten- and fifteen-cent monthlies that were less concerned with ideality and good manners. Henry then insisted that
he write a novel. Dreiser protested that he couldn't afford the time,
that he was too busy earning a living, that no novel of his would
be published—and besides, he didn't have a plot; but still he kept
pleasantly brooding over the notion. One day in October 1899, he

found himself writing two words on a clean sheet of paper: "Sister Carrie."

"My mind was a blank except for the name," he told his first biographer, Dorothy Dudley. "I had no idea who or what she was to be." Then suddenly he pictured Carrie Meeber on the train to Chicago; it was a vision that came to him, he said, "as if out of a dream." But the dream was also a memory, for much of his own life went into the novel. In one sense Carrie was Dreiser himself, just as Flaubert once said that *he* was Mme. Bovary; the little Midwestern girl had Dreiser's mixture of passivity and ambition, as well as his romantic love for cities. More definitely she resembled one of his sisters, the one who ran off to Chicago, met a successful business man, the father of two or three grown children—like Hurstwood in the novel—and eloped with him to New York. Hurstwood's degradation after losing Carrie was another memory, connected with Dreiser's misfortunes in 1895, after he lost his job on the New York *World*. Unable to find other work, he had lived in cheap lodging houses and—before he was rescued by his brother Paul—had pictured himself as sinking toward squalor and suicide. But there was more of Dreiser in the book than simply the two chief characters: there was his obsessive fear of poverty, there was his passion for gaslight and glitter, and there was his hatred for the conventional standards by which his big family of brothers and sisters had been judged and condemned. Most of all there was his feeling for life, his wonder at the mysterious fall and rise of human fortunes.

Sister Carrie had the appearance of being a Naturalistic novel and would be used as a model for the work of later Naturalists. Yet it was, in a sense, Naturalistic by default, Naturalistic because Dreiser was writing about the life he knew best in the only style he had learned. There is a personal and compulsive quality in the novel that is not at all Naturalistic. The book is felt rather than observed from the outside, like *McTeague;* and it is based on dreams rather than documents. Where *McTeague* had been a conducted tour of the depths, *Sister Carrie* was a cry from the depths, as if McTeague had uttered it.

It was a more frightening book to genteel readers than *McTeague* had been. They were repelled not only by the cheapness of the characters but even more by the fact that the author admired them. They read that Hurstwood, for example, was the manager of "a gorgeous saloon . . . with rich screens, fancy wines and a line of bar goods unsurpassed in the country." They found him an unctuous and offensive person, yet they also found that Dreiser described him as "altogether a very acceptable individual of our great

American upper class—the first grade below the luxuriously rich."
Genteel readers didn't know whether to be more offended by the
judgment or by the language in which it was expressed; and they
felt, moreover, that Hurstwood and his creator belonged to a new
class that threatened the older American culture. Most of all they
resented Carrie Meeber. They had been taught that a woman's
virtue is her only jewel, that the wages of sin are death; yet Carrie
let herself be seduced without a struggle, yielding first to a traveling
salesman, then to Hurstwood; and instead of dying in misery she
became a famous actress. *McTeague* had offended the proprieties
while respecting moral principles; every misdeed it mentioned had
been punished in the end. *Sister Carrie,* on the other hand, was a
direct affront to the standards by which respectable Americans had
always claimed to live.

The battle over Carrie started even before the book was published. Dreiser had first given the manuscript to Henry Mills Alden,
the editor of *Harper's Magazine,* who had already bought some of
his articles. Alden said he liked the novel, but he doubted that any
publisher would take it. He turned it over to the editorial readers
for Harper and Brothers, who sent it back to the author without
comment. Next the manuscript went to Doubleday, Page and Company, where it had the good fortune to be assigned to the man who
could best appreciate what Dreiser was trying to do. "It *must* be
published," Norris kept repeating to anyone who would listen. His
enthusiasm for *Sister Carrie* won over two of the junior partners,
Henry Lanier and Walter Hines Page; and with some misgiving
they signed a contract to bring it out that fall. Then Frank Doubleday, the senior partner, came back from Europe and carried the
proof sheets home with him to read over the weekend. Mrs. Doubleday read them too, and liked them not at all, but her part in the
story is not essential. Her husband could and did form his own
opinion of *Sister Carrie.* He detested the book and wanted nothing
to do with it as a publisher.

There has been a prolonged argument over what happened afterwards, but chiefly it is an argument over words like "suppression";
most of the facts are on record. Doubleday spoke to his junior
partners, who had great respect for his business judgment, and they
summoned Dreiser to a conference. Norris managed to see him first.
"Whatever happens," he said in effect, "make them publish *Sister
Carrie*; it's your right." Dreiser then conferred with the junior
partners, who tried to persuade him to surrender his contract.
"Crushed and tragically pathetic," as Lanier remembers him, he
kept insisting that the contract be observed.

It was a binding document and it *was* observed, to the letter.
Sister Carrie was printed, if only in an edition of roughly a thousand copies. It was bound, if in cheap red cloth with dull black
lettering. It was listed in the Doubleday catalogue. It was even
submitted to the press for review, if only, in most cases, through the
intervention of Frank Norris. When orders came in for it, they
were filled. It wasn't "suppressed" or "buried away in a cellar," as
Dreiser's friends afterwards complained, but neither was it displayed
or advertised or urged on the booksellers. I think it was in the
travels of Ibn Batuta that I read the account of some Buddhist
fishermen whose religion forbade them to deprive any creature of
life, even a sardine. Instead of killing fishes they merely caught
them in nets and left them to live as best they could out of water.
That is about what happened to *Sister Carrie,* which wasn't, incidentally, the first or the last book to receive such treatment from
publishing houses that changed their collective minds. One couldn't
quite say that it was killed; it was merely deprived of light and air
and left to die.

Favorable reviews might have rescued it, but with two or three
exceptions the reviews were violently adverse and even insulting.
"The story leaves a very unpleasant impression," said the Minneapolis *Journal.* "You would never dream of recommending to another
person to read it," said the *Post-Intelligencer* in Seattle. *Life,* the
humorous weekly, was serious about Carrie and warned the girls
who might think of following in her footsteps that they would "end
their days on the Island or in the gutter." *Sister Carrie,* said the
Chicago *Tribune,* "transgresses the literary morality of the average
American novel to a point that is almost Zolaesque." The *Book
Buyer* accused Dreiser of being "the chronicler of materialism in
its basest forms. . . . But the leaven of the higher life remains,"
it added, "nowhere stronger than with us."

The book-buying public, most of which yearned for the leaven
of the higher life, had no quarrel with the reviewers. The Doubleday records show that 1,008 copies of the book were bound, that
129 were sent out for review, and that only 465 were sold. After
five years the other 423 copies, with the plates from which they had
been printed, were turned over to a firm that specialized in publisher's remainders. That was the end of the story for Doubleday,
but not for Dreiser. As soon as he could scrape together five hundred dollars, he bought the plates of his own novel. He succeeded
in having it reprinted by the B. W. Dodge Company in 1907 and
by Grosset and Dunlap in 1908. Later it would be reissued in suc-
cessively larger editions by three other publishers—in 1911 by
Harper and Brothers, the firm that had first rejected it, then in 1917

by Boni and Liveright, and in 1932 by the Modern Library—and it would also be translated into most of the European languages. For Dreiser the battle over *Sister Carrie* lasted for more than a quarter-century and ended with his triumph over the genteel critics.

Yet the first years were full of disasters, in spite of the help that Dreiser and his book received from Frank Norris. One English publisher remembered Norris as a man who was "more eager for Dreiser's *Carrie* to be read than for his own novels." Besides trying to get American reviews for the book, Norris kept writing about it to England. A London edition of *Sister Carrie* appeared in 1901 and was enthusiastically praised. "At last a really strong novel has come from America," exclaimed the *Daily Mail;* and there were echoes of the judgment in other English papers.

There was a different sort of echo in New York, a buzz of angry gossip about English critics and their fantastic notions of American fiction. Without the London edition, *Sister Carrie* might have been forgotten for years, but now it was arousing a quiet wave of condemnation among persons who had never seen a copy of the novel. Dreiser found that magazine editors were suddenly uninterested in his articles and stories, which had once been widely published; the new ones were coming back with rejection slips. One editor said, "You are a disgrace to America." The *Atlantic Monthly* wrote him that he was "morally bankrupt" and could not publish there. At the office of *Harper's Monthly* Dreiser happened to meet William Dean Howells, who had always been friendly since the day when Dreiser had interviewed him for another magazine. This time Howells was cold. "You know, I don't like *Sister Carrie,*" he said as he hurried away. It was the first occasion on which he had failed to support a new work of honest American fiction.

In 1900 Howells had surrendered to the trend of the times. The great house of Harper, which had dominated American publishing, went bankrupt in that year, and Howells feared that he had lost his principal source of income. But the firm was soon reorganized, with new capital furnished through the elder J. P. Morgan and new editors for most of its magazines. Colonel Harvey, the new president, was determined to make the house yield dividends. He had an overnight conference with Howells, asked him to continue writing for *Harper's Magazine* on a yearly salary and told him, incidentally, that the battle for realism was lost.

Howells, who had been battling for realism since 1885, sadly agreed with Colonel Harvey. Whatever fire there had been in his critical writing was also lost after 1900, though perhaps that was merely because he was growing old. He still had his style, which was better than that of any other living American writer except Mark Twain. He had his almost official position as dean of American letters, but he was no longer the friend and patron of young writers in revolt.

The failure of *Sister Carrie* in its first edition was part of a general disaster that involved the whole literary movement of the 1890's. One after another the leaders of the movement had died young or else had surrendered to genteel conservatism. The first of them to go was the novelist H. H. Boyesen, a pioneer of social realism and once a famous figure, although his name is seldom mentioned now except in literature courses; Boyesen died in 1895. Next to go, in 1898, was Harold Frederic, the peppery rebel from upstate New York, who, in *The Damnation of Theron Ware,* had written the first American novel that questioned the virtue of the Protestant clergy. Stephen Crane, the one genius of the group, died in 1900, the victim of consumption, malaria, hard work, and hard living.

The dramatist James A. Herne had tried and failed to be the American Ibsen; but at least he had written the immensely popular *Shore Acres* and other plays that introduced daily American life to the American stage. He died in 1901, worn out and discouraged after the presidential campaign of the preceding year, in which he had fought for Bryan and against the annexation of the Philippines. Then Norris died in the autumn of 1902, at the beginning, so it seemed, of a grandly successful career; but he had already given signs, in *The Pit,* of abandoning his Naturalistic doctrines.

All these, except Herne, were comparatively young men and there were very few left to carry on the literary movement they had started. Hamlin Garland, after fulminating against the conservatives in art and politics, had gone over to the enemy by easy stages. Editors had taken him out to dinner and convinced him that his passion for reform was weakening his novels as works of art. Unfortunately Garland was no artist; when he lost his crusading passion he lost everything. Henry B. Fuller, the Chicago realist, remained faithful to his own standards; but his novels hadn't sold and he wrote very little for a dozen years after 1900. It was not only the rebel authors, almost all of them, who had died or fallen silent or surrendered. The little magazines that flourished in New York, Chicago, and San Francisco during the 1890's had also disappeared and the new publishing houses had become conventional or had gone out of business. Serious writing on American themes declined into a sort of subterranean existence. Speaking generally, the best

American books of the following decade would either be privately printed, like *The Education of Henry Adams,* or else they would be written in Europe.

Meanwhile Dreiser himself had narrowly escaped the fate of his brothers in arms. After *Sister Carrie* was accepted, he had begun working simultaneously on two other novels, in a frenzy of production, but slowly he had been overcome by the feeling that he was unwanted and a failure. He had destroyed one of his two manuscripts, put the other aside, sent his wife to her family in Missouri, and retired to a furnished room in Brooklyn, where he sat day after day brooding over the aimlessness of life and trying to gather enough courage to commit suicide. This time again he was rescued by his brother Paul, who gave him new clothes and sent him to a sanitarium. After his recovery he became a magazine editor and climbed rapidly in his profession, until, as head of the Butterick publications, he was earning twenty-five thousand dollars a year. It was a long time, however, before he felt strength enough in himself to write another novel.

The story of *Sister Carrie* had a curious sequel. Imperceptibly the standards of the American public had been changing in the years after 1900 and Dreiser himself had been gaining a sort of underground reputation based on his one book. When his second novel, *Jennie Gerhardt,* appeared in 1911 it was a critical and even to some extent a popular success. The struggle for Naturalism came into the open again. Dreiser had new allies in the younger writers, and by 1920 they had ceased to be rebels; instead they were the dominant faction. It was a long and finally a triumphant chapter in the history of American letters that began with the lost battle over *Sister Carrie.*

The Barbaric Naturalism of Mr. Dreiser

by Stuart P. Sherman

The layman who listens reverently to the reviewers discussing the new novels and to the novelists discussing themselves can hardly escape persuasion that a great change has rather recently taken place in the spirit of the age, in the literature which reflects it, and in the criticism which judges it. The nature of the supposed revolution may be briefly summarized.

The elder generation was in love with illusions, and looked at truth through a glass darkly and timorously. The artist, tongue-tied by authority and trammelled by aesthetic and moral conventions, selected, suppressed, and rearranged the data of experience and observation. The critic, "morally subsidized," regularly professed his disdain for a work of art in which no light glimmered above "the good and the beautiful."

The present age is fearless and is freeing itself from illusions. Now, for the first time in history, men are facing unabashed the facts of life. "Death or life," we cry, "give us only reality!" Now, for the first time in the history of English literature, fiction is become a flawless mirror held up to the living world. Rejecting nothing, altering nothing, it presents to us—let us take our terms from the bright lexicon of the reviewer—a "transcript," a "cross-section," a "slice," a "photographic" or "cinematographic" reproduction of life. The critic who keeps pace with the movement no longer asks whether the artist has created beauty or glorified goodness, but merely whether he has told the truth.

Mr. Dreiser, in his latest novel, describes a canvas by a painter of this austere modern school: "Raw reds, raw greens, dirty gray paving stones—such faces! Why, this thing fairly shouted its facts. It seemed to say: 'I'm dirty, I am commonplace, I am grim, I am shabby, but I am life.' And there was no apologizing for anything in it, no glossing anything over. Bang! Smash! Crack! came the facts one after another, with a bitter, brutal insistence on their so-ness." If you do not like what is in the picture, you are to be crushed by

"The Barbaric Naturalism of Mr. Dreiser" by Stuart P. Sherman. From *The Nation*, 101 (December 2, 1915): 648–50.

the retort that perhaps you do not like what is in life. Perhaps
you have not the courage to confront reality. Perhaps you had
better read the chromatic fairy-tales with the children. Men of
sterner stuff exclaim, like the critic in this novel, "Thank God for
a realist!"

Mr. Dreiser is a novelist of the new school, for whom we have
been invited off and on these fourteen years to thank God—a form
of speech, by the way, which crept into the language before the
dawn of modern realism. He has performed with paint. He has
presented the facts of life "one after another with a bitter, brutal
insistence on their so-ness," which marks him as a "man of the
hour," a "portent"—the successor of Mr. Howells and Mr. James.
In the case of a realist, biographical details are always relevant.
Mr. Dreiser was born of German-American parents in Terre
Haute, Indiana, in 1871. He was educated in the Indiana public
schools and at the State University. He was engaged in newspaper
work in Chicago, St. Louis, New York, and elsewhere, from 1892
to 1910. He has laid reality bare for us in five novels published as
follows: "Sister Carrie," 1901; "Jennie Gerhardt," 1911; "The
Financier," 1912; "The Titan," 1914; and "The 'Genius,'" 1915.
These five works constitute a singularly homogeneous mass of fiction. I do not find any moral value in them, nor any memorable
beauty—of their truth I shall speak later; but I am greatly impressed by them as serious representatives of a new note in American literature, coming from that "ethnic" element of our mixed
population which, as we are assured by competent authorities, is to
redeem us from Puritanism and insure our artistic salvation. They
abundantly illustrate, furthermore, the methods and intentions of
our recent courageous, veracious realism. Before we thank God for
it, let us consider a little more closely what is offered us.

I

The first step towards the definition of Mr. Dreiser's special contribution is to blow away the dust with which the exponents of the
new realism seek to becloud the perceptions of our "reverent layman." In their main pretensions, there are large elements of conscious and unconscious sham.

It should clear the air to say that courage in facing and veracity
in reporting the facts of life are no more characteristic of Theodore
Dreiser than of John Bunyan. These moral traits are not the
peculiar marks of the new school; they are marks common to every
great movement of literature within the memory of man. Each
literary generation detaching itself from its predecessor—whether it

has called its own movement Classical or Romantic or what not—has revolted in the interest of what it took to be a more adequate representation of reality. No one who is not drunken with the egotism of the hour, no one who has penetrated with sober senses into the spirit of any historical period anterior to his own, will fall into the indecency of declaring his own age preëminent in the desire to see and to tell the truth. The real distinction between one generation and another is in the thing which each takes for its master truth—in the thing which each recognizes as the essential reality for it. The difference between Bunyan and Dreiser is in the order of facts which each reports.

It seems necessary also to declare at periodic intervals that there is no such thing as a "cross-section" or "slice" or "photograph" of life in art—least of all in the realistic novel. The use of these catchwords is but a clever hypnotizing pass of the artist, employed to win the assent of the reader to the reality of the show, and, in some cases, to evade moral responsibility for any questionable features of the exhibition. A realistic novel no more than any other kind of a novel can escape being a composition involving preconception, imagination, and divination. Yet, hearing one of our new realists expound his doctrine, you might suppose that writing a novel was a process analogous to photographing wild animals in their habitat by trap and flashlight. He, if you will believe him, does not invite his subjects, nor group them, nor compose their features, nor furnish their setting. He but exposes the sensitized plate of his mind. The pomp of life goes by, and springs the trap. The picture, of course, does not teach nor preach nor moralize. It simply re-presents. The only serious objection to this figurative explanation of the artistic process is the utter dissimilarity between the blank impartial photographic plate, commemorating everything that confronts it, and the crowded inveterately selective human mind, which, like a magnet, snatches the facts of life that are subject to its influence out of their casual order and redisposes them in a pattern of its own.

In the case of any specified novelist, the facts chosen and the pattern assumed by them are determined by his central theory or "philosophy of life"; and this is precisely criticism's justification for inquiring into the adequacy of any novelist's general ideas. In vain, the new realist throws up his hands with protestations of innocence, and cries: "Search me. I carry no concealed weapons. I run life into no preconceived mould. I have no philosophy. My business is only to observe, like a man of science, and to record what I have seen." He cannot observe without a theory, nor record his observations without betraying it to any critical eye.

As it happens, the man of science who most profoundly influenced the development of the new realistic novel—Charles Darwin—more candid than the writers of "scientific" fiction—frankly declared that he could not observe without a theory. When he had tentatively formulated a general law, and had begun definitely to look for evidence of its operation, then first the substantiating facts leaped abundantly into his vision. His "Origin of Species" has the unity of a work of art, because the recorded observations support a thesis. The French novelists who in the last century developed the novel of contemporary life learned as much, perhaps, from Darwin's art as from his science. Balzac emphasized the relation between man and his social *milieu;* the Goncourts emphasized the importance of extensive collection of "human documents"; Zola emphasized the value of scientific hypotheses. He deliberately adopted the materialistic philosophy of the period as his guide in observation and as his unifying principle in composition. His theory of the causes of social phenomena, which was derived largely from medical treatises, operated like a powerful magnet among the chaotic facts of life, rejecting some, selecting others, and re-disposing them in the pattern of the *roman naturaliste.* Judicious French critics said: "My dear man," or words to that effect, "your representations of life are inadequate. This which you are offering us with so earnest an air is not reality. It is your own private nightmare." When they had exposed his theory, they had condemned his art.

Let us, then, dismiss Mr. Dreiser's untenable claims to superior courage and veracity of intention, the photographic transcript, and the unbiassed service of truth; and let us seek for his definition in his general theory of life, in the order of facts which he records, and in the pattern of his representations.

II

The impressive unity of effect produced by Mr. Dreiser's five novels is due to the fact that they are all illustrations of a crude and naïvely simple naturalistic philosophy, such as we find in the mouths of exponents of the new *Real-Politik.* Each book, with its bewildering masses of detail, is a ferocious argument in behalf of a few brutal generalizations. To the eye cleared of illusions it appears that the ordered life which we call civilization does not really exist except on paper. In reality our so-called society is a jungle in which the struggle for existence continues, and must continue, on terms substantially unaltered by legal, moral, or social conventions. The central truth about man is that he is an animal amenable to no law but the law of his own temperament, doing as he desires, subject only to the limitations of his power. The male of the species is characterized by cupidity, pugnacity, and a simian inclination for the other sex. The female is a soft, vain, pleasure-seeking creature, devoted to personal adornment, and quite helplessly susceptible to the flattery of the male. In the struggles which arise in the jungle through the conflicting appetites of its denizens, the victory goes to the animal most physically fit and mentally ruthless, unless the weaklings, resisting absorption, combine against him and crush him by sheer force of numbers.

The idea that civilization is a sham Mr. Dreiser sometimes sets forth explicitly, and sometimes he conveys it by the process known among journalists as "coloring the news." When Sister Carrie yields to the seductive drummer, Drouet, Mr. Dreiser judicially weighs the advantages and disadvantages attendant on the condition of being a well-kept mistress. When the institution of marriage is brushed aside by the heroine of "The Financier," he comments "editorially" as follows: "Before Christianity was man, and after it will also be. A metaphysical idealism will always tell him that it is better to preserve a cleanly balance, and the storms of circumstance will teach him a noble stoicism. Beyond this there is nothing which can reasonably be imposed upon the conscience of man." A little later in the same book he says: "Is there no law outside of the subtle will and the power to achieve? If not, it is surely high time that we knew it—one and all. We might then agree to do as we do; but there would be no silly illusion as to divine regulation." His own answer to the question, his own valuation of regulation, both divine and human, may be found in the innumerable contemptuous epithets which fall from his pen whenever he has occasion to mention any power set up against the urge of instinct and the indefinite expansion of desire. Righteousness is always "legal"; conventions are always "current"; routine is always "dull"; respectability is always "unctuous"; an institution for transforming schoolgirls into young ladies is presided over by "owl-like conventionalists"; families in which parents are faithful to each other lead an "apple-pie order of existence"; a man who yields to his impulses yet condemns himself for yielding is a "rag-bag moralistic ass." Jennie Gerhardt, by a facile surrender of her chastity, shows that *she could not be readily corrupted by the world's selfish lessons* on how to preserve oneself from the evil to come." Surely, this is "coloring the news."

By similar devices Mr. Dreiser drives home the great truth that man is essentially an animal, impelled by temperament, instinct, physics, chemistry—anything you please that is irrational and un-

controllable. Sometimes he writes an "editorial" paragraph in
which the laws of human life are explained by references to the
behavior of certain protozoa or by reference to a squid and a lobster fighting in an aquarium. His heroes and heroines have "cat-like
eyes," "feline grace," "sinuous strides," eyes and jaws which vary
"from those of the tiger, lynx, and bear to those of the fox, the
tolerant mastiff, and the surly bulldog." One hero and his mistress
are said to "have run together temperamentally like two leopards."
The lady in question, admiring the large rapacity of her mate,
exclaims playfully: "Oh, you big tiger! You great, big lion! Boo!"
Courtship as presented in these novels is after the manner of beasts in
the jungle. Mr. Dreiser's leonine men but circle once or twice
about their prey, and spring, and pounce; and the struggle is over.
A pure-minded serving-maid, who is suddenly held up in the hall
by a "hairy, axiomatic" guest and "masterfully" kissed upon the
lips, may for an instant be "horrified, stunned, *like a bird in the
grasp of a cat.*" But we are always assured that "through it all
something tremendously vital and insistent" will be speaking to
her, and that in the end she will not resist the urge of the *élan
vital.* I recall no one of all the dozens of obliging women in these
books who makes any effective resistance when summoned to capit-
ulate. *"The psychology of the human animal,* when confronted by
these tangles, these ripping tides of the heart," says the author of
"The Titan," "has little to do with so-called reason or logic." No;
as he informs us elsewhere with endless iteration, it is a question
of chemistry. It is the "chemistry of her being" which rouses to
blazing the ordinarily dormant forces of Eugene Witla's sympathies
in "The 'Genius.'" If Stephanie Platow is disloyal to her married
lover in "The Titan," "let no one quarrel" with her. Reason: "She
was an unstable chemical compound."

Such is the Dreiserian philosophy.

III

By thus eliminating distinctively human motives and making animal instincts the supreme factors in human life, Mr. Dreiser reduces the problem of the novelist to the lowest possible terms. I
find myself unable to go with those who admire the powerful reality of his art while deploring the puerility of his philosophy. His
philosophy quite excludes him from the field in which a great realist must work. He has deliberately rejected the novelist's supreme
task—understanding and presenting the development of character; he has chosen only to illustrate the unrestricted flow of tem-

perament. He has evaded the enterprise of representing human conduct; he has confined himself to a representation of animal behavior. He demands for the demonstration of his theory a moral vacuum from which the obligations of parenthood, marriage, chivalry, and citizenship have been quite withdrawn or locked in a twilight sleep. At each critical moment in his narrative, where a realist like George Eliot or Thackeray or Trollope or Meredith would be asking how a given individual would feel, think, and act under the manifold combined stresses of organized society, Mr. Dreiser sinks supinely back upon the law of the jungle or mutters his mystical gibberish about an alteration of the chemical formula.

The possibility of making the unvarying victoriousness of jungle-motive plausible depends directly upon the suppression of the evidence of other motives. In this work of suppression Mr. Dreiser simplifies American life almost beyond recognition. Whether it is because he comes from Indiana, or whether it is because he steadily envisages the human animal, I cannot say; I can only note that he never speaks of his men and women as "educated" or "brought up." Whatever their social status, they are invariably "raised." Raising human stock in America evidently includes feeding and clothing it, but does not include the inculcation of even the most elementary moral ideas. Hence Mr. Dreiser's field seems curiously outside American society. Yet he repeatedly informs us that his persons are typical of the American middle class, and three of the leading figures to judge from their names—Carrie Meeber, Jennie Gerhardt, and Eugene Witla—are of our most highly "cultured" race. Frank Cowperwood, the hero of two novels, is a hawk of finance and a rake almost from the cradle; but of the powers which presided over his cradle we know nothing save that his father was a competent official in a Philadelphia bank. What, if anything, Carrie Meeber's typical American parents taught her about the conduct of life is suppressed; for we meet the girl in a train to Chicago, on which she falls to the first drummer who accosts her. Eugene Witla emerges in his teens from the bosom of a typical middle-class American family—with a knowledge of the game called "post office," takes the train for Chicago, and without hesitation enters upon his long career of seduction. Jennie Gerhardt, of course, succumbs to the first man who puts his arm around her; but, in certain respects, her case is exceptional.

In the novel "Jennie Gerhardt" Mr. Dreiser ventures a disastrous experiment at making the jungle-motive plausible without suppressing the evidence of other motives. He provides the girl with pious Lutheran parents, of fallen fortune, but alleged to be of sterling character, who "raise" her with the utmost strictness. He

even admits that the family were church-goers, and he outlines the
doctrine preached by Pastor Wundt: right conduct in marriage and
absolute innocence before that state, essentials of Christian living;
no salvation for a daughter who failed to keep her chastity un-
stained or for the parents who permitted her to fall; Hell yawning
for all such; God angry with sinners every day. "Gerhardt and
his wife, and also Jennie," says Mr. Dreiser, "accepted the doctrines
of their church without reserve." Twenty pages later Jennie is
represented as yielding her virtue in pure gratitude to a man of
fifty, Senator Brander, who has let her do his laundry and in other
ways has been kind to her and to her family. The Senator suddenly
dies; Jennie expects to become a mother; Father Gerhardt is bro-
kenhearted, and the family moves from Columbus to Cleveland.
This first episode is not incredibly presented as a momentary triumph of emotional impulse over training—as an "accident." The incredible appears when Mr. Dreiser insists that an accident of this
sort to a girl brought up *under the conditions stated* is not necessarily followed by any sense of sin or shame or regret. Upon this
simple pious Lutheran he imposes his own naturalistic philosophy,
and, in analyzing her psychology before the birth of her illegitimate child, pretends that she looks forward to the event "without
a murmur," with "serene, unfaltering courage," "the marvel of life
holding her in trance," with "joy and satisfaction," seeing in her
state "the immense possibilities of racial fulfillment." This jug-
gling is probably expected to prepare us for her instantaneous
assent, perhaps a year later, when a healthy, magnetic manufacturer, who has seen her perhaps a dozen times, claps his paw upon
her and says, "You belong to me," and in a perfectly cold-blooded
interview proposes the terms on which he will set her up in New
York as his mistress. Jennie, who is a fond mother and a dutiful
daughter, goes to her pious Lutheran mother and talks the whole
matter over with her quite candidly. The mother hesitates—not
on Jennie's account, gentle reader, but because she will be obliged
to deceive old Gerhardt; "the difficulty of telling this lie was very
great for Mrs. Gerhardt"! But she acquiesces at last. "I'll help you
out with it," she concludes—"with a little sigh." The unreality of
the whole transaction shrieks.

Mr. Dreiser's stubborn insistence upon the jungle-motive results
in a dreary monotony in the form and substance of his novels. Interested only in the description of animal behavior, he constructs
his plot in such a way as to exhibit the persistence of two or three
elementary instincts through every kind of situation. He finds, for
example, a subject in the career of an American captain of industry, thinly disguised under the name of Frank Cowperwood. He has

just two things to tell us about Cowperwood: that he has a rapacious appetite for money, and that he has a rapacious appetite for women. In "The Financier" he "documents" those two truths about Cowperwood in seventy-four chapters, in each one of which he shows us how this hero made money or how he captivated women in Philadelphia. Not satisfied with the demonstration, he returns to the same theses in "The Titan," and shows us in sixty-two chapters how the same hero made money and captivated women in Chicago and New York. He promises us a third volume, in which we shall no doubt learn in a work of sixty or seventy chapters—a sort of huge club-sandwich composed of slices of business alternating with erotic episodes—how Frank Cowperwood made money and captivated women in London. Meanwhile Mr. Dreiser has turned aside from his great "trilogy of desire" to give us "The 'Genius,'" in which the hero, Witla, alleged to be a great realistic painter, exhibits in 101 chapters, similarly "sandwiched" together, an appetite for women and money indistinguishable from that of Cowperwood. Read one of these novels, and you have read them all. What the hero is in the first chapter, he remains in the hundred-and-first or the hundred-and-thirty-sixth. He acquires naught from his experience but sensations. In the sum of his experiences there is nothing of the impressive mass and coherence of activities bound together by principles and integrated in character, for all his days have been but as isolated beads loosely strung on the thread of his desire. And so after the production of the hundredth document in the case of Frank Cowperwood, one is ready to cry with fatigue: "Hold! Enough! We believe you. Yes, it is very clear that Frank Cowperwood had a rapacious appetite for women and for money."

If at this point you stop and inquire why Mr. Dreiser goes to such great lengths to establish so little, you find yourself once more confronting the jungle-motive. Mr. Dreiser, with a problem similar to De Foe's in "The Apparition of Mrs. Veal," has availed himself of De Foe's method for creating the illusion of reality. The essence of the problem and of the method for both these authors is the certification of the unreal by the irrelevant. If you wish to make acceptable to your reader the incredible notion that Mrs. Veal's ghost appeared to Mrs. Bargrave, divert his incredulity from the precise point at issue by telling him all sorts of detailed credible things about the poverty of Mrs. Veal's early life, the sobriety of her brother, her father's neglect, and the bad temper of Mrs. Bargrave's husband. If you wish to make acceptable to your reader the incredible notion that Aileen Butler's first breach of the seventh article in the decalogue was "a happy event," taking place "much as a marriage might have," divert his incredulity by describ-

ing with the technical accuracy of a fashion magazine not merely
the gown that she wore on the night of Cowperwood's reception,
but also with equal detail the half-dozen other gowns that she
thought she might wear, but did not. If you have been for three
years editor-in-chief of the Butterick Publications, you can probably perform this feat with unimpeachable versimilitude; and
having acquired credit for expert knowledge in matters of dress and
millinery, you can now and then emit unchallenged a bit of philosophy such as "Life cannot be put in any one mould, and the
attempt may as well be abandoned at once. . . . Besides, whether
we will or no, theory or no theory, the large basic facts of chemistry and physics remain." None the less, if you expect to gain
credence for the notion that your hero can have any woman in
Chicago or New York that he puts his paw upon, you had probably better lead up to it by a detailed account of the street-railway
system in those cities. It will necessitate the loading of your pages
with a tremendous baggage of irrelevant detail. It will not sound
much like art. It will sound more like one of Lincoln Steffens's special articles. But it will produce an overwhelming impression of
reality, which the reader will carry with him into the next chapter where you are laying bare the "chemistry" of the human animal.

IV

It would make for clearness in our discussions of contemporary
fiction if we withheld the title of "realist" from a writer like Mr.
Dreiser, and called him, as Zola called himself, a "naturalist."
While asserting that all great art in every period intends a
representation of reality, I have tried to indicate the basis for a
working distinction between the realistic novel and the naturalistic
novel of the present day. Both are representations of the life of man
in contemporary or nearly contemporary society, and both are presumably composed of materials within the experience and observation of the author. But a realistic novel is a representation based
upon a theory of human conduct. If the theory of human conduct
is adequate, the representation constitutes an addition to literature
and to social history. A naturalistic novel is a representation based
upon a theory of animal behavior. Since a theory of animal behavior can never be an adequate basis for a representation of the
life of man in contemporary society, such a representation is an
artistic blunder. When half the world attempts to assert such a
theory, the other half rises in battle. And so one turns with relief
from Mr. Dreiser's novels to the morning papers.

The Dreiser Bugaboo

by H. L. Mencken

Dr. William Lyon Phelps, the Lampson professor of English at Yale, opens his chapter on Mark Twain in his "Essays on Modern Novelists" with a humorous account of the critical imbecility which pursued Mark in his own country down to his last years. The favorite national critics of that era (and it extended to 1895, at the least) were wholly anaesthetic to the fact that he was a great artist. They admitted him, somewhat grudgingly, a certain low dexterity as a clown, but that he was an imaginative writer of the first rank, or even of the fifth rank, was something that, in their insanest moments, never so much as occurred to them. Phelps cites, in particular, an ass named Professor Richardson, whose "American Literature," it appears, "is still a standard work" and "a deservedly high authority"—apparently in colleges. In the 1892 edition of this *magnum opus*, Mark is dismissed with less than four lines, and ranked below Irving, Holmes and Lowell—nay, actually below Artemus Ward, Josh Billings and Petroleum V. Nasby! The thing is fabulous, fantastic—but nevertheless true. Lacking the "higher artistic or moral purpose of the greater humorists" (*exempli gratia*, Rabelais, Molière, Aristophanes!), Mark is put off by this Prof. Balderdash as a laborious buffoon . . . But stay! Do not laugh yet! Phelps himself, indignant at the stupidity now proceeds to prove that Mark was really a great moralist, and more, a great optimist . . . Turn to "The Mysterious Stranger" and "What Is Man?"! . . .

College professors, alas, never learn anything. The identical pedagogue who achieved this nonsense about old Mark in 1910 now seeks to dispose of Theodore Dreiser in the precise manner of Richardson. That is to say, he essays to finish him by putting him into Coventry, by loftily passing him over. "Do not speak of him," said Kingsley of Heine; "he was a wicked man." Search the latest volume of the Phelps revelation, "The Advance of the Eng-

"The Dreiser Bugaboo" by H. L. Mencken. From *The Seven Arts*, 2 (August 1917): 507-17. Copyright 1917 by *The Seven Arts*. Reprinted 1964 by AMS Press. Reprinted by permission of the publisher.

lish Novel," and you will find that Dreiser is not once mentioned
in it. The late O. Henry is hailed as a genius who will have "abiding
fame"; Henry Sydnor Harrison is hymned as "more than a clever
novelist," nay, "a valuable ally of the angels" (the right-thinker
complex! art as a form of snuffling!), and an obscure Pagliaccio
named Charles D. Stewart is brought forward as "the American
novelist most worthy to fill the particular vacancy caused by the
death of Mark Twain"—but Dreiser is not even listed in the index.
And where Phelps leads with his baton of birch most of the other
drovers of rah-rah boys follow. I turn, for example, to "An Introduction to American Literature," by Henry S. Pancoast, A.M.,
L.H.D., dated 1912. There are kind words for Richard Harding
Davis, for Amelie Rives, and even for Will N. Harben, but not a
syllable for Dreiser. Again there is "A History of American Literature," by Reuben Post Halleck, A.M., LL.D., dated 1911. Lew
Wallace, Marietta Holley, Owen Wister and Augusta Evans Wilson
have their hearings, but not Dreiser. Yet again, there is "A History
of American Literature Since 1870," by Prof. Fred. Lewis Pattee, instructor in "the English language and literature" somewhere in
Pennsylvania. Fred has praises for Marion Crawford, Margaret
Deland and F. Hopkinson Smith, and polite bows for Richard
Harding Davis and Robert W. Chambers, but from end to end of
his fat tome I am unable to find the slightest mention of Dreiser.

So much for one group of heroes of the new Dunciad. That it
includes most of the acknowledged heavyweights of the craft—the
Babbitts, Mores, Brownells and so on—goes without saying; as Van
Wyck Brooks has pointed out in *The Seven Arts,* these magnificoes
are austerely above any consideration of the literature that is in
being. The other group, more courageous and more honest, proceeds by direct attack; Dreiser is to be disposed of by a moral *at-
tentat.* Its leaders are two more professors, Stuart P. Sherman and
H. W. Boynton, and in its ranks march the lady critics of the
newspapers with much shrill, falsetto clamor. Sherman is the only
one of them who shows any intelligible reasoning. Boynton, as always, is a mere parroter of conventional phrases, and the objec-
tions of the ladies fade imperceptibly into a pious indignation
which is indistinguishable from that of the professional suppres-
sors of vice.

What, then, is Sherman's complaint? In brief, that Dreiser is a
liar when he calls himself a realist; that he is actually a naturalist,
and hence accursed. That "he has evaded the enterprise of representing human conduct, and confined himself to a representation
of animal behavior." That he "imposes his own naturalistic philosophy" upon his characters, making them do what they ought not

to do, and think what they ought not to think. That he "has just two things to tell us about Frank Cowperwood: that he has a rapacious appetite for money, and a rapacious appetite for women." That this alleged "theory of animal behavior" is not only incorrect, but immoral, and that "when one half the world attempts to assert it, the other half rises in battle." [*The Nation,* Dec. 2, 1915.]

Only a glance is needed to show the vacuity of all this irate flubdub. Dreiser, in point of fact, is scarcely more the realist or the naturalist, in any true sense, than H. G. Wells or the later George Moore, nor has he ever announced himself in either the one character or the other—if there be, in fact, any difference between them that anyone save a pigeon-holing pedagogue can discern. He is really something quite different, and, in his moments, something far more stately. His aim is not merely to record, but to translate and understand; the thing he exposes is not the empty event and act, but the endless mystery out of which it springs; his pictures have a passionate compassion in them that it is hard to separate from poetry. If this sense of the universal and inexplicable tragedy, if this vision of life as a seeking without a finding, if this adept summoning up of moving images, is mistaken by college professors for the empty, meticulous nastiness of Zola in "Pot-Bouille"—in Nietzsche's phrase, for "the delight to stink"—then surely the folly of college professors, as vast as it seems, has been underestimated. What is the fact? The fact is that Dreiser's attitude of mind, his manner of reaction to the phenomena he represents, the whole of his alleged "naturalistic philosophy," stem directly, not from Zola, Flaubert, Augier and the younger Dumas, but from the Greeks. In the midst of democratic cocksureness and Christian sentimentalism, of doctrinaire shallowness and professorial smugness, he stands for a point of view which at least has something honest and courageous about it; here, at all events, he is a realist. Let him put a motto to his books, and it might be:

O ye deathward-going tribes of men!
What do your lives mean except that they go to nothingness?

If you protest against that as too harsh for Christians and college professors, right-thinkers and forward-lookers, then you protest against "Oedipus Rex."

As for the animal behavior prattle of the learned headmaster, it reveals on the one hand only the academic fondness for seizing upon high-sounding but empty phrases and using them to alarm the populace, and on the other hand, only the academic incapacity for observing facts correctly and reporting them honestly. The truth is, of course, that the behavior of such men as Cowperwood and Eugene Witla and of such women as Carrie Meeber and Jennie Gerhardt, as Dreiser describes it, is no more merely animal than the behavior of such acknowledged and undoubted human beings as Dr. Woodrow Wilson and Dr. Jane Addams. The whole point of the story of Witla, to take the example which seems to concern the horrified watchmen most, is this: that this life is a bitter conflict between the animal in him and the aspiring soul, between the flesh and the spirit, between what is weak in him and what is strong, between what is base and what is noble. Moreover, the good, in the end, gets its hooks into the bad: as we part from Witla he is actually bathed in the tears of remorse, and resolved to be a correct and godfearing man. And what have we in "The Financier" and "The Titan"? A conflict, in the ego of Cowperwood, between aspiration and ambition, between the passion for beauty and the passion for power. Is either passion animal? To ask the question is to answer it.

I single out Dr. Sherman, not because his pompous syllogisms have any plausibility in fact or logic, but simply because he may well stand as archetype of the booming, indignant corrupter of criteria, the moralist turned critic. A glance at his paean to Arnold Bennett [New York *Evening Post,* Dec. 31, 1915] at once reveals the true gravamen of his objection to Dreiser. What offends him is not actually Dreiser's shortcomings as an artist, but Dreiser's shortcomings as a Christian and an American. In Bennett's volumes of pseudo-philosophy—e.g., "The Plain Man and His Wife" and "The Feast of St. Friend"—he finds the intellectual victuals that are to his taste. Here we have a sweet commingling of virtuous conformity and complacent optimism, of sonorous platitude and easy certainty—here, in brief, we have the philosophy of the English middle classes—and here, by the same token we have the sort of guff that the half-educated of our own country can understand. It is the calm, superior numskullery that was Victorian; it is by Samuel Smiles out of Hannah More. The offense of Dreiser is that he has disdained this revelation and gone back to the Greeks. Lo, he reads poetry into "the appetite for women"—he rejects the Pauline doctrine that all love is below the diaphragm! He thinks of Ulysses, not as a mere heretic and criminal, but as a great artist. He sees the life of man, not as a simple theorem in Calvinism, but as a vast adventure, an enchantment, a mystery. It is no wonder that respectable schoolteachers are against him. . . .

The Comstockian attack upon "The 'Genius' " seems to have sprung out of the same muddled sense of Dreiser's essential hostility to all that is safe and regular—of the danger in him to that mellowed Methodism which has become the national ethic. The book, in a way, was a direct challenge, for though it came to an end upon a note which even a Methodist might hear as sweet, there were provocations in detail. Dreiser, in fact, allowed his scorn to make off with his taste—and *es ist nichts fürchtlicher als Einbildungskraft ohne Geschmack.* The Comstocks arose to the bait a bit slowly, but none the less surely. Going through the volume with the terrible industry of a Sunday-school boy dredging up pearls of smut from the Old Testament, they achieved a list of no less than 89 alleged floutings of the code—75 described as lewd and 14 as profane. An inspection of these specifications affords mirth of a rare and lofty variety; nothing could more cruelly expose the inner chambers of the moral mind. When young Witla, fastening his best girl's skate, is so overcome by the carnality of youth that he hugs her, it is set down as lewd. On page 51, having become an art student, he is fired by "a great warm-tinted nude of Bouguereau"— lewd again. On page 70 he begins to draw from the figure, and his instructor cautions him that the female breast is round, not square —more lewdness. On page 151 he kisses his girl on mouth and neck and she cautions him: "Be careful! Momma may come in"—still more. On page 161, having got rid of mamma, she yields "herself to him gladly, joyously" and he is greatly shocked when she argues that an artist (she is by way of being a singer) had better not marry —lewdness double damned. On page 245 he and his bride, being ignorant, neglect the principles laid down by Dr. Sylvanus Stall in his great works on sex hygiene—lewdness most horrible! But there is no need to proceed further. Every kiss, hug and tickle of the chin in the chronicle is laboriously snouted out, empanelled, exhibited. Every hint that Witla is no vestal, that he indulges his unchristian fleshliness, that he burns in the manner of I Corinthians, VII, 9, is uncovered to the moral inquisition.

On the side of profanity there is a less ardent pursuit of evidence, chiefly, I daresay, because their unearthing is less stimulating. (Besides, there is no law prohibiting profanity in books: the whole inquiry here is but so much *lagniappe.*) On page 408, describing a character called Daniel C. Summerfield, Dreiser says that the fellow is "very much given to swearing, more as a matter of habit than of foul intention," and then goes on to explain somewhat lamely that "no picture of him would be complete without the interpolation of his various expressions." They turn out to be *God Damn* and *Jesus Christ*—three of the latter and five or six of the former. All go down; the pure in heart must be shielded from the knowledge of them. (But what of the immoral French? They call the English *Goddams.*) Also, three plain *damns,* eight *hells,* one *my God,* five *by Gods,* one *go to the devil,* one *God Almighty* and one plain

God. Altogether, 31 specimens are listed. "The 'Genius'" runs to 350,000 words. The profanity thus works out to somewhat less than one word in 10,000. . . . Alas, the Comstockian proboscis, feeling for such offendings, is not as alert as when uncovering more savoury delicacies. On page 191 I find an overlooked *by God.* On page 372 there are *Oh, God, God curses her,* and *God strike her dead.* On page 373 there are *Ah, God, Oh, God,* and three other invocations of God. On page 617 there is *God help me.* On page 720 there is *as God is my judge.* On page 723 there is *I'm no damned good.* . . . But I begin to blush.

When the Comstock Society began proceedings against "The 'Genius'," a group of English novelists, including Arnold Bennett, H. G. Wells, W. L. George and Hugh Walpole, cabled an indignant caveat. This bestirred the Authors' League of America to activity, and its executive committee issued a minute denouncing the business. Later a protest of American *literati* was circulated, and more than 400 signed, including such highly respectable authors as Winston Churchill, Percy Mackaye, Booth Tarkington and James Lane Allen, and such critics as Lawrence Gilman, Clayton Hamilton and James Huneker, and the editors of such journals as the *Century,* the *Atlantic Monthly* and the *New Republic.* Among my literary lumber is all the correspondence relating to this protest, not forgetting the letters of those who refused to sign, and some day I hope to publish it, that posterity may not lose the joy of an extremely diverting episode. Meanwhile, the case moves with stately dignity through the interminable corridors of jurisprudence, and the bulk of the briefs and exhibits that it throws off begins to rival the staggering bulk of "The 'Genius'" itself.

In all this, of course, there is a certain savoury grotesquerie; the exposure of the Puritan mind makes life, for the moment, more agreeable. The danger of the combined comstockian professorial attack, to Dreiser as artist, is not that it will make a *muss*-Presbyterian of him, but that it will convert him into a professional revolutionary, spouting stale perunas for all the sorrows of the world. Here Greenwich Village pulls as Chautauqua pushes; already, indeed, the passionate skepticism that was his original philosophy begins to show signs of being contaminated by various so-called "radical" purposes. The danger is not one to be sniffed in. Dreiser, after all, is an American like the rest of us, and to be an American is to be burdened by an ethical prepossession, to lean toward causes and remedies. Go through "The 'Genius'" or "A Hoosier Holiday" carefully, and you will find disquieting indications of what might be called a democratic trend in thinking—that is, a trend toward short cuts, easy answers, glittering theories. He is bemused, off and on, by all the various poppycock of the age, from Christian Science to spiritism, and from the latest guesses in eschatology and epistemology to *art pour l'art.* A true American, he lacks a solid culture, and so he yields a bit to every wind that blows, to the inevitable damage of his representation of the eternal mystery that is man.

Joseph Conrad, starting out from the same wondering agnosticism, holds to it far more resolutely, and it is easy to see why. Conrad is, by birth and training, an aristocrat. He has the gift of emotional detachment. The lures of facile doctrine do not move him. In his irony there is a disdain which plays about even the ironist himself. Dreiser is a product of far different forces and traditions, and is capable of no such escapement. Struggle as he may to rid himself of the current superstitions, he can never quite achieve deliverance from the believing attitude of mind—the heritage of the Indiana hinterland. One half of the man's brain, so to speak, wars with the other half. He is intelligent, he is thoughtful, he is a sound artist—but always there come moments when a dead hand falls upon him, and he is once more the Indiana peasant, snuffing absurdly over imbecile sentimentalities; giving a grave ear to quackeries, snorting and eye-rolling with the best of them. One generation spans too short a time to free the soul of man. Nietzsche, to the end of his days, remained a Prussian pastor's son, and hence two-thirds a Puritan; he erected his war upon holiness, toward the end, into a sort of holy war. Kipling, the grandson of a Methodist preacher, reveals the tin-pot evangelist with increasing clarity as youth and its ribaldries pass away and he falls back upon his fundamentals. And that other English novelist who springs from the servants' hall—let us not be surprised or blame him if he sometimes writes like a bounder.

As for Dreiser, as I hint politely, he is still, for all his achievement, in the transition stage between Christian Endeavor and civilization; between Warsaw, Indiana, and the Socratic grove; between being a good American and being a free man; and so he sometimes vacillates perilously between a moral sentimentalism and a somewhat extravagant revolt. "The 'Genius,'" on the one hand, is almost a tract for rectitude, a Warning to the Young; its motto might be *Scheut die Dirnen!* And on the other hand, it is full of a laborious truculence that can be explained only by imagining the author as heroically determined to prove that he is a plain-spoken fellow and his own man, let the chips fall where they may. So, in spots, in "The Financier" and "The Titan," both of them far better books. There is an almost moral frenzy to expose and riddle what passes for morality among the stupid. The isolation of irony is never reached; the man is still a bit evangelical; his ideas are still novelties to him; he is as solemnly absurd in some of his floutings of the code American as he is in his respect for Bouguereau, or in his flirtings with New Thought, or in his naive belief in the importance of novel-writing. . . .

But his books remain, particularly his earlier books—and not all the ranting of the outraged orthodox will ever wipe them out. They were done in the stage of wonder, before self-consciousness began to creep in and corrupt it. The view of life that got into "Sister Carrie," the first of them, was not the product of a deliberate thinking out of Carrie's problem. It simply got itself there by the force of the artistic passion behind it; its coherent statement had to wait for other and more reflective days. This complete rejection of ethical plan and purpose, this manifestation of what Nietzsche used to call moral innocence, is what brought up the guardians of the national tradition at the gallop, and created the Dreiser bugaboo of today. All the rubber-stamp formulae of American fiction were thrown overboard in these earlier books; instead of reducing the inexplicable to the obvious, they lifted the obvious to the inexplicable; one could find in them no orderly chain of causes and effects, of rewards and punishments; they represented life as a phenomenon at once terrible and unintelligible, like a stroke of lightning. The prevailing criticism applied the moral litmus. They were not "good"; *ergo,* they were "evil."

The peril that Dreiser stands in is here. He may begin to act, if he is not careful, according to the costume forced on him. Unable to combat the orthodox valuation of his place and aim, he may seek a spiritual refuge in embracing it, and so arrange himself with the tripe-sellers of heterodoxy, and cry wares that differ from the other stock only in the bald fact that they are different. . . . Such a fall would grieve the judicious, of whom I have the honor to be one.

The Art of Theodore Dreiser

by Randolph Bourne

Theodore Dreiser has had the good fortune to evoke a peculiar quality of pugnacious interest among the younger American intelligentsia such as has been the lot of almost nobody else writing to-day unless it be Miss Amy Lowell. We do not usually take literature seriously enough to quarrel over it. Or else we take it so seriously that we urbanely avoid squabbles. Certainly there are none of the vendettas that rage in a culture like that of France. But Mr. Dreiser seems to have made himself, particularly since the suppression of "The 'Genius',", a veritable issue. Interesting and surprising are the reactions to him. Edgar Lee Masters makes him a "soul-enrapt demi-urge, walking the earth, stalking life"; Harris Merton Lyon saw in him a "seer of inscrutable mien"; Arthur Davison Ficke sees him as master of a passing throng of figures, "labored with immortal illusion, the terrible and beautiful, cruel and wonder-laden illusion of life"; Mr. Powys makes him an epic philosopher of the "life-tide"; H. L. Mencken puts him ahead of Conrad, with "an agnosticism that has almost passed beyond curiosity." On the other hand, an unhappy critic in *The Nation* last year gave Mr. Dreiser his place for all time in a neat antithesis between the realism that was based on a theory of human conduct and the naturalism that reduced life to a mere animal behavior. For Dreiser this last special hell was reserved, and the jungle-like and simian activities of his characters were rather exhaustively outlined. At the time this antithesis looked silly. With the appearance of Mr. Dreiser's latest book, "A Hoosier Holiday," it becomes nonsensical. For that wise and delightful book reveals him as a very human critic of very common human life, romantically sensual and poetically realistic, with an artist's vision and a thick, warm feeling for American life.

This book gives the clue to Mr. Dreiser, to his insatiable curi-

"The Art of Theodore Dreiser." From Randolph Bourne, *History of a Literary Radical* (New York: The Viking Press, Inc., 1948). Copyright © 1920 by B. W. Huebsch, renewed 1948 by The Viking Press, Inc. Reprinted by permission of The Viking Press, Inc.

osity about people, about their sexual inclinations, about their
dreams, about the homely qualities that make them American. His
memories give a picture of the floundering young American that
is so typical as to be almost epic. No one has ever pictured this
lower middle-class American life so winningly because no one has
had the necessary literary skill with the lack of self-consciousness.
Mr. Dreiser is often sentimental, but it is a sentimentality that
captivates you with its candor. You are seeing this vacuous, wistful,
spiritually rootless, Middle-Western life through the eyes of a
naïve but very wise boy. Mr. Dreiser seems queer only because he
has carried along his youthful attitude in unbroken continuity. He
is fascinated with sex because youth is usually obsessed with sex.
He puzzles about the universe because youth usually puzzles. He
thrills to crudity and violence because sensitive youth usually recoils from the savagery of the industrial world. Imagine incorrigible, sensuous youth endowed with the brooding skepticism of the
philosopher who feels the vanity of life, and you have the paradox
of Mr. Dreiser. For these two attitudes in him support rather than
oppose each other. His spiritual evolution was out of a pious,
ascetic atmosphere into intellectual and personal freedom. He seems
to have found himself without losing himself. Of how many American writers can this be said? And for this much shall be forgiven
him,—his slovenliness of style, his lack of *nuances,* his apathy to
the finer shades of beauty, his weakness for the mystical and the
vague. Mr. Dreiser suggests the over-sensitive temperament that
protects itself by an admiration for crudity and cruelty. His latest
book reveals the boyhood shyness and timidity of this Don Juan
of novelists. Mr. Dreiser is complicated, but he is complicated in
a very understandable American way, the product of the uncouth
forces of small-town life and the vast disorganization of the wider
American world. As he reveals himself, it is a revelation of a certain broad level of the American soul.

Mr. Dreiser seems uncommon only because he is more naïve than
most of us. It is not so much that his pages swarm with sexful
figures as that he rescues sex for the scheme of personal life. He
feels a holy mission to slay the American literary superstition that
men and women are not sensual beings. But he does not brush
this fact in the sniggering way of the popular magazines. He takes
it very seriously, so much so that some of his novels become carica-
tures of desire. It is, however, a misfortune that it has been Brieux
and Freud and not native Theodore Dreiser who has saturated
the sexual imagination of the younger American intelligentsia. It
would have been far healthier to absorb Mr. Dreiser's literary
treatment of sex than to go hysterical over its pathology. Sex has

little significance unless it is treated in personally artistic, novelistic terms. The American tradition had tabooed the treatment of those infinite gradations and complexities of love that fill the literary imagination of a sensitive people. When curiosity became too strong and reticence was repealed in America, we had no means of articulating ourselves except in a deplorable pseudo-scientific jargon that has no more to do with the relevance of sex than the chemical composition of orange paint has to do with the artist's vision. Dreiser has done a real service to the American imagination in despising the underworld and going bravely to the business of picturing sex as it is lived in the personal relations of bungling, wistful, or masterful men and women. He seemed strange and rowdy only because he made sex human, and American tradition had never made it human. It had only made it either sacred or vulgar, and when these categories no longer worked, we fell under the dubious and perverting magic of the psycho-analysts.

In spite of his looseness of literary gait and heaviness of style Dreiser seems a sincere groper after beauty. It is natural enough that this should so largely be the beauty of sex. For where would a sensitive boy, brought up in Indiana and in the big American cities, get beauty expressed for him except in women? What does Mid-Western America offer to the starving except its personal beauty? A few landscapes, an occasional picture in a museum, a book of verse perhaps! Would not all the rest be one long, flaunting offense of ugliness and depression? "The 'Genius',," instead of being that mass of pornographic horror which the Vice Societies repute it to be, is the story of a groping artist whose love of beauty runs obsessingly upon the charm of girlhood. Through different social planes, through business and manual labor and the feverish world of artists, he pursues this lure. Dreiser is refreshing in his air of the moral democrat, who sees life impassively, neither praising nor blaming, at the same time that he realizes how much more terrible and beautiful and incalculable life is than any of us are willing to admit. It may be all *apologia,* but it comes with the grave air of a mind that wants us to understand just how it all happened. "Sister Carrie" will always retain the fresh charm of a spontaneous working-out of mediocre, and yet elemental and significant, lives. A good novelist catches hold of the thread of human desire. Dreiser does this, and that is why his admirers forgive him so many faults.

If you like to speculate about personal and literary qualities that are specifically American, Dreiser should be as interesting as any one now writing in America. This becomes clearer as he writes more about his youth. His hopelessly unorientated, half-educated boy-

hood is so typical of the uncritical and careless society in which
wistful American talent has had to grope. He had to be spiritually
a self-made man, work out a philosophy of life, discover his own
sincerity. Talent in America outside of the ruling class flowers
very late, because it takes so long to find its bearings. It has had
almost to create its own soil, before it could put in its roots and
grow. It is born shivering into an inhospitable and irrelevant
group. It has to find its own kind of people and piece together its
links of comprehension. It is a gruelling and tedious task, but those
who come through it contribute, like Vachel Lindsay, creative work
that is both novel and indigenous. The process can be more easily
traced in Dreiser than in almost anybody else. "A Hoosier Holiday"
not only traces the personal process, but it gives the social background. The common life, as seen throughout the countryside, is
touched off quizzically, and yet sympathetically, with an artist's
vision. Dreiser sees the American masses in their commonness and
at their pleasure as brisk, rather vacuous people, a little pathetic
in their innocence of the possibilities of life and their optimistic
trustfulness. He sees them ruled by great barons of industry, and
yet unconscious of their serfdom. He seems to love this countryside, and he makes you love it.

Dreiser loves, too, the ugly violent bursts of American industry,
—the flaming steel-mills and gaunt lakesides. "The Titan" and
"The Financier" are unattractive novels, but they are human documents of the brawn of a passing American era. Those stenographic
conversations, webs of financial intrigue, bare bones of enterprise,
insult our artistic sense. There is too much raw beef, and yet it all
has the taste and smell of the primitive business-jungle it deals
with. These crude and greedy captains of finance with their wars
and their amours had to be given some kind of literary embodiment,
and Dreiser has hammered a sort of raw epic out of their lives.

It is not only his feeling for these themes of crude power and
sex and the American common life that makes Dreiser interesting.
His emphases are those of a new America which is latently expressive and which must develop its art before we shall really have
become articulate. For Dreiser is a true hyphenate, a product of
that conglomerate Americanism that springs from other roots than
the English tradition. Do we realize how rare it is to find a talent
that is thoroughly American and wholly un-English? Culturally
we have somehow suppressed the hyphenate. Only recently has he
forced his way through the unofficial literary censorship. The vers-
librists teem with him, but Dreiser is almost the first to achieve a
largeness of utterance. His outlook, it is true, flouts the American
canons of optimism and redemption, but these were never anything

but conventions. There stirs in Dreiser's books a new American quality. It is not at all German. It is an authentic attempt to make something artistic out of the chaotic materials that lie around us in American life. Dreiser interests because we can watch him grope and feel his clumsiness. He has the artist's vision without the sureness of the artist's technique. That is one of the tragedies of America. But his faults are those of his material and of uncouth bulk, and not of shoddiness. He expresses an America that is in process of forming. The interest he evokes is part of the eager interest we feel in that growth.

Reality in America: Part II

by Lionel Trilling

This belief in the incompatibility of mind and reality is exemplified by the doctrinaire indulgence which liberal intellectuals have always displayed toward Theodore Dreiser, an indulgence which becomes the worthier of remark when it is contrasted with the liberal severity toward Henry James. Dreiser and James: with that juxtaposition we are immediately at the dark and bloody crossroads where literature and politics meet. One does not go there gladly, but nowadays it is not exactly a matter of free choice whether one does or does not go. As for the particular juxtaposition itself, it is inevitable and it has at the present moment far more significance than the juxtaposition which once used to be made between James and Whitman. It is not hard to contrive factitious oppositions between James and Whitman, but the real difference between them is the difference between the moral mind, with its awareness of tragedy, irony, and multitudinous distinctions, and the transcendental mind, with its passionate sense of the oneness of multiplicity. James and Whitman are unlike not in quality but in kind, and in their very opposition they serve to complement each other. But the difference between James and Dreiser is not of kind, for both men addressed themselves to virtually the same social and moral fact. The difference here is one of quality, and perhaps nothing is more typical of American liberalism than the way it has responded to the respective qualities of the two men.

Few critics, I suppose, no matter what their political disposition, have ever been wholly blind to James's great gifts, or even to the grandiose moral intention of these gifts. And few critics have ever been wholly blind to Dreiser's great faults. But by liberal critics James is traditionally put to the ultimate question: of what use, of what actual political use, are his gifts and their intentions? Granted that James was devoted to an extraordinary moral perceptiveness, granted too that moral perceptiveness has something to do with politics and the social life, of what possible practical value in our world of impending disaster can James's work be? And James's style, his characters, his subjects, and even his own social origin and the manner of his personal life are adduced to show that his work cannot endure the question. To James no quarter is given by American criticism in its political and liberal aspect. But in the same degree that liberal criticism is moved by political considerations to treat James with severity, it treats Dreiser with the most sympathetic indulgence. Dreiser's literary faults, it gives us to understand, are essentially social and political virtues. It was Parrington who established the formula for the liberal criticism of Dreiser by calling him a "peasant": when Dreiser thinks stupidly, it is because he has the slow stubbornness of a peasant; when he writes badly, it is because he is impatient of the sterile literary gentility of the bourgeoisie. It is as if wit, and flexibility of mind, and perception, and knowledge were to be equated with aristocracy and political reaction, while dullness and stupidity must naturally suggest a virtuous democracy, as in the old plays.

The liberal judgment of Dreiser and James goes back of politics, goes back to the cultural assumptions that make politics. We are still haunted by a kind of political fear of the intellect which Tocqueville observed in us more than a century ago. American intellectuals, when they are being consciously American or political, are remarkably quick to suggest that an art which is marked by perception and knowledge, although all very well in its way, can never get us through gross dangers and difficulties. And their misgivings become the more intense when intellect works in art as it ideally should, when its processes are vivacious and interesting and brilliant. It is then that we like to confront it with the gross dangers and difficulties and to challenge it to save us at once from disaster. When intellect in art is awkward and dull we do not put it to the test of ultimate or immediate practicality. No liberal critic asks the question of Dreiser whether *his* moral preoccupations are going to be useful in confronting the disasters that threaten us. And it is a judgment on the proper nature of mind, rather than any actual political meaning that might be drawn from the works of the two men, which accounts for the unequal justice they have received from the progressive critics. If it could be conclusively demonstrated—by, say, documents in James's handwriting—that James explicitly intended his books to be understood as pleas for co-operatives, labor unions, better housing, and more equitable taxation, the American critic in his liberal and progressive character would still be worried by James because his work shows so many of the electric qualities of mind. And if something like the opposite were proved of Dreiser, it would be brushed aside—as his doctrinaire anti-Semitism has in fact been brushed aside—because his books have the awkwardness, the chaos, the heaviness which we associate with "reality." In the American metaphysic, reality is always material reality, hard, resistant, unformed, impenetrable, and unpleasant. And that mind is alone felt to be trustworthy which most resembles this reality by most nearly reproducing the sensations it affords.

In *The Rise of American Civilization*, Professor Beard uses a significant phrase when, in the course of an ironic account of James's career, he implies that we have the clue to the irrelevance of that career when we know that James was "a whole generation removed from the odors of the shop." Of a piece with this, and in itself even more significant, is the comment which Granville Hicks makes in *The Great Tradition* when he deals with James's stories about artists and remarks that such artists as James portrays, so concerned for their art and their integrity in art, do not really exist: "After all, who has ever known such artists? Where are the Hugh Verekers, the Mark Ambients, the Neil Paradays, the Overts, Limberts, Dencombes, Delavoys?" This question, as Mr. Hicks admits, had occurred to James himself, but what answer had James given to it? "If the life about us for the last thirty years refused warrant for these examples," he said in the preface to volume XII of the New York Edition, "then so much the worse for that life. . . . There are decencies that in the name of the general self-respect we must take for granted, there's a rudimentary intellectual honor to which we must, in the interest of civilization, at least pretend." And to this Mr. Hicks, shocked beyond argument, makes this reply, which would be astonishing had we not heard it before: "But this is the purest romanticism, this writing about what ought to be rather than what is!"

The "odors of the shop" are real, and to those who breathe them they guarantee a sense of vitality from which James is debarred. The idea of intellectual honor is not real, and to that chimera James was devoted. He betrayed the reality of what is in the interests of what ought to be. Dare we trust him? The question, we remember, is asked by men who themselves have elaborate transactions with what ought to be. Professor Beard spoke in the name of a growing, developing, and improving America. Mr. Hicks, when he wrote *The Great Tradition*, was in general sympathy with a nominally radical movement. But James's own transaction with what ought to be is suspect because it is carried on through what I have called the electrical qualities of mind, through a complex and rapid imagination and with a kind of authoritative immediacy. Mr. Hicks knows that Dreiser is "clumsy" and "stupid" and "bewildered" and "crude in his statement of materialistic monism"; he knows that Dreiser in his personal life—which is in point because James's personal life is always supposed to be so much in point—was not quite emancipated from "his boyhood longing for crass material success," showing "again and again a desire for the ostentatious luxury of the successful business man." But Dreiser is to be accepted and forgiven because his faults are the sad, lovable, honorable faults of reality itself, or of America itself—huge, inchoate, struggling toward expression, caught between the dream of raw power and the dream of morality.

"The liability in what Santayana called the genteel tradition was due to its being the product of mind apart from experience. Dreiser gave us the stuff of our common experience, not as it was hoped to be by any idealizing theorist, but as it actually was in its crudity." The author of this statement certainly cannot be accused of any lack of feeling for mind as Henry James represents it; nor can Mr. Matthiessen be thought of as a follower of Parrington— indeed, in the preface to *American Renaissance* he has framed one of the sharpest and most cogent criticisms of Parrington's method. Yet Mr. Matthiessen, writing in the *New York Times Book Review* about Dreiser's posthumous novel, *The Bulwark,* accepts the liberal cliché which opposes crude experience to the mind and establishes Dreiser's value by implying that the mind which Dreiser's crude experience is presumed to confront and refute is the mind of gentility.

This implied amalgamation of mind with gentility is the rationale of the long indulgence of Dreiser, which is extended even to the style of his prose. Everyone is aware that Dreiser's prose style is full of roughness and ungainliness, and the critics who admire Dreiser tell us it does not matter. Of course it does not matter. No reader with a right sense of style would suppose that it does matter, and he might even find it a virtue. But it has been taken for granted that the ungainliness of Dreiser's style is the only possible objection to be made to it, and that whoever finds in it any fault at all wants a prettified genteel style (and is objecting to the ungainliness of reality itself). For instance, Edwin Berry Burgum, in a leaflet on Dreiser put out by the Book Find Club, tells us that Dreiser was one of those who used—or, as Mr. Burgum says, utilized—"the diction of the Middle West, pretty much as it was spoken, rich in colloquialism and frank in the simplicity and directness of the pioneer tradition," and that this diction took the place of "the

literary English, formal and bookish, of New England provincialism
that was closer to the aristocratic spirit of the mother country than
to the tang of everyday life in the new West." This is mere fantasy.
Hawthorne, Thoreau, and Emerson were for the most part remarkably colloquial—they wrote, that is, much as they spoke; their
prose was specifically American in quality, and, except for occasional lapses, quite direct and simple. It is Dreiser who lacks the
sense of colloquial diction—that of the Middle West or any other.
If we are to talk of bookishness, it is Dreiser who is bookish; he is
precisely literary in the bad sense; he is full of flowers of rhetoric
and shines with paste gems; at hundreds of points his diction is
not only genteel but fancy. It is he who speaks of "a scene more
distingué than this," or of a woman "artistic in form and feature,"
or of a man who, although "strong, reserved, aggressive, with an
air of wealth and experience, was *soi-disant* and not particularly
eager to stay at home." Colloquialism held no real charm for him
and his natural tendency is always toward the "fine":

> . . . Moralists come and go; religionists fulminate and declare the
> pronouncements of God as to this; but Aphrodite still reigns. Em-
> bowered in the festal depths of the spring, set above her altars of
> porphyry, chalcedony, ivory and gold, see her smile the smile that
> is at once the texture and essence of delight, the glory and despair
> of the world! Dream on, oh Buddha, asleep on your lotus leaf, of an
> undisturbed Nirvana! Sweat, oh Jesus, your last agonizing drops over
> an unregenerate world! In the forests of Pan still ring the cries of
> the worshippers of Aphrodite! From her altars the incense of adora-
> tion ever rises! And see, the new red grapes dripping where votive
> hands new-press them!

Charles Jackson, the novelist, telling us in the same leaflet that
Dreiser's style does not matter, remarks on how much still comes
to us when we have lost by translation the stylistic brilliance of
Thomas Mann or the Russians or Balzac. He is in part right. And
he is right too when he says that a certain kind of conscious, super-
vised artistry is not appropriate to the novel of large dimensions.
Yet the fact is that the great novelists have usually written very
good prose, and what comes through even a bad translation is
exactly the power of mind that made the well-hung sentence of
the original text. In literature style is so little the mere clothing of
thought—need it be insisted on at this late date?—that we may say
that from the earth of the novelist's prose spring his characters,
his ideas, and even his story itself.[1]

---

[1] The latest defense of Dreiser's style, that in the chapter on Dreiser in the
Literary History of the United States, is worth noting: "Forgetful of the
integrity and power of Dreiser's whole work, many critics have been distracted

To the extent that Dreiser's style is defensible, his thought is also defensible. That is, when he thinks like a novelist, he is worth following—when by means of his rough and ungainly but no doubt cumulatively effective style he creates rough, ungainly, but effective characters and events. But when he thinks like, as we say, a philosopher, he is likely to be not only foolish but vulgar. He thinks as the modern crowd thinks when it decides to think: religion and morality are nonsense, "religionists" and moralists are fakes, tradition is a fraud, what is man but matter and impulses, mysterious "chemisms," what value has life anyway? "What, cooking, eating, coition, job holding, growing, aging, losing, winning, in so changeful and passing a scene as this, important? Bunk! It is some form of titillating illusion with about as much import to the superior forces that bring it all about as the functions and gyrations of a fly. No more. And maybe less." Thus Dreiser at sixty. And yet there is for him always the vulgarly saving suspicion that maybe, when all is said and done, there is Something Behind It All. It is much to the point of his intellectual vulgarity that Dreiser's anti-Semitism was not merely a social prejudice but an idea, a way of dealing with difficulties.

No one, I suppose, has ever represented Dreiser as a masterly intellect. It is even commonplace to say that his ideas are inconsistent or inadequate. But once that admission has been made, his ideas are hustled out of sight while his "reality" and great brooding pity are spoken of. (His pity is to be questioned: pity is to be judged by kind, not amount, and Dreiser's pity—*Jennie Gerhardt* provides the only exception—is either destructive of its object or it is self-pity.) Why has no liberal critic ever brought Dreiser's ideas to the bar of political practicality, asking what use is to be made of Dreiser's dim, awkward speculation, of his self-justification, of his

---

into a condemnation of his style. He was, like Twain and Whitman, an organic artist; he wrote what he knew—what he was. His many colloquialisms were part of the coinage of his time, and his sentimental and romantic passages were written in the language of the educational system and the popular literature of his formative years. In his style, as in his material, he was a child of his time, of his class. Self-educated, a type or model of the artist of plebeian origin in America, his language, like his subject matter, is not marked by internal inconsistencies." No doubt Dreiser was an organic artist in the sense that he wrote what he knew and what he was, but so, I suppose, is every artist; the question for criticism comes down to *what* he knew and *what* he was. That he was a child of his time and class is also true, but this can be said of everyone without exception; the question for criticism is how he transcended the imposed limitations of his time and class. As for the defense made on the ground of his particular class, it can only be said that liberal thought has come to a strange pass when it assumes that a plebeian origin is accountable for a writer's faults through all his intellectual life.

lust for "beauty" and "sex" and "living" and "life itself," and of
the showy nihilism which always seems to him so grand a gesture
in the direction of profundity? We live, understandably enough,
with the sense of urgency; our clock, like Baudelaire's has had the
hands removed and bears the legend, "It is later than you think."
But with us it is always a little too late for mind, yet never too
late for honest stupidity; always a little too late for understanding,
never too late for righteous, bewildered wrath; always too late for
thought, never too late for naive moralizing. We seem to like to
condemn our finest but not our worst qualities by pitting them
against the exigency of time.

But sometimes time is not quite so exigent as to justify all our
own exigency, and in the case of Dreiser time has allowed his
deficiencies to reach their logical, and fatal, conclusion. In *The
Bulwark* Dreiser's characteristic ideas come full circle, and the
simple, didactic life history of Solon Barnes, a Quaker business
man, affirms a simple Christian faith, and a kind of practical mysticism, and the virtues of self-abnegation and self-restraint, and
the belief in and submission to the hidden purposes of higher
powers, those "superior forces that bring it all about"—once, in
Dreiser's opinion, so brutally indifferent, now somehow benign.
This is not the first occasion on which Dreiser has shown a tenderness toward religion and a responsiveness to mysticism. *Jennie
Gerhardt* and the figure of the Reverend Duncan McMillan in *An
American Tragedy* are forecasts of the avowals of *The Bulwark,*
and Dreiser's lively interest in power of any sort led him to take
account of the power implicit in the cruder forms of mystical per-
formance. Yet these rifts in his nearly monolithic materialism cannot quite prepare us for the blank pietism of *The Bulwark,* not
after we have remembered how salient in Dreiser's work has been
the long surly rage against the "religionists" and the "moralists,"
the men who have presumed to believe that life can be given any
law at all and who have dared to suppose that will or mind or faith
can shape the savage and beautiful entity that Dreiser liked to call
"life itself." Now for Dreiser the law may indeed be given, and
it is wholly simple—the safe conduct of the personal life requires
only that we follow the Inner Light according to the regimen of
the Society of Friends, or according to some other godly rule. And
now the smiling Aphrodite set above her altars of porphyry, chal-
cedony, ivory, and gold is quite forgotten, and we are told that the
sad joy of cosmic acceptance goes hand in hand with sexual absti-
nence.

Dreiser's mood of "acceptance" in the last years of his life is not,
as a personal experience, to be submitted to the tests of intellectual

validity. It consists of a sensation of cosmic understanding, of an overarching sense of unity with the world in its apparent evil as well as in its obvious good. It is no more to be quarreled with, or reasoned with, than love itself—indeed, it is a kind of love, not so much of the world as of oneself in the world. Perhaps it is either the cessation of desire or the perfect balance of desires. It is what used often to be meant by "peace," and up through the nineteenth century a good many people understood its meaning. If it was Dreiser's own emotion at the end of his life, who would not be happy that he had achieved it? I am not even sure that our civilization would not be the better for more of us knowing and desiring this emotion of grave felicity. Yet granting the personal validity of the emotion, Dreiser's exposition of it fails, and is, moreover, offensive. Mr. Matthiessen has warned us of the attack that will be made on the doctrine of *The Bulwark* by "those who believe that any renewal of Christianity marks a new 'failure of nerve.' " But Dreiser's religious avowal is not a failure of nerve—it is a failure of mind and heart. We have only to set his book beside any work in which mind and heart are made to serve religion to know this at once. Ivan Karamazov's giving back his ticket of admission to the "harmony" of the universe suggests that *The Bulwark* is not morally adequate, for we dare not, as its hero does, blandly "accept" the suffering of others; and the Book of Job tells us that it does not include enough in its exploration of the problem of evil, and is not stern enough. I have said that Dreiser's religious affirmation was offensive; the offense lies in the vulgar ease of its formulation, as well as in the comfortable untroubled way in which Dreiser moved from nihilism to pietism.[2]

   The Bulwark is the fruit of Dreiser's old age, but if we speak of it as a failure of thought and feeling, we cannot suppose that with age Dreiser weakened in mind and heart. The weakness was always there. And in a sense it is not Dreiser who failed but a whole way of dealing with ideas, a way in which we have all been in some degree involved. Our liberal, progressive culture tolerated Dreiser's vulgar materialism with its huge negation, its simple cry of "Bunk!," feeling that perhaps it was not quite intellectually ade-

   [2] This ease and comfortableness seem to mark contemporary religious conversions. Religion nowadays has the appearance of what the ideal modern house has been called, "a machine for living," and seemingly one makes up one's mind to acquire and use it not with spiritual struggle but only with a growing sense of its practicability and convenience. Compare *The Seven Storey Mountain*, which Monsignor Sheen calls "a twentieth-century form of the *Confessions* of St. Augustine," with the old, as it were original, *Confessions* of St. Augustine.

quate but certainly very *strong*, certainly very *real*. And now, almost as a natural consequence, it has been given, and is not unwilling to take, Dreiser's pietistic religion in all its inadequacy.

Dreiser, of course, was firmer than the intellectual culture that accepted him. He *meant* his ideas, at least so far as a man can mean ideas who is incapable of following them to their consequences. But we, when it came to his ideas, talked about his great brooding pity and shrugged the ideas off. We are still doing it. Robert Elias, the biographer of Dreiser, tells us that "it is part of the logic of (Dreiser's) life that he should have completed *The Bulwark* at the same time that he joined the Communists." Just what kind of logic this is we learn from Mr. Elias's further statement. "When he supported left-wing movements and finally, last year, joined the Communist Party, he did so not because he had examined the details of the party line and found them satisfactory, but because he agreed with a general program that represented a means for establishing his cherished goal of greater equality among men." Whether or not Dreiser was following the logic of his own life, he was certainly following the logic of the liberal criticism that accepted him so undiscriminatingly as one of the great, significant expressions of its spirit. This is the liberal criticism, in the direct line of Parrington, which establishes the social responsibility of the writer and then goes on to say that, apart from his duty of resembling reality as much as possible, he is not really responsible for anything, not even for his ideas. The scope of reality being what it is, ideas are held to be mere "details," and, what is more, to be details which, if attended to, have the effect of diminishing reality. But ideals are different from ideas; in the liberal criticism which descends from Parrington ideals consort happily with reality and they urge us to deal impatiently with ideas—a "cherished goal" forbids that we stop to consider how we reach it, or if we may not destroy it in trying to reach it the wrong way.

Dreiser's Moral Seriousness

by Gerald Willen

As a conscious thinker there is no doubt that Dreiser believed the individual to be incapable of making a free choice; as a novelist, however, he invariably projected his characters into situations calling for the exercise of the will. Perhaps as a conscious thinker he might have thought that the decisions made by his characters at critical moments illustrated their inability to act in any but a predetermined way. It is true that the choices taken by the central figures in Dreiser's novels are, in a sense, forced upon them by the pattern of circumstances out of which their lives are woven; that is to say, their decisions are more or less predictable, given their environments, their desires, and their characters.

But given all these factors, there is nothing in the novels to suggests that the actions taken by any individual are the only actions open to him—that he must, of necessity, act as he does. Hurstwood does not *have* to run off with Carrie, stealing his employers' money in order to do so; Jennie does not *have* to accept Lester Kane's proposal, nor is her seduction by Senator Brander inevitable; Clyde Griffiths does not *have* to plot Roberta Alden's death, and there is no absolutely compelling reason why he must change his mind about drowning her.

In a curious way Dreiser obliges his reader to adopt the moral view toward his work. For by having his characters take what he considers to be the only course of action open to them, he gives them their moral histories, histories that are unusual rather than ordinary. Where the ordinary person might be tempted to act, Dreiser's characters act; where the ordinary person fears to tread, Dreiser's characters enter. In other words, Dreiser's people act freely in situations in which the ordinary person, for one reason or another, is inhibited. And really, by giving his characters their heads, Dreiser is pleading for more freedom in moral matters rather than

"Dreiser's Moral Seriousness" by Gerald Willen. From *University of Kansas City Review*, 23 (March 1957): 181–87. Copyright © 1957 by *University of Kansas City Review*. Reprinted by permission of the author and *The University Review*.

saying that the individual cannot help what he does. In real life the number of people who are tempted to act on their desires must be great, yet the numbers who act on them, as Dreiser's characters almost invariably do, must be comparatively small. Therefore, because Dreiser's fiction is replete with incidents wherein unusual choices involving moral considerations are made, the reader must evaluate the work from the moral point of view.

There is a sense, after all, in which Dreiser's novels are contrasted with life as it is actually lived by the kind of people they deal with. These people, as Conrad pointed out in "Heart of Darkness," live in fear of the butcher, the policeman, of their neighbors' opinion, and of being put away in the insane asylum; and their fears prevent them from acting on their desires as they would like. Because Dreiser's characters act on their desires, they differ from the ordinary run of people, and thus they acquire their moral histories. However, what they do have in common with the living is a desire to be free of the restrictions imposed on behavior. When the author has them act, inevitably as he supposes, he is functioning as Aristotle said the poet should function: he relates not what has happened, but what may happen according to the law of probability or necessity. And, to return for the moment to Dreiser the conscious thinker, he was wrong in supposing that his characters had to act as they do, for they do have alternative modes of action; history and life are full of people moved by the same desires and unable to act on them. As an artist he was right in having his characters act as they do, for he was showing, as the artist should, what may happen according to the law of probability or necessity.

In western literature human freedom has always been shown as limited; in it Fate, the gods, or God has operated to restrict man's freedom to act as he chooses. Yet western man has always thought of himself as having a will of his own. The very conflict upon which dramatic literature depends originates in the opposition between the decrees of Fate, the wills of the gods, or the purpose of God and the will of man to assert his own independence. And tragedy, as a literary form, stems from man's powerlessness to assert his will successfully in the face of forces stronger than himself. In his fiction Dreiser shifts only slightly from the traditional conception of man's position in the universe. For the will he substitutes desire, for supernatural forces the demands of society. Thus the conflict in his novels is based on the opposition between the force of desire and the demands of society.

Dreiser may think that these elements are impersonal, and to a certain extent, if we accept his terms, they are: desire has a biological basis; society is a collective order. But because in fiction these factors must be embodied in the individual, of necessity they become personal. Thus Dreiser's protagonists are all moved by strong personal desires, to rise in the social order, to be wealthy, to possess many women, and even to love. They are opposed not by social factors, but by people and, paradoxical as it may seem, by conflicting elements within themselves. The romantic Hurstwood is opposed by the conventional Hurstwood, the amoral Cowperwood by the moral Edward Malia Butler, Jennie Gerhardt and Lester Kane by members of the Kane family, the ambitious Clyde Griffiths by the passionate Clyde Griffiths. Dreiser may talk all he wants about "the force of sex," "chemisms," "varietism," and the like, but they remain abstractions until they are embodied in the individual. Once they are so embodied, they become subject to moral, as well as philosophical, interpretation.

Dreiser, as a matter of fact, without himself passing moral judgment, asks that we do so. We may say that it is wrong of society to make it impossible for Jennie Gerhardt and Lester Kane to marry, but by society we mean the Kane family. It is true that, in opposing the marriage, members of the Kane family act in accord with the social demands of their class; yet they also act as individuals. As individuals they represent the particulars, as agents the universals. Their particular actions are subject to moral evaluation; the universals for which they are the agents will condition and inform their actions, but they do not make their actions inevitable. Dreiser says they do, because according to his view the individual acts in conformity with his conditioning when it is not in conflict with anything else. When, however, a conflict between conditioning and desire arises, Dreiser then claims that the individual will act in accordance with desire. Yet as inevitable as this pattern of action appears to Dreiser, under certain conditions it is reversible, because the author sees the twin forces of convention and desire as being of equal strength.

Hence Lester Kane is torn between his love for Jennie and the necessity of retaining his social and financial position. He can act at first on the force of his desire, but when he is later threatened with being virtually disinherited, he acts in conformity with the force of convention. If he can reverse his actions, it must be said that he is a free agent insofar as his choices are concerned. When he chooses not to be declassed, he has in mind the consequences that will result from whatever line of action he takes. Any choice made in terms of consequences is a free choice, as we understand the term, and as such it is subject to moral evaluation. We can say of it that it has led to a desired end and therefore was good, or that it failed to lead to the desired end and was therefore bad.

Kane himself evaluates the consequences of his decision when he says to Jennie just prior to his death, " 'It wasn't the right thing, after all.' "

The novels in which the choices made by the protagonists are irreversible are those in which the law, either moral or legal, has been broken. Hurstwood's theft of his employers' money, Cowperwood's illegal use of the city's funds, Clyde Griffiths' not-so-ambiguous attitude toward Roberta Alden at the moment of her drowning—these are irrevocable; that is to say, they prevent the characters involved from returning to prior conditions. By stealing, Hurstwood cuts himself off from his class, and in consequence his slow decline sets in; by his shady dealings, Cowperwood finds himself isolated, although his setbacks result in good part from his involvements with women; by "not wanting" to save Roberta, Clyde Griffiths becomes vulnerable to legal prosecution. In each of these cases the protagonist involved is doing something that he knows to be prohibited by law or moral custom; because they act freely in these prohibited situations, Hurstwood, Cowperwood, and Clyde Griffiths can be held accountable for what they do.

To be sure, Dreiser points out that the situations in which they find themselves are difficult and that the choices they make offer them "a way out" that not only is painless but also advantageous; but it is precisely because they act for their own advantage in these situations that they must be held morally responsible for their actions. We may sympathize with them as Dreiser does, we may recognize in them motives that are all too human as Dreiser also does; but all our sympathy and our recognition cannot lift from them the burden of personal responsibility. It is to be doubted that Dreiser himself absolves them of it; he sees them as impelled to act as they do because of the circumstances of their lives, and he is very careful to dwell at great length on the reasons for their actions. He may see them as trapped, but he also endows them with wills of their own, and because he does, the case for the inevitability of their decisions is not an absolute one. Alternate actions are open to them; consequently, the moral law applies to them.

The success of Dreiser's novels depends to a large extent on the fact that his characters are free agents living in a middle-class society that both restricts the individual from acting on his desires and also puts great stress on the achievement by the individual of his objectives. In this society class lines are loosely drawn, with the result that the individual is able to rise or descend in the social scale, and his success will depend to some extent on his ability to better his original position. Money is the most important means of measurement, and if the individual is to rise, he must, somehow, gain possession of enough of it to secure him a place in the class he desires to enter. A good number of Dreiser's characters begin with nothing; hence, their first problem is to acquire the means with which to satisfy their social ambitions. Complicating, and even complementing, the situations in which they find themselves is another strong factor, sexual activity.

In every one of the novels sexual activity, usually of the kind not sanctioned by society, is the means by which the central characters succeed or fail in their quest for social and financial security. Carrie Meeber and Jennie Gerhardt are projected into the middle class by their relationships with Drouet and Hurstwood on the one hand, and with Lester Kane on the other. Cowperwood's financial defeats result partially from his tampering with the daughters and wives of his associates. Eugene Witla's personal problems and consequent inability to paint originate in his sexual dissatisfaction with marriage. Clyde Griffiths' failure stems directly from his strongly passionate nature. And finally, Solon Barnes's world disintegrates completely because of the sexual activity of his younger son.

Dreiser's use of sex as a force is the means by which he individualizes his characters' search for a more satisfactory way of life, and it is also the means by which he introduces conflict. On the one hand, his characters find that only through unsanctioned sexual activity can they reach their objectives or satisfy their desires; on the other hand, the personal relationships they enter into run contrary to the standards established by society for the guidance of conduct. With the dilemma thus set up, Dreiser's novels begin. If his characters had been endowed with the unconventional attitudes with which they could synchronize their unconventional behavior, their problems would be comparatively minor. But with the exception of Cowperwood and Aileen Butler, Dreiser's people are basically conventional in their outlook. They want to be members in good standing of the society whose values they flaunt. Because they fail to understand that their unconventional behavior automatically sets them apart, banishes them, so to speak, from the orthodox group, they fail in the end where at first they had succeeded.

Hurstwood is the most obvious example. In running off with Carrie, he satisfies his desire; because in other respects his values are those of the middle class, he cannot make the adjustments necessary to his changed condition in life. He hopes to pick up in New York where he had left off in Chicago. His reputation means a good deal to him, and when he realizes that he cannot re-establish it, he lacks the resources with which to build a different kind of life, and so his disintegration sets in.

Only when Dreiser's characters realize that continued unorthodox behavior will cause them to be exiled permanently from the group with which they are in sympathy and with which they need to be identified, and when they take the necessary action, can they once more be accepted. But in conforming to the demands of society, they find it necessary to act contrary to their inclinations. Neither Jennie Gerhardt nor Lester Kane wants to give the other up, yet they both know that their continued association with each other would be catastrophic. Jennie is willing enough to accept social ostracism, but Kane would be destroyed by it, and it is with this realization that they part.

All of Dreiser's novels are based on the dreams of their major protagonists, and all of the protagonists, with the exception of Solon Barnes, are willing to break the moral code in order to achieve their dreams. Carrie dreams of a station in life commensurate with her estimate of herself and her needs, Jennie of a life devoted to the welfare of the people she loves, Cowperwood of economic power and the possession of many women, Eugene Witla of the freedom that he thinks will enable him to become a great artist, Clyde Griffiths of a life of grace and ease. Only Solon Barnes is satisfied with what he has and can be ill at ease when he becomes wealthy; but at the end of his life, even he can dream of a return to the values he has seen smashed by various members of his family and by his business associates.

With the exception of Cowperwood, all of Dreiser's people are working toward a goal approved by society, namely the bettering of their original social position in life. Cowperwood must be excepted, because, although his search for tremendous wealth is of itself acceptable to society, the means he employs are frowned upon; curiously enough, however, once he amasses his great wealth and acquires the power that automatically goes with it, society and Dreiser as well begin to regard him with awe and esteem. The other characters, lacking Cowperwood's ruthlessness, are faced with a much more difficult struggle. For sooner or later they discover that if they are to realize their dreams, they are going to have to compromise with the moral code; once they do so, society withdraws approval of their aims. Dreiser, in other words, seems to have adopted the view that the struggle for a more comfortable way of life, while it is approved in principle by society, calls for methods that society condemns. And, in a sense, his work can be taken as an attack on the American success dream which, as he sees it, both sanctions and even demands dissatisfaction on the part of the individual with his original status in life, and also disapproves of the methods necessary to the individual who aims to better his status.

To Dreiser, then, American middle-class society is immoral, and it might be logical to think that he would treat as hypocrites the individuals in whom the prevailing attitudes are embodied. But as a rule he does not. Only in the cases of several of Cowperwood's fellow financiers does he openly develop people as less honest than they make themselves out to be; moreover, Cowperwood's most important antagonist, Edward Malia Butler, who represents what can be called the normal world, is as honest as he can be in his financial activities and strongly convinced of the essential rightness of his religious position. Angela Blue Witla, Samuel Griffiths, and the Reverend Mr. Duncan McMillan, to name but a few upholders of the conventional order, are sincere in their beliefs and genuinely troubled by any deviation from the moral code. Dreiser may be critical of their values, but he always treats the individual with dignity and understanding, reserving his attacks for the ideas that lie behind behavior. And in his last completed novel, *The Bulwark,* he laments the fact that in a world devoted to the pursuit of money and indiscriminate pleasure, it is no longer possible to live according to an honorable code of ethics.

It is possible and, in fact, necessary, if we are to understand Dreiser's view of the moral situation, to read the earlier novels in the light of the ideas expressed in *The Bulwark.* If we do so, we find not that Dreiser is a naturalist, but that he envisions the individual as caught between the ideal and the actual. Endowed with desires that conflict with the ideals of society, but at the same time pushed by society to satisfy these desires, he finds himself punished if he does so, socially and personally frustrated if he does not. To live with any degree of satisfaction in such a world, he must be completely ruthless, as was Cowperwood, or equipped with unassailable integrity, as was Solon Barnes. And even Barnes's integrity cannot preserve him from the decay that is implicit in the new world's values. Cowperwood's ruthlessness is admirably suited to the new spirit, and it is significant that he should be the only one of Dreiser's figures to achieve any lasting satisfaction.

To a certain extent Carrie Meeber arrives also at satisfaction of sorts, in that her success as an actress assures her of the money she needs; perhaps she is not ruthless in quite the same way as Cowperwood, yet her success is dependent on the degree to which she can remain emotionally aloof from the men in her life. All the other major characters in the novels fail in their attempts to realize their dreams because, although their objectives are approved by society, they can be achieved only at the cost of antagonizing this very same society; and since these people are so constituted that they need social approval, they are unable to survive once they have been condemned. Hurstwood, Jennie Gerhardt, Lester Kane, Eugene Witla, and Clyde Griffiths are all people who, once their desires or activities are disapproved of by society, must either abandon their objectives or resort to violent methods that alienate them even further from the group with which they need to be identified.

Thus Dreiser's novels take place in a society that is itself constantly passing judgment on its members. It is a society in conflict with itself over the values it actually lives by and those it thinks it lives by. From it Dreiser isolates a number of representative individuals, sets them in motion, and renders their lives in terms of the difficulties they encounter with the problems arising from the moral ambiguities that envelop their activities. By dwelling so insistently on moral questions, by endowing his characters with wills of their own, and by confronting them with real choices, Dreiser enables the reader to pass moral judgment on the characters themselves as well as on the society in which they live. Whatever importance Dreiser's novels have derives from his moral seriousness. This moral seriousness appears again and again in the rendering of his characters' lives and in the social context into which they are projected.

Theodore Dreiser and the Divided Stream

by *Charles Child Walcutt*

The Divided Stream of American transcendentalism is the source and indeed the being of what is called the naturalistic movement in our fiction. The essence of transcendentalism is to be found in Emerson's assertion that Nature is the symbol of Spirit. This means that what is Ideal or Absolute as Spirit is translated into physical laws and perfectly embodied (or incarnated) as Nature. But Spirit and Nature are not actually separate for the transcendentalist. They are terms he devises to identify two aspects of the One. Spirit lives in Nature; Nature reveals and embodies Spirit. Modern physicists have come to the same monistic position through their discovery that matter and energy are not different things but only different forms or expressions of the same thing. What seems ultimately to be an electric charge expresses itself as all the forms of the physical universe. Both energy and law are "superior" to matter, but they appear only in or through matter.

Now the transcendentalist called the same elements Spirit and Nature. The former was accessible to Intuition or inspiration; the latter to scientific investigation. Emerson said, "Nature is the symbol of Spirit," and "The axioms of physics translate the law of ethics." Here is the whole system. But the system did not stay whole. The monist stream did not stay One. Just as the language of analysis initially divided it with two words, so time and experience divided it into poles of optimism and pessimism, freedom and determinism, will and fate, social reformism and mechanistic despair. The optimism and idealism of Spirit could not remain identified with the dazzling but terrifying preoccupation with the forces of alien nature, for the Nature which was assumed to be a version of man's spirit and therefore of his will appeared under

"Theodore Dreiser and the Divided Stream" by Charles Child Walcutt. From Alfred Kazin and Charles Shapiro, eds., *The Stature of Theodore Dreiser* (Bloomington: The University of Indiana Press, 1955), pp. 246–69. A definitive, longer version appears in Walcutt's *American Literary Naturalism, A Divided Stream* (Minneapolis: University of Minnesota Press, 1956). Copyright © 1956 by the University of Minnesota Press. Reprinted by permission of the University of Minnesota Press.

scientific analysis as a force which first controlled man's will and presently made it seem that his freedom was an illusion, that there was no such thing as will but only chemicals performing reactions which could (theoretically, at least) be predicted.

This is the divided stream. It accounts, originally, for America's devotion to facts, to things, to order, efficiency, and knowledge, for her belief that the liberation of the human spirit will be accomplished through the mastery of nature. And it thus accounts for the manner in which our devotion to science and fact has led us to the point where natural law seems to deny freedom and indeed the very concept of Spirit. It accounts for the fact that naturalism has been described, by competent critics, as both "optimistic progressivism" and "mechanistic determinism." Surprisingly enough, it can be both, for a novel that shows a hapless individual destroyed by social or hereditary forces over which he has no control can at the same time and through this very action express outraged idealism and demonstrate the need for reform through either social or scientific knowledge. A step further, however, and we come to the point where naturalism moves through a meaningless cosmos where non-human law is king and the individual can watch and experience and perhaps be destroyed, but cannot finally convince himself that human will or reason can dominate nature.

Theodore Dreiser drank his inspiration from both branches of the divided stream. He has been described as a pessimist, a socialist, a communist; he has been said to embody the antithesis of American transcendentalism; he has himself acknowledged beliefs in the meaninglessness of life, in the moral autonomy of the superman, in the ultimate value and dignity of the individual. In his later works he has placed mind above matter. And even while he was writing his early books he believed in a mystical Cosmic Consciousness that one would hardly have suspected from reading those books. His mixture of despair and idealism, of wonder and fear, of pity and guilt, of chemistry and intuition has given us the most moving and powerful novels of the naturalistic tradition. Examined chronologically, they reveal naturalistic ideas struggling to find a structure by which the novel could move without turning upon crucial ethical choices. They also reveal a continuous *ethical* questioning of tradition, dogma, received morality and social "justice." Thus they always contain the antithesis of their materialistic premises. Between the poles of this tension is Dreiser's "naturalism." It moves during his literary career, through phases of objectivity, resignation, and protest toward the groping affirmation of spirit that presides over and, oddly, defeats his final work.

Psychologically, Dreiser is his own divided stream of pity and guilt, of wonder and terror, of objectivity and responsibility. He observes a world without meaning, yet he also responds to a compelling need to believe. Misery in any form moved the young Dreiser to tears. Throughout *A Book About Myself* one of the dominant notes is Dreiser's wondering sympathy for the pain which life inflicts in the form of hunger, weariness, and uncertainty on those whom poverty and suffering have already rendered inarticulate.

Dreiser's repeated references in his early books to the "chemical compound which is youth," the "chemic force" within the mind, "the chemic formula which works to reproduce the species," show that he believed in a sort of mechanistic psychology. He did not pretend to comprehend the workings of the mind, but he was *apparently* sure that there is nothing transcendental in it. This real but as yet unexplained phenomenon of human thought and vitality he deprived of some of its mystery by naming it "chemic." The notion that mental activity is a chemical reaction is not, of course, a full explanation of that activity, and nowhere does Dreiser suggest that it does constitute such a full explanation. He still recognized some wonderful mystery, some all-important force, which gives life its wonder and terror and meaning. Again and again in his autobiography, *A Book About Myself* (1922), he broods over the impermanence of life and his conviction that only living is of absolute value.

> When one was dead one was dead for all time. Hence the reason for the heartbreak over failure here and now; the awful tragedy of a love lost, a youth never properly enjoyed. Think of living and yet not living in so thrashing a world as this, the best of one's hours passing unused or not properly used. Think of seeing this tinkling phantasmagoria of pain and pleasure, beauty and all its sweets, go by, and yet being compelled to be a bystander, a mere onlooker, enhungered but never satisfied.

This yearning is everywhere in his books; it is a part of his temperament which we must feel in order to understand the peculiar qualities that he brought to his writing. As a materialist, then, he recognized, in *The "Genius"* (1915), that man is not in control of his destiny:

> Most of these young men (reporters) looked upon life as a fierce, grim struggle in which no quarter was either given or taken, and in which all men laid traps, lied, squandered, erred through illusion; a conclusion with which I now most heartily agree.

In this connection the account he gives of his first acquaintance with the works of Herbert Spencer, in about 1893, is worthy of quotation:

> I fear that I cannot make you feel how these things came upon me in the course of a few weeks' reading and left me numb, my gravest fears as to the unsolvable disorder and brutality of life eternally verified . . . There was of course this other (note the dichotomy) matter of necessity, internal chemical compulsion, to which I had to respond whether I would or no. I was daily facing a round of duties which now more than ever verified all that I had suspected and that these books proved. With a gloomy eye I began to watch how the chemical —and their children, the mechanical—forces operated through man and outside him, and this under my very eyes . . . and when I read Spencer I could only sigh. All I could think of was that since nature would not or could not do anything for man, he must, if he could, do something for himself; and of this I saw no prospect, he being a product of these selfsame accidental, indifferent and bitterly cruel forces.

Science did not appeal to Dreiser. He had had so much experience with human misery that it did not seem to him possible to achieve any reasoned explanation of the riddle of life. On the contrary he was endlessly impressed by the instances he saw of life's steady and purposeless flux: "What a queer, haphazard, disconnected thing this living was!" ". . . life is haphazard and casual and cruel; to some lavish, to others niggardly." "But as I wandered about I realized . . . that life was a baseless, shifting thing, its seeming ties uncertain and unstable and that that which one day we held dear was tomorrow gone, to come no more." "The tangle of life, its unfairness and indifference to the moods and longings of any individual, swept over me once more weighing me down far beyond the power of expression." This wonder at the ceaseless, confusing flux of life is elaborated in his book of "philosophy," the very title of which—*Hey, Rub-a-Dub-Dub; A Book of the Mystery and Terror and Wonder of Life* (1919)—is an expression of his characteristic attitude toward cosmic forces.[1]

The combination of his observations with his philosophy could produce only moral and ethical agnosticism; and indeed if his au-

---

[1] Dreiser's wide and sympathetic vision of life, his willingness to see and think about its sordid side, make one respect him for failing to arrive at a categorical explanation for the meaning of it all. If the philosopher must withdraw into an ivory tower in order to round out his system, the man who deals with the whole moving pathos of life-as-it-is should not be without some admiration. The practice among academic critics of disposing of Dreiser as a "peasant" or a "journalist" who could not think things through is based, if it has a base, upon ignorance of his personal experience.

tobiography is to be relied upon Dreiser had lost faith in conventional moral codes long before he had come upon the writings of Spencer. We find him declaring, in *A Book About Myself,* that "I am inclined to suspect that the monogamous standard to which the world has been tethered much too harshly for a thousand years or more now is entirely wrong. I do not believe that it is Nature's only or ultimate way of continuing or preserving itself. Nor am I inclined to accept the belief that it produces the highest type of citizen." And not only did he distrust the unthinking Christian repression of sex—he was concerned with the importance of the sexual urge in normal human life and with the impossibility of giving an authentic or rounded picture of human activity without taking full cognizance of its ubiquitous pressure and stimulation. "Via sex gratification—or perhaps better, its ardent and often defeated pursuit—comes most or all that is most distinguished in art, letters and our social economy, but underneath each and every one of such successes must primarily be written a deep and abiding craving for women, or some one woman, in whom the sex desires of any one person for the time being are centered. 'Love' or 'lust' (and the one is but an intellectual sublimation of the other) moves the seeker in every field of effort," he wrote in *Hey, Rub-a-Dub-Dub.*[2]

A warm, boundless human sympathy; a tremendous vital lust for life with a conviction that man is the end and measure of all things in a world which is nevertheless without purpose or standards; moral, ethical, and religious agnosticism; contact with the scientific thought of the late nineteenth century which emphasized the power and scope of mechanical laws over human desires; belief in a chemical-mechanistic explanation of the human machine; plus an overarching yearning for faith—these are the elements which Dreiser brought to the writing of his novels. Determinism did not attract him as a working hypothesis because he was more interested in the mystery and terror and wonder of life itself than in tracing those forces which might account for and so dispel the mystery.

Knowing Dreiser's life and character one avoids the pitfalls of assuming that his naturalism is derived primarily from other writers. Of literary "influences" it is sufficient to indicate that Dreiser had been urged to read Zola but had not read him when he wrote *Sister Carrie,* although he had been considerably impressed by a Zolaesque novel composed by one of his friends on a

---

[2] This book was written in 1919 and consequently shows evidence of familiarity with the Freudian approach to sex. It may be remarked, however, that Dreiser's attitude toward problems of sex is substantially the same in all of his novels from 1900 to 1925.

Chicago newspaper. On the other hand, he had gorged on Balzac as early as 1893-4. If literary influences were to be pursued, they would obviously point toward realism; but our concern here is to analyze the form which the naturalistic impulse received in his novels, rather than to search out the exact sources of that impulse in his reading.

Dreiser's "naturalism" found expression in four distinct stages. Different ideas about the body of theory just presented appear in succeeding novels and give them different significant forms,—until we come to his last novels, where the predominance of materialistic, non-teleological theory has gone, and in its place appears a solid affirmation of tradition and moral restraint as the values capable of resisting the deteriorating effects of modern society.

II

In the first stage, Dreiser was expounding his conviction of the essential purposelessness of life and attacking the conventional ethical codes which to him seemed to hold men to standards of conduct that had no rational basis in fact, while they condemned others without regard to what Dreiser thought might be the real merits of their situations. The first half of this program—expounding the purposelessness of life—is the backbone of his first novel, *Sister Carrie,* published in 1900. Through a queer juxtaposition of incidents, and with only small regard for the worthiness of their impulses, one character achieves fame and comfort while another loses his wealth, social position, pride, and finally his life.

Into this novel Dreiser has brought all the vivid reality of his own experience with the dreary, beaten, downtrodden life of those who have no money, background, sophistication, and no special talent. With a deep compassion that never assumes the right to pass moral judgment upon the actions of his characters, he shows Carrie Meeber coming to Chicago from the country, drearily passing from one ill-paid and health-breaking job to another, and at length, jobless and depressed by the thought of having to return defeated to the country, setting up housekeeping with Drouet, a "drummer" whom she had met on the train as she first entered the city.

With this social and financial advance, Carrie begins to recognize class differences, to long for "better" things, even to sense Drouet's limitations. Drouet's friend Hurstwood represents the next higher level of culture and wealth. He is manager of a prosperous saloon, he owns a fine house, and his family is eagerly climbing the social ladder. When he meets Carrie he falls desperately in love with her and, in what almost amounts to an abduction, he abandons his family, steals $10,000 from his employer, and flees with her through Canada and into New York.

From this point the fall of Hurstwood and the rise of Carrie are depicted in antiphonal relationship. Hurstwood's degeneration is a remarkable representation of the meaninglessness, almost unmotivated sort of tragedy that art had, until then, conspired to ignore. His wife's grasping jealousy and pettiness impel him towards Carrie, and his being seen with her gives his wife grounds for a divorce action. It is by the merest chance that he finds the safe open on the very night when he had planned to disappear. His theft of the money results from a frantic impulse which he is too weak to resist. When he tries to return the cash to the safe, he finds that the lock has clicked shut. So the theft is consummated by an accident. He is later forced to return the money, but he never recovers his self-esteem. In New York he takes a half interest in a second-rate saloon and after a time loses his investment. Then he dawdles, first looking for jobs, finally sitting in hotels instead of looking; at length he stays home, reading newspapers endlessly and hoarding the little money he has left. The change in his character from an affluent good-fellow to a seeedy miser is convincing and pathetic. Carrie stays with him as long as she can; but when she gets a place in a stage chorus she leaves him in order to room with a girl who is dancing in the same chorus. Hurstwood goes down—to poverty, destitution, begging, starvation, and finally suicide.

As he is drawing nearer to his sordid death, Carrie climbs rapidly until she is earning what was to her an unheard-of salary, living in one of the finest hotels in the city, and receiving proposals and attentions from men as far superior to Hurstwood at his best as he had been to the flashy Drouet: "Even had Hurstwood returned in his original beauty and glory, he could not have allured her." The book ends on a note of uncertainty. Carrie is not to be thought of as having attained any final goal. She is still longing and wondering, "an illustration of the devious way by which one who feels rather than reasons may be led in the pursuit of beauty. Though often disillusioned, she was still waiting for that halcyon day when she should be led forth among dreams become real."

Contemporary reviewers denounced the sordid content and the amoral attitude. They saw no inevitable punishment for transgression and no suggestion that there ought to be, but they missed the moral overtones; for although Dreiser appeals to Nature and rejects conventional moral codes, he also gropes beyond Nature toward a Transcendental concept of Spirit. He defends Drouet's "natural" pursuit of Carrie and suggests that his "conscience" is society's imposition: "He would need to delight himself with Carrie as surely as he would need to eat his heavy breakfast. He might suffer the least rudimentary twinge of conscience in whatever he did, and *in just so far he was evil and sinning"* (italics are mine). But Drouet's spontaneity reflects—or at least promises—something higher than impulse. "We have but an infantile perception of morals. There is more in the subject than mere conformity to a law of evolution. It is yet deeper than conformity to things of earth alone." Later he writes that man will be free when the conflict within him between instinct and will has been resolved,—that is, when the division between imperfect impulse and imperfect reason has been transcended into what the Transcendalists called Reason or Intuition. This development would erase the distinction between Nature and Spirit.

A consciously scientific use of detail appears when Dreiser brings chemical physiology to the explanation of Hurstwood's mental condition as he is beginning his final downward plunge:

> Constant comparison between his old state and his new showed a balance for the worse, which produced a constant state of gloom or, at least, depression. Now it has been shown experimentally that a constantly subdued frame of mind produces certain poisons in the blood, called katastates, just as virtuous feelings of pleasure and delight produce helpful chemicals called anastates. The poisons generated by remorse inveigh against the system, and eventually produce marked physical deterioration. To these Hurstwood was subject.

This, in small compass, is a clear-cut instance of the influence of science upon Dreiser's method: he is approaching his problem with a new set of instruments. The chemical explanation for mental conditions is of a piece with the amoral outlook and change of focus away from ethical plot-conflict toward the dispassionate *observation* of life. This latter problem brings one to the heart of what is new in the form of *Sister Carrie*.

Structurally, the novel consists of the two life cycles which are opposed to each other in studied balance. What *Sister Carrie* exhibits that is most characteristically naturalistic is the complete absence of ethical plot-complication. The movement of the novel does not depend upon acts of will by the central figures. It is the movement of life—skillfully selected and represented by the artist, to be sure, but still a movement which has little resemblance to the typical plot that begins with a choice or crucial action and ends with the satisfaction of the forces set in motion by that choice. There is no suspense created because the art of the novelist is directed by an entirely different motive. It is the quality of the lives represented that moves the reader, not the excitement of what the characters do. Here Dreiser reflects the impressionism of Crane and strikes a note that we have later in the work of Sherwood Anderson, where a very different sort of writer has in a different way presented the qualities of experience instead of choices and results. Having deprived his novel of the conventional structure, Dreiser supplies the two cycles —Carrie's rise and Hurstwood's descent. These two cycles embody the principle of change which Dreiser finds fundamental to all life and all natural processes. In a naïve mechanist's novel they would pretend to embody social laws. Not so with Dreiser.

Dreiser, primarily a novelist, never subordinates human values to philosophical implications. The reader is interested in Carrie as a person who faces problems comparable to his own; and if the reader is not to be offended by the course of the story, the successes and failures of the characters must in some way answer to the reader's notion of their worth as human beings. Because of this fact, ethical standards can hardly be eliminated from any novel. Carrie's rise, even though accidental, and not, by conventional standards, "deserved," is welcome because she is an appealing character; and Hurstwood's degeneration, distressing though it may be, is not unbearably offensive because Hurstwood has qualities which cause him to lose some of the reader's sympathy. The philosopher in Dreiser makes concessions to the novelist because his heart is in league with humanity. This is another way of saying that what happens in a piece of fiction must be probable, and probability includes the satisfactions, to some degree, of the moral sense. Hardy's *Return of the Native* appears to turn upon the cruellest coincidences, and yet each character in it experiences a morally probable fate. So with Dreiser. One cannot write stories in which, just as the crisis is approaching, the villain is killed by a falling meteor. Such things may occur in life, but they cannot in novels, which in their design and organization depict a truth that is free from the outrageous accidents of actuality. With these reservations, we may return to the assertion that *Sister Carrie* is organized to demonstrate the essential purposelessness of life. The plot structure of conventional fiction is abandoned for the new organization that answers to Dreiser's view of life.

But though he recognizes the operation of external forces, he is not, in *Sister Carrie,* concerned with an experimental demonstration of the nature of that operation. Rather he is concerned with the pathos of human life and with the constant inscrutable change that attends it. We come, in the last analysis, to a matter of emphasis: one may study the way external forces operate upon men, attempting to lay bare the secrets of their action; or one may see life through the eyes of the objects of these forces, with the wonder and terror of the changes unexplained. Dreiser does a little of both:

he shows clearly enough how Hurstwood and Carrie change as they do; but mostly he is concerned with bringing out the shifting, uncertain, mysterious nature of experience as it appears when being acted upon by forces which it cannot fathom and which—most terrible truth—have no purpose that can be related to the purposes of men.

Dreiser believes in a determinism which destroys or modifies the moral view of conduct. He is, further, impressed by the inscrutability of fortune, the lack of meaning and purpose in the action of external forces. Between these two smothering convictions flourishes his affirmation—his belief in the vitality and importance of life. It is upon the latter that one's attention is directed in *Sister Carrie*. The inscrutable variations of fortune serve chiefly to underline the positive quality of life—shifting, elusive, unaccountable—that holds our attention, rather than the spectacle of carefully analyzed forces operating under "experimental" conditions.[3]

Jennie Gerhardt (1911) is a sort of companion-piece to *Sister Carrie*, with the same major ideas but a shift in emphasis. In the latter, conventional moral codes are assumed to be invalid, while the action is concerned with demonstrating the unpredictable flux of life. In *Jennie Gerhardt* this unpredictable flux is assumed, and the action turns upon the moral and ethical standards according to which society (supposedly) operates. We see how the life of a lovely and sympathetic woman is blighted because her conduct is "officially" immoral; and the effect of the story is to suggest that standard Christian morality is inadequate either to guide or to judge conduct in a world that does not, as Dreiser sees it, answer to the assumptions underlying that code.

Jennie is a girl to whom life "is a true wonderland. . . . From her earliest youth goodness and mercy had molded her every impulse." A wealthy and distinguished Senator discovers her scrubbing floors in his hotel and, enchanted by her beauty and charm, decides to marry her; but he dies suddenly, before the marriage, leaving Jennie pregnant. After the child is born, the disgraced family moves to Cleveland where Jennie presently meets Lester Kane, scion of a wealthy Cincinnati family. He is generous, forceful, direct, and the slightest bit coarse-grained. In spite of his wealth

---

[3] The gap between Dreiser's work and the experimental novel of Zola is a wide one, for Dreiser does not make even a pretense of controlling his conditions and discovering truths about the nature of human psychology and physiology. Just where Zola, for example, would theoretically put most emphasis —i.e. in the extraction of laws about human nature—Dreiser is most uncertain and most sure that no certainty can be attained. To him such laws would be fruitless for the very reason that external conditions cannot ever be controlled —a fact of which all his experiences had convinced him.

and good breeding, the reader is made to feel that he is, emotionally, less beautifully constructed than Jennie, though he is capable of appreciating her fine nature and is, indeed, worlds beyond her culturally. Most of the book is devoted to their changing relations. He keeps her in various apartments, supplying her liberally with money, always half intending to marry her but never quite making up his mind to disturb the comfortable *status quo*.

Then forces conspire to take Lester away from her. His father dies, leaving Lester's inheritance contingent upon his abandoning Jennie. His family brings all its persuasive force to bear. And, to sweep aside the last hesitation, Lester is attracted by a cultivated and wealthy widow who is deeply in love with him. As always, Jennie is wholly unselfish in wanting Lester to do what is best for himself—and it is he who is uncertain which way to turn, drawn at once by loyalty to Jennie, fascination for Mrs. Gerald, the desire to retain his accustomed wealth and to be active in his father's business, and the influence exerted by his family and the polite society which wants him to become finally "respectable." Social ostracism, combined with the loss of a large part of his independent fortune, which makes Lester's need for a share in his father's estate more pressing, finally turn the balance against Jennie—though it is she who urges him to go.

At a subsequent meeting he tries to explain his feelings:

> "I was just as happy with you as I ever will be. It isn't myself that's important in this transaction apparently; the individual doesn't count much in the situation . . . All of us are more or less pawns. We're moved about like chessmen by circumstances over which we have no control. . . .
>
> "After all, life is more or less of a farce," he went on a little bitterly. "It's a silly show. The best we can do is to hold our personality intact. It doesn't appear that integrity has much to do with it." [4]

Stricken with a fatal illness, he calls her to his death bed, where he tells her,

> "I haven't been satisfied with the way we parted. It wasn't the right thing, after all. I haven't been any happier. I'm sorry. I wish now, for my own peace of mind, that I hadn't done it. . . . It wasn't right. The thing wasn't worked out right from the start; but that wasn't your fault. I'm sorry. I wanted to tell you that. I'm glad I'm here to do it."

The story ends with Jennie at the station for a last glimpse of the coffin. Her child has died, Lester is gone, she is destitute.

---

[4] This passage is notable as the most explicit statement of belief in the novel. It comes from Lester, but it represents Dreiser's own attitude because it is virtually the thesis of his novel.

A novel with a "kept woman" for its central figure would be somewhat unusual, but when that kept woman is presented as good and admirable, as possessing positive virtues which raise her quite above the general run of socially minded people, we recognize a novel in which conventional values are challenged, in which an unusual approach is taken to the problem of man in society.

In Jennie's world good intention and beauty of character are not necessarily rewarded. Nor is what is conventionally called evil punished. Hence standard ethics are discredited because they do not represent a realistic interpretation of social relations. They do not constitute the genuine forces which make for social cohesion and regulate the conduct of civilized men. This assumption is fundamental in *Jennie Gerhardt*. As the hero says, "The best we can do is to hold our personality intact." Jennie's goodness is valued more highly than the society which destroys her chance for happiness. Dreiser does not show that there may be extenuating circumstances to pardon the sinfulness of the "fallen woman." He denies that she is sinful; he deplores the moral codes which, failing to restrain her first slip, inflict a consciousness of guilt upon her ever after; he considers her good and beautiful, and the reader is led to conclude that Lester Kane was foolish (or very unlucky) not to have married her. These conclusions suggest that Dreiser believes in a spiritual truth which exists above the flux and error of actuality. He does not account for it, but he affirms its presence in Jennie and he deplores through his novel the social conditions which blight its growth and free expression.

But the pathos of Jennie's life is the outstanding fact of the novel, the fact upon which may depend any ideas that the reader may gather. As a work of art *Jennie Gerhardt* is highly successful; the ideas upon which it is based serve first of all to create a certain aesthetic effect and do not obtrude themselves in the way of that effect. It is too bad that Jennie should suffer, and the system is to be deplored for making her suffer, but that is not tantamount to saying that the institution of marriage, for example, should be rejected. It would indeed detract from the pathos of Jennie's situation if the author were crusading for change. The conditions which crush her must, for the purpose of the novel, be regarded as unchangeable.

III

In the second stage of his development Dreiser added the idea of the superman to the two main ideas which I have described. When one had found that life was meaningless and morals absurdly inadequate, the next step was to conclude that the only good lay in exercising one's will to power. The philosophy of the superman was conveniently available to enable Dreiser to take this step; and he wrote four novels about the activities of supermen in the modern business world. Nietzsche's philosophy saw in the superman the only hope for the betterment of mankind. Dreiser may have known this aspect of Nietzsche's thought, he may even have begun *The Financier* with the intention of demonstrating some such idea, but his study of the activities of one of the Robber Barons of the late nineteenth century seems finally to have drawn him away from the notion that the financial superman was an indispensable agent in the development of a capitalistic society.

Dreiser's "Trilogy of Desire," composed of *The Financier* (1912), *The Titan* (1914), and *The Stoic* (1947), represents his efforts to set forth the life of a modern financial superman. Although written from the point of view of the superman and begun as a celebration rather than an indictment of him, these novels virtually accomplished Jack London's avowed but unfulfilled purpose in writing the *Sea Wolf*—to show that "the superman cannot be successful in modern life . . . , he acts like an irritant in the social body." This cannot be called Dreiser's purpose, however, for he never arrived at that degree of conviction which would permit him to organize a portion of the social scene and write about it as if he had thought his way through to a final conclusion about its meaning. It is the planlessness and inconclusiveness of life that interested Dreiser. On the other hand, nearly all critics have ceased accusing him of being merely a patient recorder who copied his books tediously from newspaper records. The organizing hand of the artist is always present, but its purpose is not to reduce the complexity of life to a prettily simplified pattern that answers all one's questions about cause and effect, design and purpose.

The Financier and *The Titan* contain perhaps the greatest mass of documentation to be found in any American novels in the naturalistic tradition. They are records of an epoch of American life. The career of Charles T. Yerkes, traction magnate of Philadelphia and Chicago, supplied Dreiser with the materials for his two books. Yerkes is transformed into Frank Algernon Cowperwood, and the novels record his economic and amorous affairs in minutest detail. *The Financier* takes Cowperwood from boyhood up to the panic of 1873. A "superman" devoid of ethical restraints, he goes from business to business, gaining control of the Philadelphia street-railway network, and becoming involved with political graft. He becomes a millionaire and is laying plans to make a billion when the Chicago fire in 1871 causes a panic which wipes out his fortune. Because he seduced the daughter of the political boss, he is at this time abandoned by those in control and made a scapegoat for an indignant populace. After thirteen months in prison he is pardoned just in time to regain his fortune by selling short in the panic of 1873. Here ends *The Financier*.

The Titan is longer and more detailed. It tells how Cowperwood moves to Chicago and, through bribes and cleverness, gains a number of franchises for the distribution of suburban gas. After this coup he launches into a long fight to gain control of all the Chicago street railways. The facts are all there, vividly realized and brought to life. And since the affairs of Cowperwood are part and parcel of this vast economic complex, the recording of its intricacies is documentation in the closest naturalistic tradition. It is setting, condition, and material for the novel; none of it is extraneous, none gratuitous, because it is all a part of Cowperwood's career.

It has been shown in the discussion of both *Sister Carrie* and *Jennie Gerhardt* that Dreiser's determinism is determinism *after the fact*. That is, he does not pretend to go behind an act of so-called will and show all the conditions and pressures of which it is composed. In *The Financier* and *The Titan* there is the same attitude toward man and society, but the situation is greatly altered by a change in one of the factors of the problem. The factor of course is Frank Algernon Cowperwood. Instead of being relatively weak like Carrie, Hurstwood, Jennie, and Lester Kane, Cowperwood is endowed with tremendous energy and ability. He is born to conquer, and he knows it. Toward the end of *The Titan* he is still strong:

> he seemed a kind of superman, and yet also a bad boy—handsome, powerful, hopeful . . . impelled by some blazing internal force which harried him on and on.

He is the apotheosis of individualism, the man who moves the mass, which "only moves forward because of the services of the exceptional individual." He answers to the Nietzschean wish "that the significant individual will always appear and will always do what his instincts tell him to do."

At the end of *The Financier* Cowperwood has asserted himself stupendously, made and lost a great fortune, complicated the life of every banker and politician in Philadelphia, and yet, like Jennie and Lester Kane and Hurstwood, has been swept back and forth by environing forces more powerful than even his intelligence and resolution. Being a larger figure, he moves in a more elaborate complex of forces; but the forces elude his foresight and generalship and temporarily strip him of freedom and fortune.

At the end of the great struggle related in *The Titan,* when

Cowperwood is temporarily defeated by the enmity his power has evoked, Dreiser expatiates upon the spectacle of his superman's career:

> Rushing like a great comet to the zenith, his path a blazing trail, Cowperwood did for the hour illuminate the terrors and wonders of individuality. But for him also the eternal equation—the pathos of the discovery that even giants are but pygmies, and that an ultimate balance must be struck. Of the strange, tortured, terrified reflection of those who, caught in his wake, were swept from the normal and the commonplace, what shall we say? Legislators by the hundreds were hounded from politics into their graves; a half-hundred aldermen of various councils who were driven grumbling or whining into the limbo of the dull, the useless and the commonplace.

These sentences repeat the philosophy outlined earlier in connection with *Sister Carrie* and *Jennie Gerhardt*. The action of the books involves the same wondering uncertainty, the same vision of life as purposeless and unpredictable, the same denial of ethical codes, the same recognition of external pressures which determine the courses of our lives. What distinguishes *The Financier* and *The Titan* from the two previous novels is, as we have seen, the different weight given in them to the human factor in Dreiser's equation of change. Cowperwood is a greater force than Dreiser's earlier characters, but his position in the cosmos is essentially the same.

In conclusion we may consider the ethical import of these books. Hearing about them, one's reaction is that Dreiser must have composed them as an indictment of the business methods of the Robber Barons—to show that they were social menaces who should have been extirpated. Doubtless some such conclusion comes to the reader after he has finished the novels; but so long as he is reading them Cowperwood is the hero. His morals may not be held up as exemplary for American society, but his intelligence and energy make him the center of attention and concern. Further than this, Dreiser is frequently at pains to cast doubt upon the judgments which condemn Cowperwood. Early in *The Financier,* young Cowperwood gets his first lesson in the law of tooth and fang by catching a lobster devour a squid that was placed in a tank with him in a store window. The same novel ends with a parable about the Black Grouper, a fish which survives by virtue of its ability to change color and so deceive enemy and prey alike. We are asked,

> What would you say was the intention of the over-ruling, intelligent constructive force which gives to Mycteroperca this ability? To fit it to be truthful? To permit it to present an unvarying appearance which all honest, life-seeking fish may know? Or would you say that

subtlety, chicanery, trickery, were here at work? . . . The indictment is fair.

Would you say, in the face of this, that a beatific, beneficent, creative overruling power never wills that which is either tricky or deceptive?

The conclusion is that Christian ethics are illusory, that people should not be blamed for disobeying a code which, if followed, would render them unfit to survive.

It does not follow from this denial of conventional ethics that a Cowperwood is a boon to society. He may "move the mass," but Dreiser's own story shows that he does not move it to any good end. There is no paradox here. The point is that Dreiser is thinking in terms of the individual without sufficiently considering his social function. He is condemning "Divine Law" without apparently realizing that it often corresponds to natural law. Cowperwood cannot reasonably be condemned to hell-fire for following his natural bent, and it is natural for him to strive for power; but his social value is another matter. Dreiser denies a beneficent guiding Purpose, and so removes moral blame; but he does not investigate the social function of Cowperwood. If he did, he would unquestionably recognize society's need to restrain such individuals. And he has done so since then.

The "Genius" (1915) is cut from the same block as *The Financier* and *The Titan*. Both in form and thesis it resembles those novels so closely that an extended analysis of it is unnecessary. Eugene Witla, the hero of *The "Genius,"* is a superman like Cowperwood. He is an artist rather than a financier, but otherwise he is much the same sort of person. Like Cowperwood, again, he is set loose in the turbulence of modern life and permitted to exercise his superior cunning and resourcefulness untrammeled by moral restraints or inhibiting consideration for others. Like Cowperwood he has his successes and his failures, the forces which thwart his intentions frequently being the combination of weaker people who unite in defiance of his superman self-assertion. And again, Witla's amours occupy a large portion of the story, represent the superabundance of his artistic "genius," and are responsible for several of his misfortunes. Like *The Financier* and *The Titan*, *The "Genius"* consists of a loosely connected sequence of events related by chronology and by the fact that Eugene Witla participates in them all. The book, furthermore, ends upon a note of wonder and uncertainty which we have found to be characteristics of Dreiser's attitude of life at this stage. And finally, the superman hero is the center of reference and attention throughout the story. His effect upon society is not considered, for Dreiser is still brooding over the place of the individual in his meaningless cosmos. *The "Genius"* is probably also the most personal of Dreiser's books. Revelation replaces theory to a considerable degree.

IV

The third stage in Dreiser's naturalism is marked by his conversion to socialism. Here the ideas that signalized his first stage remain, but instead of advocating individual anarchy, as he tended to do under the aegis of Nietzsche, he has come to believe that something can be accomplished toward the amelioration of social evils if men will unite in a concerted attack upon those evils. *An American Tragedy* (1925) is founded upon this point of view, although we must remember that this, like Dreiser's other novels, is first of all a human story.

An American Tragedy is the story of how Clyde Griffiths goes from singing hymns on the streets of Kansas City, to working as a bellhop in Chicago, to prospering in the collar factory of his wealthy uncle, and, just as he has been taken up by a rich and fascinating society girl, to discovering that his factory girl-friend is pregnant. In desperation, after weeks of torturing worry, he plans to take her boating in the country and "accidentally" drown her. At the final moment he lacks courage to overturn the boat, but Chance—or the situation produced by the two personalities in their particular relation—completes the design in another way: seeing his despairing and horrified expression, Roberta comes toward him in the boat. He strikes out desperately to fend her off and unintentionally hits her with a camera. The boat capsizes, striking Roberta as she falls into the water, and Clyde refrains from saving her.

The rest of the story is devoted to the apprehension, trial, conviction, and execution of Clyde for the murder of Roberta. As the passage referred to above indicates, Clyde himself is not perfectly sure whether or not he is guilty. Before Roberta arose and came toward him in the rowboat, he had certainly decided that he would not commit the crime he had planned. On the other hand, he instituted the expedition with murder in his heart—a fact which exerted great influence upon the final decision of the jury. The prosecution brings dozens of witnesses and traces Clyde's movements minutely. Clyde's only defense is his last-minute change of heart, for which there is no evidence and which is easily counterbalanced by the absolute proof of his murderous intentions.

From an objective point of view one can hardly blame Clyde for an action in which he was largely a weak and helpless participant. Clyde did not wilfully produce the dilemma which called forth his attempt to resolve it. His craving for wealth and social position can be understood—like his complementary lack of ethical standards—in the light of his upbringing. His weakness is contemptible to some readers, but Dreiser certainly does not condemn it. Clyde has a certain power of choice, to be sure, which Dreiser does not reduce to its ultimate chemical constituents as the first naive naturalists thought they might finally be able to do; but that power of choice, though accepted as a factor in the problem, is shown to be conditioned by the many forces among which it exists.

In *An American Tragedy,* however, there is a difference of emphasis which is intimately associated with the structure of the novel. To begin with, Clyde is doubtless the weakest of Dreiser's heroes; he has least of the inexplicable inner drive which makes a commanding personality. He begins, further, with a pitifully meager background and narrow view of life. He is no Cowperwood or Witla superman—he has not even the charm of Carrie or Jennie. And as the novel proceeds there is so careful an attention to detail and so complete a delineation of the various experiences which add to Clyde's miserable store of ideas and ideals that the reader seems to be gaining a full insight into the forces which account for the nature of Clyde's personality. It is because of the simplicity of Clyde's character and the narrowness of his initial outlook that Dreiser is able to go so far behind the phenomenon of his "will" and explain its constituents.

This greater penetration of character goes hand in hand with a considerable difference in structure; for whereas the very essence and meaning of the earlier novels is to be found in the confused and inconclusive buffeting that makes up the lives of Carrie, Jennie, or even Cowperwood, the story of Clyde Griffiths takes its integrated and undeviating way through murder, arrest, trial, and execution. This unity is characteristic of tragedy, which can occur even in a naturalist's world and give form (and even some dignity) to what would otherwise be a dreary and meaningless life.

Although this difference in structure might be attributed merely to its content, there is, furthermore, a difference between the philosophy of the *American Tragedy* and the earlier novels which justifies the assertion that it marks a third distinct stage in Dreiser's naturalism. In *The Financier, The Titan,* and *The "Genius"* Dreiser saw life through the eyes of a superman, to whom it appeared as a welter of forces among which he must try somehow to work out his individual salvation. The damage to society in the career of a Cowperwood may be discovered in the books; but the purpose of those books is not to dwell upon the social evil of his career. Similarly, Eugene Witla's career is seen as an individual's

struggle, without particular social implications. In Clyde Griffiths'
progress, on the contrary, social implications abound. Dreiser had
been converted to socialism since writing *The "Genius"*; his American tragedy is a tragedy brought about by the society in which
we live. That society is responsible, as the immediate cause, for
Clyde's actions. This social consciousness marks the third stage of
Dreiser's naturalism. This is not to say that *An American Tragedy*
is an indictment of our social order. It is first of all a work of art,
the tragedy of Clyde Griffiths, a picture of a life that is tragic because the protagonist is at once responsible (as any human being
feels another to be) and helpless (as the philosopher views event).
. . . Clyde's tragedy is a tragedy that depends upon the American
social system. It shows the unfortunate effects of that system more,
for example, than did the defeat of Cowperwood at the end of
The Titan. In the latter instance a "superman" was battling the
opposition aroused by his will to power. In Clyde's case the whole
of the American social order, in its normal activity, is brought into
the picture.

V

I have deferred discussion of *The Stoic* because, although it completes the "Trilogy of Desire," taking up Cowperwood's career after
the Chicago débâcle, it was not published until 1947, thirty-three
years after *The Titan*. Dreiser had most of the book written shortly
after publication of *The Titan*, but he kept it by him because he
could not, apparently, work it through to a satisfactory conclusion.
In the meantime he wrote new sorts of novels which took him into
new spheres of thought where it became increasingly difficult to
carry through the implications of ideas which were still growing
while he wrote the two earlier volumes.

The opening chapters discover Cowperwood taking stock after his
expulsion from the Chicago scene. Love and business as usual are
interwoven, on this occasion when Berenice Fleming, the most
charming and talented woman he has known, whom he has supported through her adolescence, now in the bloom of young woman-
hood gives herself to him and persuades him also to undertake a
new and grander venture in the world of finance. Renewed by the
consummation of his love for Berenice, he lays plans to invade the
traction business of London, and very soon has set in motion a
gigantic scheme to unify and modernize the London underground
system.

Complications appear by virtue, as usual, of the impingement of

sex upon business. Lord Stane, who is to launch Cowperwood socially as well as bring his large Underground holdings into the
financial pool, falls in love with Berenice. On a money-raising trip
to America, Cowperwood enters a brief but intense affair with a
young dancer. When his wife, Aileen, who has been temporarily
shelved, reads of this she threatens to expose Cowperwood in a
scandal that will ruin his British operations. But now, when the
elements of a highly dramatic involvement are set before us, the
story comes to an abrupt and inconclusive ending.

Cowperwood dies of Bright's disease.

Following his death, his fortune of some $12,000,000 is quickly
eaten away by taxes, litigation, assessments, litigation, and more
litigation. His great house and art collection are auctioned off to
pay claims. There is no money to build the hospital he had arranged to leave to the City of New York. Aileen is put out of her
house, forced to take an absurdly small settlement, and dies of
pneumonia. We hear nothing of what happens to the great London Underground unification. Cowperwood is treated somewhat
unkindly by the press, as his enormous fortune and influence
evaporate when he is no longer present to maintain them. If he has
been a "superman," he has made no permanent impression on society, and his material contribution of street railway systems will
not provide alms for oblivion. Any larger significance of his demise
is lost because Dreiser devotes most of his attention to the sordid
vanity of Aileen, who deserts Cowperwood on his death bed when
she learns that Berenice is seeing him.

But most striking and extraordinary of culminations is the turning of Berenice to Yogi in the concluding chapters. Here the divided
stream of American transcendentalism does astonishing things.
Wandering in a chaos of pure materialistic flux, Dreiser allows his
heroine in these closing chapters to leap to pure Spirit, to Brahma,
and to the contemplation and realization of Divine Love. And
Dreiser too seems to make the leap, because it appears beyond any
question that Berenice carries his thoughts and convictions. She is
the most sensitive and intelligent of his characters; she is the only
one who makes significant discoveries about the folly and selfishness of even the most cultivated materialistic life; her four years of
study with a Guru in India are presented with utter seriousness.
This leap of Dreiser's from pure matter to pure Spirit invites various speculations and comments. The philosophical abysses of
Brahmanism, with its concepts of unknowable mysteries and endless cosmic cycles of repetition, are psychologically not un-related
to the abysses of purposeless flux which terrify the devoted materialist. Nor has it ever been possible to say that Dreiser denied the

existence of mysteries. Always in league with humanity, from his earliest book he presented the mazes of the human quest as pathetic and compelling. He sought through his love of men to express the sense of an ideal pattern for which he had sought vainly in nature.

Viewed in artistic terms, however, Dreiser's conclusion of *The Stoic* must be considered grotesque. Berenice is too utterly brilliant and dazzling to be quite real. Her love of fine things, her absorption with herself, her whimsical intelligence, and her courageous defiance of convention in becoming Cowperwood's mistress—these are too many traits to fuse into a convincing personality. In India she ascends through all the levels of Yogi to a direct experience of the supreme Reality—a level from which it is hardly probable that she would return to New York, make the amazing discovery that there is poverty there just as in India, and so devote herself to building and working in the hospital that Cowperwood had planned. The birth of a social consciousness comes naïvely twinned to the discovery of Brahma. Another false start occurs when Berenice finds herself drawn by the culture and charm of Lord Stane. He seems to have the background that Cowperwood lacks. His interests, to, are much broader. And Cowperwood who had sworn undying love for Berenice, has just been revealed as having a new love affair in New York. But nothing comes of this potential conflict (a favorite in American fiction, by the way), for Berenice decides that Cowperwood's attraction is irresistible. We see her at one moment shrewdly calculating a liaison of vengeance but at the next giving in to pure passion and fascination. After Berenice returned from India to discover that Cowperwood's fortune had vanished into the pockets of lawyers, she "was filled with sorrow as she inwardly viewed the wreckage of all of his plans." Now Cowperwood's plans were largely predacious and materialistic. After her years of study with the Guru, Berenice would have known that Cowperwood's desire to perpetuate his name by leaving a museum, was not to be confused with the charity which suffereth all. Yet this is what she appears to do. These are all indications of Dreiser's failure to adapt his materials into an effective pattern. Too many ideas wander about the marches of his action without actually being involved in it.

What finally identifies the structural failure of this book is Dreiser's failure to manage the problem of *scale*. He began by describing financial transactions in a detail that would have carried the volume to 600 pages, but these are casually abandoned in the midst of the barest beginnings of the great London venture. The love entanglements, likewise, are given here and there such minute detail that they create the expectation of an exhaustive presentation; but they turn out to be only samples of a whole that does not take shape. The point of view shifts loosely from person to person at least a dozen times during the story. Minds are invaded and then abandoned with little regard for the values of a controlled point of view. The tired and grainy fragments of the story fall apart. The architectonics of naturalism have disappeared. Having liberated Dreiser's talent, naturalism left him with a cumbersome technique which he could not use for his newer ideas.

If Dreiser's novel appears wooden, it is because the mixture of new ideas and old is grotesque; the style and the techniques of characterization have not accommodated the new ideas. His characters are introduced and described formally—background, occupation, financial status, followed by a few words of generalization about personality or character. For example:

> Also present were Lord and Lady Bosvike, both young and smart and very popular. They were clever at all sports, enjoyed gambling and the races, and were valuable in any gathering because of their enthusiasm and gaiety. Secretly they laughed at Ettinge and his wife, though at the same time they valued their position and deliberately set themselves out to be agreeable to them.

This writing has not made use of modern techniques of characterization or modern concepts of personality. It illustrates rather Dreiser's consistent use of the formal Victorian categories, like honesty, diligence, and piety. This makes *The Stoic* seem old-fashioned in 1949; if "naturalism" is new and unusual, then naturalism has vanished from *The Stoic*. Where it most clearly appears is in Dreiser's treatment of love. This is anything but Victorian, for to him love is dependent upon all the social, financial, and personal forces that operate at any moment. It is a tension of lust, ambition, vanity, insecurity, and hate; an alteration in any of these elements will unbalance the tension and set it moving toward a new relationship. Dreiser is not able to exhibit this idea dramatically, but it appears again and again in the thoughts of his characters. Anyone making a new acquaintance of the opposite sex wonders what it would be like to be in love with him and adds up the various financial and social complications. Even in their moments of passion, lovers are busy assessing the *status* of their relation, for nothing is permanent and every action initiates irreversible changes. This fragment of the old Dreiser struggles rather feebly in *The Stoic* with Yogi, traces of socialism, and the writer's weariness. The return to Spirit, although it completes the broken arc of the transcendental tradition, does not furnish here a pattern for coherent fiction.

Dreiser's final novel, although published a year earlier than *The*

Stoic was conceived many years later and written long after the greater part of *The Stoic* was finished. *The Bulwark* (1946) appears to represent a transitional stage between the materialism of his earlier work and the Brahminism which appears in the closing pages of *The Stoic*. It deals with three generations of Quakers in Pennsylvania. They go from piety to prosperity to perdition. The protagonist is Solon, of the middle generation, who gets rich, clings to the Inner Light, but sees his children drawn away into various forms of vice and vanity because they cannot resist the material attractions of fine clothes and automobiles or the physical attractions of sex. The novel has a double theme. Sociologically, it shows that the control exercised by a religion of simplicity like Quakerism is powerless against the lures of American materialism. Within Solon it shows the same conflict: Solon contributes to the downfall of his children because he thinks he can serve both God and Mammon. By serving Mammon he makes a lot of money, which opens up the world of ostentation and vice to his children. If they had all lived in poverty, they would not have been tempted. Yet, paradoxically, it is Solon's Quaker background that makes him sober, industrious, and trustworthy—so that he can rise to affluence as a banker. (I do not know what to say about the unquestioned fact that there have been and still are many Quaker families where wealth and simplicity do go together without difficulty, even through several generations. They do not appear in the argument of *The Bulwark*.)

The Bulwark does not reveal the mixture and confusion of communism and Yogi that appear in *The Stoic*. When Solon becomes a successful banker, rich enough to give his children the luxuries they crave, it is not suggested that he is exploiting the poor or living on the unearned increment of usury. His rise is presented as the reward of diligence and devotion. It appears in time that he has erred in believing that the moral sobriety of Quakerism could carry him through financial maneuvers unscathed; but his error is, depending upon how one regards it, either a fatal error that was inescapable under the circumstances or the error of judgment of a man who could not foresee where his commercial involvements would take him. Any Marxian analysis of his experiences much be supplied by the reader. The frivolous outlooks of his children are not attributed to the class struggle but are presented *sub specie aeternitatis;* here, he seems to say, are children growing up with false human values,—values that do not call forth the good of which these children are capable. Their lives are wasted in ostentation and frivolity.

The early Dreiser would have stressed the idea that they were not responsible for their standards; he would have implied that any standards were relative and therefore questionable. Latterly he hurried past these old and easy assumptions to consider what values are good and where they can be found. The Inner Light of Quakerism is not said to be the perfect guide, but it is a guide which made the old people strong and which sustained Solon until he meddled with such powerful gods as Mammon and Moloch. Although Quakerism is not contrasted with Buddhism or Yogi or Platonism, it is clearly presented as a way which made strong Americans; and its strength lies in its qualities of tradition and myth. These compel belief, fidelity, and discipline—without which it would appear that man is not capable of leading a coherent life. The whole book asserts that man must be guided—that is, man in modern America—by powerful attachments to an Authority that he accepts on faith. The rigid morality of Quakerism dampens spontaneity and snubs impulse. To the early Dreiser such repression was bad. Now it is good, for it is a discipline that strengthens the will and quickens the spirit. Dreiser has turned from materialistic monism to Christian dualism, from impulse to control, from nature to spirit, from iconoclasm to traditionalism, from flux to myth.

This is the first novel in which Dreiser has been confronted with the problem of advancing four or five separate actions, instead of concentrating on one person, as in his early novels, and the result is not fortunate. It is, to begin with, difficult for a writer of Dreiser's diffuseness to deal with the birth, early education, adolescence, and "end" of five children and their parents in less than 400 pages. He has performed this task through the small end of a telescope: occasional incidents are dramatized, but most are recounted hastily, in a succession of two and three-page chapters. Characters are developed only to be dropped; others live and die without ever coming to life; others are introduced, forgotten, and then embarrassingly revived for a new occasion. This failure of form reveals a literary artistry that could not keep pace with the changing times. In the historical context of 1900, a straight-line presentation of one incident after another was striking and powerful. Given a prevailing notion of form in the novel, the denial of it becomes a form. The movement of Dreiser's early novels had such a form. But without that-from-which-it-revolts the same work would be either chaotic or commonplace. Here the latter is true, for there is, in this matter, a dialectic at work; whereas in 1900 Dreiser expressed a powerful antithesis, in 1946 the same kind of form is irrelevant because several new syntheses have nullified the tension in which it formerly participated. Nor, in view of the confusion of its plots, can we say that *The Bulwark* is as well constructed as *Sister Carrie*. Today it will be asked, with genuine bewilderment, whether *The*

Bulwark is naturalistic. The question would not have been asked in 1900, when it would have struck the pious reader that here was a shockingly detached presentation of moral issues: a boy who strays into vice because he has been repressed at home, who commits suicide rather than bear the shame of having been in jail, who has, in fine, not been equipped to judge wisely and so is not judged by the author. To the world of 1900 this would have seemed an attack upon the very concept of moral responsibility. Today it is commonplace.

As I have already said, Dreiser's greatness as a novelist cannot be accounted for by his naturalism. His greatness is in his insight, his sympathy, and his tragic view of life. Although *The Bulwark* reveals major shifts in his beliefs, and although it is very clumsily contrived, it could still have had all the power and greatness of *Jennie Gerhardt* or *An American Tragedy* if Dreiser had succeeded, to use James's term, in "rendering" his idea. I would not suggest that *The Bulwark* fails because Dreiser abandoned some of his old theories, for much the same view of life is there. Dreiser was bewildered because the world was too complicated and he was not equipped to understand it. Sister Carrie seeks a meaning in her experience, which she cannot find. Solon Barnes has a meaning but cannot live by it, and at the end of the book he is not unlike Carrie in wondering why events have happened as they have.

Thus the fourth stage of Dreiser's naturalism is not naturalism, after all, and it is indeed most instructive to see how easily the style, the method, and the attitudes of the early Dreiser are entirely converted in these final novels to the uses of Authority and Spirit. Having brooded long and sadly over the materialist's world, he turns away from it at the end without greatly changing his tone.

An American Tragedy

by Robert Penn Warren

Theodore Dreiser once said that his philosophy of love might be called "Varietism." But there was one mistress to whom he remained faithful, after his fashion, all his life. That mistress was the bitch-goddess Success. He knew all her failings and falsities. He knew that her sweetest kiss would turn to dust on the tongue. But he could never forget her face. And all his stories are about her.

Dreiser was born in Terre Haute, Indiana, in 1871, of an immigrant German father and an illiterate Moravian mother. The father was a Catholic, pious, rigid, and totally incompetent, "a thin grasshopper of a man, brooding wearily." The mother was warm-hearted and full of unjudging sympathy for the defeated, maimed, and erring, but had little capacity to make up for the father's practical failure. Dreiser knew a boyhood of poverty, ignorance, rejection, sad yearnings, and grandiose daydreams. In his youth he was, as he says in his autobiography, "blazing with sex, as well as with a desire for material and social supremacy," but his anger at the frustration of this "materialistic lust of life" was sometimes transmuted into a pity for others deprived like himself, for "life in all its helpless degradation and poverty, the unsatisfied dreams of people." He saw that pain is pain, even when it is pain at the frustration of unworthy desire. He saw, for instance, his father's impotence in the face of the booming economic system he could never understand; he saw one brother jailed for forgery, and another hit the road to die, by the time he was forty, of dissipation and defeat; he saw one sister early seduced by a political bigshot of Terre Haute, and later another sister come home to give birth to an illegitimate child.

But Dreiser, still a boy, saw also the brother who had been jailed turn up as Paul Dresser, a successful song-writer and theatre man, elegant in a fur coat, to snatch the family out of starvation and establish them in a house owned by his current sweetheart—the prototype of Sal in his song "My Gal Sal" and a successful whore-momma of Evansville, Indiana.

And the young Dreiser, who saw the fur coat and silk hat of Paul Dresser, was soon to see the rambunctious, brutal energy of Chicago on the make. So success was possible, too. Dreiser was, in fact, the child of the Gilded Age, but the gilding he knew was the glitter of gaslight on rhinestone, red plush, and saloon art; and this glitter remained, in one part of his being, the image of the highest beauty, even when, in some of the novels, the glitter of rhinestone is officially replaced by the cold fire of the diamond and the saloon art by genuine oils attributed to Bouguereau.

Into the worship of success entered another notion—the notion, derived from observation and from reading Balzac, Zola, Spencer, and Huxley, that life is merely the blind collision of "accidental, indifferent, and bitterly cruel forces." In this world the virtues of neither Christianity nor Horatio Alger could be closely depended upon to prevail. But there was something worse than the prospect of surrendered virtue. Of his discovery of Huxley and Spencer, he says: "Up to this time there had been in me a blazing and un-checked desire to get on, the feeling that in doing so we did get somewhere; now in its place was the definite conviction that spirit-ually one got nowhere. . . ."

One got nowhere, there was blankness; but for all men there was, nevertheless, the doom of desire, the compulsion blazing un-checked and beyond the tutelage of any philosophy; and for Drei-ser himself that doom was compounded by a second, the doom of having to record the saga of desire and thus relive its pathos.

Dreiser's saga of desire has two forms. The first form is the story of the superman, like Cowperwood of *The Titan* and *The Finan-cier* or Witla of *The 'Genius'*, the brutal realist who sees through the shams of the world and ruthlessly applies the force of his own superior "chemism"—to use another of Dreiser's infelicitous words, like "varietism"—in that collision of "bitterly cruel forces" which is life. In these stories, we find some documentary value, the value of old photographs and newspaper clippings, the color of a period, the shock that the idea of the survival of the fittest made on the old-fashioned world, a notion of what some of the Titans and Geniuses of the period may have thought, in their deepest selves, of themselves, and even moments of dramatic force. But all in all, there is a dreary and mechanical repetitiousness in these tales of the triumph of superior "chemisms" in the collision of "accidental, indifferent, and bitterly cruel forces."

Here we see the stultifying effects of Dreiser's philosophy when directly applied to the materials of life. The trouble, let us hasten to say, does not lie in the basic nature of the philosophy itself. Dreiser's philosophy, though crudely put and grossly naked of any decent professional draperies, is but another example of nineteenth-century materialism—the vision of the God-abandoned and sanction-stripped world of natural process. The trouble, for fiction at least, is not even that Dreiser has no subtle dialectic to develop the logical implications of the vision. The trouble is the spirit in which Dreiser applies the idea to the materials of life. The ideas of Zola or Hardy are not, at root, greatly different from those of Dreiser. The difference between *Nora* or *Tess* and *The Titan* is the spirit in which the ideas are related to experience. This is a spirit that tends to schematize those materials deductively, to delimit arbitrarily the range of human experience, to deny the constructive and idealizing function of imagination in his characters and, in the end, in himself.

There is, furthermore, another kind of trouble in these tales of success. Dreiser, looking back on the life-hating God of his grasshopper-thin, brooding father, and hating that father for his life-failure, could, in part of his being, vindictively rejoice in the death of God, and vicariously fulfill, in the triumph of his Lucky Jims, those energies which he had feared that God and the father, in their several ways, had robbed him of. The vindictive rejoicing and the vicarious fulfilment combine to deprive these stories of emotional resonance. These qualities, despite the scrupulous documentation, infect the work with abstraction. They give, instead of the richness and suggestiveness of life, an impression of dreary compulsion and mechanical repetition. Ultimately we miss the human awareness. These tales of success are, we may say, the work done under the aegis of the father; and they fail.

The second form of the saga of desire is the stories of failure; and they do not fail. *Sister Carrie, Jennie Gerhardt,* and *An American Tragedy* are the work done, to pursue our conceit, under the aegis of the mother. Something of that unjudging warmth of heart which Dreiser reports of her enables him to transmute the bitterness of his own recollected failures and chronic fears of the future into a tenderness toward creatures doomed, for whatever reason, to fail. His approach is not deductive here; he lives, and relives, their failure. The "chemisms" may blindly and cruelly collide and the great machine of the universe grind blankly on, but the fact of the blindness and blankness of the process does not abolish the pain of a victim. Nor does it abolish that mysterious sense of triumph which Jennie Gerhardt feels at the end of her story, in the midst of her failure. It may be argued that Sister Carrie herself does not "fail," that she rises in the world. But her success is as much

a part of the world of blind accident as is Hurstwood's failure, and
the image of Carrie at the end, in her rocking chair, is the image
of someone who, in getting somewhere, has gone nowhere.

In these tales the human awareness is set over against the natural process of which the human creature is a part, and the unre-
solvable paradox of that confrontation is the drama. It is the drama
in which we all live—or at least the drama which we must take
as a starting point for whatever our interpretation of our living
and whatever effort to resolve the paradox. It is the drama, too, in
which Dreiser's imagination stirs to life.

Dreiser's tales of failure are his successes, and *An American
Tragedy,* in which failure is unalleviated, is his greatest success.
Published in 1925, it is the work in which he could look backward
from the distance of middle-age and evaluate his own experience
of success and failure. We feel, in this book, the burden of the
personal pathos, the echo of the personal struggle to purge the
unworthy aspirations. We also feel, in this book, the burden of a
historical moment, the moment of the Great Boom which climaxed
the period from Grant to Coolidge, the half century in which the
new America of industry and finance capitalism was hardening into
shape and its secret forces were emerging to dominate all life. In
other words, *An American Tragedy* can be taken as a document,
both personal and historical, and it is often admired, and defended,
in these terms.

As a document it is indeed powerful, but such documentary
power is derivative: an artifact dug from the Sumerian tomb moves
us whether it is beautiful or not simply because some human
hand, nameless and long since dust, had fashioned it; and a book
may move us because we know what, of a man's life or of a moment in history, it represents. But the power of *An American
Tragedy* is not derivative. The weight of Dreiser's experience and
of the historical moment are here, but they are here as materials;
in the strange metabolism of creation, they are absorbed and
transmuted into fictional idea, fictional analogy, fictional illusion.
The book is "created," and therefore generates its own power, mul-
tiplying the power implicit in the materials.

The thing in *An American Tragedy* most obviously created
is Clyde Griffiths himself. The fact that Dreiser, in his characteristic way, chose a model for Clyde—one Chester Gillette, who, in
1906, had drowned his sweetheart, Grace Brown, in Moose Lake,
Herkimer County, N. Y.—does not make Clyde less of a creation.
Rather, it emphasizes that he is a creation; and the contrast between the dreary factuality of an old newspaper account and the

anguishing inwardness of the personal story may well have served as a mirror for the contrast that always touched Dreiser's feelings and fired his imagination—the contrast between the grinding impersonality of the machine of the world and the pathos of the personal experience. In fact, the novel begins and ends with an image of this contrast: the family of street preachers, in the beginning with the boy Clyde and in the end with the illegitimate son of Clyde's sister Esta, stand lost between the "tall walls of the commercial heart of an American city" and lift up their hymn "against the vast skepticism and apathy of life." The image of the boy Clyde looking up at the "tall walls" of the world is the key image of the novel.

The creation of the character of Clyde is begun by a scrupulous accretion of detail, small indications, and trivial events. We are early caught in the dawning logic of these details. We see the sidewise glances of yearning. We see how, when he discovers his sister Esta in the secret room, pregnant and abandoned, his first reaction is selfish; how only when she refers to "poor Mamma" does his own sympathy stir; how this sympathy is converted suddenly into a sense of world-pathos, and then, in the end, turns back into self-pity. We see him staring at the rich house of his uncle, and again when for the first time he lays eyes on Sondra, with "a curiously stinging sense of what it was to want and not to have." We see his real sadness at Roberta's jealousy, which he, also one of the deprived, can feel himself into, but we know that his pity for her is, at root, self-pity. We see him open the *Times-Union* to see the headline: *Accidental Double Tragedy at Pass Lake*. We see all this, and so much more, and remember his mother's letter to him after his flight from Kansas City: ". . . for well I know how the devil tempts and pursues all of us mortals, and particularly just such a child as you." And what a stroke it is to fuse the reader's foreboding interest with the anxiety of the mother!

For Dreiser's method of presenting the character is far deeper and more subtle than that of mere accretion. The method is an enlargement and a clarifying, slow and merciless, of a dimly envisaged possibility. We gradually see the inward truth of the mother's clairvoyant phrase, "such a child as you"; and the story of Clyde Griffiths is the documentation of this.

A thousand strands run backward and forward in this documentation, converting what is a process in time into a logic outside of time. When back in Kansas City, we see Clyde's sexual fear and masochism in relation to the cold, cunning Hortense, we are laying the basis for our understanding of what will come later, the repetition with Sondra of the old relationship and the avenging of it on the defenseless Roberta. When in the room of women where Clyde is foreman, he looks wistfully out the window on the summer river, we are being prepared for the moment when he first encounters Roberta at the pleasure lake, and for the grimmer moment to come on Big Bittern Lake. When, on the night after the first meeting with Sondra, Clyde does not go to Roberta, we know that this is a shadowy rehearsal for the last betrayal and murder.

It is not only that we find, in an analytic sense, the logic of character displayed; in such instances we find this logic transliterated into a thousand intermingling images, and in this transliteration the logic itself becoming the poetry of destiny. We see the process moving toward climax when, on the train, on the death ride with Roberta, Clyde flees from his own inner turmoil into the objective observations which, in their irrelevancy, are the mark of destiny: *Those nine black and white cows on that green hillside,* or *Those three automobiles out there running almost as fast as the train.* And we find the climax of the process in the "weird, contemptuous, mocking, lonely" call of the weir-weir bird which offers a commentary on the execution, as it had on the birth, of the murderous plan.

This transliteration of logic into a poetry of destiny is what accounts for our peculiar involvement in the story of Clyde. What man, short of saint or sage, does not understand, in some secret way however different from Clyde's way, the story of Clyde and does not find it something deeper than a mere comment on the values of American culture? Furthermore, the mere fact that our suspense is not about the *what* but about the *how* and the *when* emphasizes our involvement. No, to be more specific, our *entrapment*. We are living out a destiny, painfully waiting for a doom. We live into Clyde's doom, and in the process live our own secret sense of doom which is the backdrop of our favorite dramas of the will.

How deep is our involvement—or entrapment—is indicated by the sudden sense of lassitude, even relief, once the murder is committed; all is now fulfilled, and in that fact the drawstring is cut. So we may even detach ourselves, at least for the moment, from the youth now "making his way through a dark, uninhabited wood, a dry straw hat upon his head, a bag in his hand . . ."

As a commentary on Dreiser's art, we can note how, after this sentence that closes Book II, Dreiser jerks back his camera from that lonely figure and begins Book III by withdrawing into magisterial distance for a panoramic sweep of the lens: "Cataraqui County extending from the northernmost line of the village known as Three Mile Bay on the south to the Canadian border, on the

north a distance of fifty miles. Its greater portion covered by uninhabited forests and . . ." The whole effect is that of detachment;
and with this we are restored, after a long painful while, to the
role of observer, uninterested and critical, not involved.

But we shall not be long permitted to keep this comfortable
role. Soon the camera will come close to the cell where Clyde waits,
the focus will be sharpened. And in this alternation of focus, and
shift from involvement to detachment, we find one of the deep
art-principles of the work, one of the principles of its compelling
rhythm. It is compelling because the shift of focus is never arbi-
trary; it grows out of the expressive needs of the narrative as Dreiser has conceived it, and out of the prior fact that the narrative is
conceived in a drama between the individual and the universe.

Randolph Bourne once said that Dreiser had the "artist's vision
without the sureness of the artist's technique." This is true of
most of Dreiser's books, and in a limited sense may be true of *An
American Tragedy*. I have used the phrase "Dreiser's art" in full
awareness that most critics, even critics as dangerous to disagree
with as Lionel Trilling, will find it absurd; and in full awareness
that even those who admire Dreiser will, with few exceptions,
concede a point on "art," or apologetically explain that Dreiser's
ineptitudes somehow have the value of stylistic decorum and can
be taken as a manifestation of his groping honesty, and will then
push on to stake their case on his "power" and "compassion."

But ultimately how do we know the "power" or the "compassion"—know them differently, that is, from the power or compassion we may read into a news story—except by Dreiser's control?
Except, in other words, by his grasp of the human materials and
his rhythmic organization of them, the vibrance which is the life
of fictional illusion, that mutual interpenetration in meaning
of part and whole which gives us the sense of preternatural fulfilment? Except, in short, by art?

There is a tendency to freeze the question of Dreiser as an artist
at the question of prose style. As for prose style, Dreiser is a split
writer. There is the "literary" writer whose style is abominable.
But there is another writer, too, a writer who can write a scene with
fidelity if not always with felicity. But sometimes there is the
felicity, a felicity of dramatic baldness: the letters of Mrs. Griffiths
or Roberta; the scene of Roberta back home, in her mother's
house, looking out at the ruined fields; or the scene when Clyde
first sees Sondra, with that "curiously stinging sense of what it is
to want and not to have."

Words are what we have on the page of a novel, and words are

not only a threshold, a set of signs, but a fundamental aspect of
meaning, absorbed into everything else. Words, however, are not
the only language of fiction. There is the language of the unfolding
scenes, the language of the imagery of enactment, with all its primitive massiveness—the movie in our heads, with all the entailed
questions of psychological veracity and subtlety, of symbolic densities and rhythmic complexities. I am trying here to indicate
something of the weight of this language, or better, languages, as
an aspect of Dreiser's art.

With this intention we can return to the question of the rhythm
between detachment and involvement, which manifests itself in
shifts of pace and scale. But we may find the basis for another
rhythm in the fact that the personal story of Clyde is set in a whole
series of shifting perspectives. By perspective I do not mean a point
of view in the ordinary technical sense. I mean what may be called
an angle of interest. For instance, the picture of the organization
of the collar factory in Lycurgus gives a perspective on life, and
on the fate of Clyde; this is another contrast between a mechanism
and man, a symbolic rendering of the ground idea of the novel.

But there are many perspectives. There is the perspective of the
religious belief of the family, which returns in the end to frame
the whole story; that of the world of the bell-hop's bench in the
hotel; that of sex and "chemism"; that of the stamping room in
the factory with its mixture of sex, social differences, power, and
money; that of the economic order of Lycurgus which stands as
a mirror for the world outside; that of the jealousies and intrigues
of the young social set of the town, jealousies and intrigues which,
ironically enough, make it possible for Clyde to enter that charmed
circle; that of justice and law in relation to the political structure
of Cataraqui County; that of the death house.

Sometimes a perspective comes as an idea boldly stated, sometimes as implicit in a situation or person. In fact, all the persons
of the novel, even the most incidental, are carriers of ideas and
represent significant perspectives in which the story may be viewed.
In the enormous cast there are no walk-ons; each actor has a role
in the structure of the unfolding dialectic. And it is the pervasive
sense of this participation, however unformulated, that gives the
novel its density, the weight of destiny.

If, as a matter of fact, the dialectic were insisted upon as dialectic we should not find this weight. We find it only because the
dialectic unfolds in personality, in the presentation of personality
not as a carrier of idea but as a thing of inner vibrance. The mother,
for instance, is a small masterpiece of characterization. She is the
carrier of "religion," but with her own inner contradictions, exists

in her full and suffering reality, a reality which, at the end when she comes to join Clyde, affirms itself by her effect on everyone around. Roberta is fully rendered, not only in her place in the social and economic order and in her role as victim, but with the complexity of her humanity. When her friend Grace catches her in a lie about Clyde, she stiffens with "resentment." She does not quite tell the truth to her mother about why she moves out of her first room. In the midst of her as yet submerged moral struggle she deceives even herself as to why she selects a room downstairs and with an outside door in the new house. She is a sufferer, but she is not beyond the flash of jealous anger when Clyde, with unconscious brutality, remarks that Sondra dresses well: "If I had as much money as that I could too." And the scene in which Clyde tries to persuade her to let him come to her room is of extraordinary depth, coming to climax when he turns sullenly away, and she, overwhelmed by her fear and pain at her own rebelliousness, feels the "first, flashing, blinding, bleeding stab of love."

Even minor characters have more than their relation to the dialectic. The prosecuting attorney and the defending lawyers have their own depth, and their roles are defined by their personal histories. A character like Hortense may be merely sketched in, but she takes on a new significance when we see her, like Rita, as an earlier avatar of Sondra, who is—and let us dwell on the adjectives —"as smart and vain and sweet a girl as Clyde had ever laid eyes on." And if at first Sondra herself seems scarcely more than another example of the particular type of *femme fatale* destined to work Clyde's ruin, let us remember how Clyde, in his cell, receives the letter beginning: "Clyde—This is so that you will not think someone once dear to you has utterly forgotten you. . . ." The letter, typewritten, is unsigned, but with it, in all the mixture of human feeling and falsity, Sondra, retroactively as it were, leaps to life.

As every person enters the story with a role in the dialectic, so every person enters with a human need which seeks fulfilment in the story. The delineation of this need—for instance, the portrait of the socially ambitious clerk in Lycurgus or the history of the prosecuting attorney Mason—serves to distract our interest from Clyde's personal story, another kind of distancing of the main line of narrative. At the same time, in the extraordinary coherence of the novel, we finally see that such apparent digressions are really mirrors held up to Clyde's story, in fact to Clyde himself: in this world of mirrors complicity is the common doom. So here we have —in the distraction of interest and realization of complicity— another version of the rhythm of approach and withdrawal.

There is, indeed, another sense in which the delineation of each new need compensates, in the end, for the distraction it has provoked. Each new need serves as a booster to the thrust of narrative, and in the rhythm of these thrusts we find another principle of the organization of the whole. Or to change our image, in the braiding together of these needs with the need of Clyde, we find acceleration, the pulse of creative life. To put it still another way, the delineation of each new perspective, each new person, each new need acts as a kind of "unmasking" of the dynamism of the story, in individual and social terms; and something of our own resistance to unmasking enters into the whole response to the story. This resistance, set against our natural commitment to the narrative, creates another sort of frustrating tension, and another sort of rhythm of withdrawal and approach. Furthermore, over against the unmasking of the mechanism of life is set the feel of life itself being lived in the urgency of its illusions; and this contrast gives us, if we choose to regard it as such, another principle of rhythm, another principle by which the form unfolds.

We have spoken of the marked moment of withdrawal at the beginning of Book III, after we have left Clyde walking away from the scene of Roberta's death, into the forest. Our commitment to the movement of narrative leading to the death of Roberta has been so complete that now, with it accomplished, we feel a sense of let-down, of the end. The sense of an end is so strong that the story of the now accomplished crime seems, for the moment at least, to split off from the subsequent story of consequences; and Dreiser, by the moment of withdrawal into distance, emphasizes the split. The split, coming about two-thirds of the way through the novel, has been felt, by some readers, as a grave flaw in the structure. The split is indeed real—a real break in emotional continuity. But we must ask ourselves whether or not this split serves, as the similar "split" in Conrad's *Lord Jim* or Shakespeare's *Julius Caesar,* to emphasize a deeper thematic continuity.

The story is one of crime and punishment. In the first two Books we see the forces that converge toward the death of Roberta, and in Book III we see the forces that are triggered into action by her death; that is, we see as a continuing theme the relation of the individual personality and individual fate to such forces. What, in other words, is the nature of responsibility in this world of shadowy complicities, where all things conspire in evil? The shadowiness of the outer world is matched by the shadowiness of the inner world; at the very last moment in the boat Clyde does not "will" to strike Roberta—even her death is an accident. Then after the "accident" this shadowiness of the inner world merges again with that of the outer. For instance, Jephson, one of the lawyers defending Clyde, creates a version of the accident; and then Clyde is persuaded, without much resistance, to testify to a "lie" in order to establish, as Jephson put it, the "truth."

This scene of the "persuasion" of Clyde is matched by a later scene in which, after Clyde's conviction, the young preacher Mc-Millan strips Clyde of all his alibis and equivocations, and prepares him for repentance and salvation. But just before the execution, even as Clyde assures his mother that God has heard his prayers, he is asking himself: "Had he?" And Clyde goes to his death not knowing what he really knows or feels, or what he has done. The theme of complicity and ambiguity, in varying manifestations, runs throughout.

The fact that Dreiser divides the novel into only three Books falsifies the real structure. There are really four basic movements, and there should be four Books: the story up to the flight from Kansas City, the story of the preparation; the story of the temptation leading to the death of Roberta; the story of the conviction, that of the ambiguities of justice; and the story of the search for salvation as death draws near. And in the last phase another theme, related to the others but more deeply grounded, appears, the theme of identity. If in this world of complicities and ambiguities it is hard to understand responsibility, then how, ultimately, can one understand the self? In fact, in this world of shadows Clyde has always sought to flee from the self. In all his self-absorption and selfishness, he has sought to repudiate the deepest meaning of self. He had longed to enter the "tall walls" of the world and find there a dream-self, a self-to-be-created, a role to play in the rich and thrilling world—a role, we may say, to take the place of a self. The very end of Book I, which has described Clyde's first attempt to enter the world, shows him fleeing from the wreck of the borrowed car: ". . . he hoped to hide—to lose himself and so escape . . ." He wishes to escape responsibility and punishment; he does "lose himself," and early in Book II we learn that he has lost his name, to reassume it only when he can use it to advantage with his rich uncle from Lycurgus.

All the rest of Clyde's grim, sleazy story can be regarded as an attempt to repudiate the old self. And the repudiation of self is associated with Clyde's readiness to repudiate others: he is ashamed of his family; he drops new friends—Dillard and Rita, for example —as soon as he makes contact with his rich relations; he ends by murdering Roberta. Or it may be put that Clyde, having no sense of the reality of self, has no sense of the reality of others, and even his pity for others is always a covert self-pity.

At the end, in a last desperate hope, Clyde is forced by McMillan to face the truth that he has fled from responsibility and self. But even now, as Clyde tries to accept the self, he cannot be sure of who or what he is. His "tragedy" is that of namelessness, and this is one aspect of its being an American tragedy, the story of the individual without identity, whose responsible self has been absorbed by the great machine of modern industrial secularized society. I say "secularized" because the only persons who offer a notion of self that Dreiser can set against the machine of the world are Clyde's mother and the Reverend McMillan. This is not to say that Dreiser is offering a doctrinal solution, but it is to say that only in the image drawn from religion does he, ironically enough, with all his ambivalences, find an image of the responsible self.

Many critics, by way of blame or praise, have emphasized the mechanistic view informing Dreiser's work. Critics who make the emphasis by way of blame are usually referring to his notion of "chemisms," of blind forces in the blood. Those who do so by way of praise are usually referring to some notion of social determinism. James Farrell succinctly put this view: "To him, evil is social: all his novels are concerned with social history, the social process of evil. Ambition, yearning, aspiration—these all revolve around this problem, and it in turn revolves around the role of money. He has related social causation . . . to the individual pattern of destiny."

He has indeed. And this fact is part of his great power and enduring importance as a novelist. But it is only a part, however original and essential a part. The real drama, which finally gives value to the whole and makes that greater than the sum of the parts, lies in the fact that in the full context of "social causation," as in that of the "chemisms," the individual story, in all its throbbing consciousness, is paradoxically and anguishingly enacted. The last anguish is the yearning for identity. And this yearning is the last mystery, the story in which Dreiser has, to use Mencken's words, "lifted the obvious to the inexplicable."

Dreiser and Tragedy:
The Stature of Theodore Dreiser

by Irving Howe

Do I exaggerate in saying that Theodore Dreiser has dropped
out of the awareness of cultivated Americans? If so, it is but a slight
exaggeration. Few young writers now model themselves on his
career, and not many readers think of him as one of those literary
figures whose word can transform the quality of their experience.
Dreiser has suffered the fate that often besets writers caught up in
cultural dispute: their work comes to seem inseparable from what
has been said about it, their passion gets frozen into history.

Mention Dreiser to a bright student of literature, mention him
to a literate older person, and only seldom will the response be
a swift turning of memory to novels that have brought pleasure and
illumination. Far more likely is a series of fixed associations—to a
cragged, brooding, bear-like figure who dragged himself out of 19th
Century poverty and provincialism, and in *Sister Carrie* composed
a pioneering novel of sexual candor; or to a vague notion that the
author of *The Financier* and *The Titan* turned out quantities of
illtuned and turgid social documentation; or to a prepared judgment against a writer taken to be sluggish in thought and language,
sluggishly accumulating data of destruction and failure, but deaf
to the refinements of consciousness, dull to the play of sensibility,
and drab, utterly and hopelessly drab in the quality of his mind.

The decline of Dreiser's reputation has not been an isolated event.
It has occurred in the context, and surely as a consequence, of the
counter-revolution in American culture during the past few decades.
For readers educated in these years, Dreiser often became a symbol
of everything a superior intelligence was supposed to avoid. For
the New Critics, to whom the very possibility of a social novel
seemed disagreeable; for literary students trained in the fine but
narrow school of the Jamesian sensibility; for liberals easing into
a modest gentility and inclined to replace a belief in social com-

"Dreiser and Tragedy: The Stature of Theodore Dreiser" by Irving Howe.
From *The New Republic*, 151 (July 25 and August 22, 1964): 19–21, 25–28.
Copyright © 1964 by Irving Howe. Reprinted by permission of the author.

mitment with a search for personal distinction; for intellectuals delighted with the values of ambiguity, irony, complexity and impatient with the pieties of radicalism—for all such persons Dreiser became an object of disdain. He stood for an earlier age of scientism, materialism, agnosticism: all of which were now seen as hostile to the claims of moral freedom and responsibility. He represented the boorishness of the populist mentality, as it declined into anti-Semitism or veered toward a peculiarly thoughtless brand of Communism. He could not think: he could only fumble with the names of ideas. He could not write: he could only pile words on top of each other. He cared not for art as such, but only for the novel as a vehicle of social and "philosophical" ideas. He was uneducated, insensitive—the novelist as mastodon.

So the indictment went, frequently right in its details, and when coming from so temperate a critic as Lionel Trilling often persuasive in result. If a few literary men, like the novelist James T. Farrell and the critic Alfred Kazin, continued to praise Dreiser as a writer of massive and poignant effects, if they insisted that attention be paid to the novels he wrote rather than his foolish public declamations, they were not much heeded in the last few decades.

But now, when Dreiser's prejudices have begun to be forgotten and all that remains—all that need remain—are his three or four major novels, it is time for reconsideration. The early praise these books received may have been undiscriminating: we are not obliged to repeat it. Dreiser's role in assaulting the taboos of gentility can no longer excite us as once it did his admirers. And as for his faults, no great critical insight is required to identify them, since they glare out of every chapter, especially his solemnities as a cosmic voice and his habit of crushing the English language in a leaden embrace. Yet these faults are interwoven with large creative powers, and it can be argued that for the powers to be released there had first to be the triggering presence of the faults. Let me cite an example.

As a philosopher, Dreiser can often be tiresome; yet his very lust for metaphysics, his stubborn insistence upon learning "what it's all about," helped to deepen the emotional resources from which he drew as a novelist. For he came to feel that our existence demands from us an endless contemplativeness, even if—perhaps because—we cannot think through our problems or solve our mysteries. In the frustrations he encountered when trying to extract some conceptual order from the confusion and trouble of existence, he grew more closely involved, more *at one*, with the characters he created, also confused and troubled.

In the first task of the novelist, which is to create an imaginary social landscape both credible and significant, Dreiser ranks among the American giants, the very few American giants we have had. Reading *An American Tragedy* once again, after a lapse of more than twenty years, I have found myself greatly moved and shaken by its repeated onslaughts of narrative, its profound immersion in human suffering, its dredging up of those shapeless desires which lie, as if in fever, just below the plane of consciousness. How much more vibrant this book is than the usual accounts of it in recent criticism might lead one to suppose! It is a masterpiece, nothing less.

Dreiser published *An American Tragedy* in 1925. By then he was 54 years old, an established writer with his own fixed and hard-won ways, who had written three first-rate novels: *Sister Carrie, Jennie Gerhardt* and *The Financier*. These books are crowded with exact observation—observation worked closely into the grain of narrative—about the customs and class structure of American society in the phase of early finance capitalism. No other novelist has absorbed into his work as much knowledge as Dreiser had about American institutions: the mechanisms of business, the stifling rhythms of the factory, the inner hierarchy of a large hotel, the chicaneries of city politics, the status arrangements of rulers and ruled. For the most part Dreiser's characters are defined through their relationships to these institutions. They writhe and suffer to win a foothold in the slippery social world or to break out of the limits of established social norms. They exhaust themselves to gain success, they destroy themselves in acts of impulsive deviancy. But whatever their individual lot, they all act out the drama of determinism—which, in Dreiser's handling, is not at all the sort of listless fatality that hostile critics would make it seem, but is rather a fierce struggle by human beings to discover the limits of what is possible to them and thereby perhaps to enlarge those limits by an inch or two. That mostly they fail is Dreiser's tribute to reality.

This controlling pattern in Dreiser's novels has been well described by Bernard Rosenberg, a sociologist with a literary eye:

"Emile Durkheim had suggested in Dreiser's day that when men speak of a force external to themselves which they are powerless to control, their subject is not God but social organization. This is also Dreiser's theme, and to it he brings a sense of religious awe and wonder. 'So well defined,' he writes, 'is the sphere of social activity, that he who departs from it is doomed.' . . . Durkheim identified social facts, i.e., the existence of norms, precisely as Dreiser did: by asking what would happen if they were violated. . . . Norms develop outside the individual consciousness and exist prior to it; we

internalize them and are fully aware of their grip only when our behavior is deviant. Durkheim illustrated this proposition in a dozen
different ways, and so did Dreiser."

In Dreiser's early novels most of the central characters are harried
by a desire for personal affirmation, a desire they can neither
articulate nor suppress. They suffer from a need that their lives
assume the dignity of dramatic form, and they suffer terribly, not
so much because they cannot satisfy this need, but because they do
not really understand it. Money, worldly success, sensual gratification are the only ends they know or can name, but none of these
slakes their restlessness They grapple desperately for money, they
lacerate themselves climbing to success, yet they remain sullen and
bewildered, always hopeful for some unexpected sign by which to
release their bitter craving for a state of grace or, at least, illumination. Dreiser's characters are romantics who behave as if the Absolute can be found, immaculately preserved, at the very summit
of material power. Great energies can flow from this ingrained
American delusion, both for the discharge of ambition and the
aggressiveness of ego. And Dreiser too, because he had in his own
experience shared these values and struggled, with varying effectiveness, to burn them out of his system—Dreiser too lived out the
longings and turmoil of his characters.

Yet there is usually present in his early novels a governing intelligence more copious and flexible than that of the characters.
This governing intelligence is seldom revealed through direct statement, either by characters or author. Taking upon himself the
perils and sharing in the miseries of his characters, he leaves the
privilege of admonition to others. Yet there is never really a question as to what his novels "mean," nor any serious possibility that
the characters will usurp control. Through the logic of the narrative, we are enabled to grasp with an almost visceral intensity how
shallow are the standards by which the characters live.

In these early novels society figures largely as a jungle; and with
good reason—the capitalism of the early 20th Century closely
resembled a jungle. The characters may begin with a hard struggle
for survival, but far more quickly than most of Dreiser's critics
allow, they leave it behind them. Having emerged from the blunt
innocence of their beginnings, they are now cursed with a fractional
awareness. They can find neither peace nor fulfillment. In their
half-articulate way, Dreiser's characters are beset by the same yearnings that trouble the characters of Fitzgerald and many other
American novelists: a need for some principle of value by which to
overcome the meanness, the littleness of their lives. To know, however, that the goals to which one has pledged one's years are trivial,

yet not to know in what their triviality consists—this is a form of suffering which overcomes Dreiser's characters again and again. In all its dumb misery, it is the price, or reward, of their slow crawl to awareness. One sometimes feels that in the novels of Dreiser there is being reenacted the whole progression of the race toward the idea of the human.

The prose in these early novels is often as wretched as unsympathetic critics have said. Dreiser had little feeling for the sentence as a rhythmic unit (though he had a strong intuitive grasp of the underlying rhythm of narrative as a system of controlled variation and incremental development). He had a poor ear for the inflections of common speech, or even for the colloquial play of language. And worst of all, he had a weakness, all too common among the semi-educated, for "elegant" diction and antique rhetoric. Yet, despite the many patches of grey and the occasional patches of purple prose, Dreiser manages to accumulate large masses of narrative tension; he pulls one, muttering and bruised, into the arena of his imagination; and finally there is no recourse but surrender to its plenitude, its coarse and encompassing reality.

Not even Dreiser's philosophical excursions—bringing together nativist American prejudice with the very latest ideas of 1900— can break the thrust of these narratives. Dreiser's thought has by now been analyzed, mauled and ridiculed: his distortion of social life through metaphors of brute nature, his reduction of human motive to the malignant pressure of "chemisms," his toying with "the superman" in the Cowperwood novels. But it hardly matters. One brushes all this aside, resigned to the malice of a fate that could yoke together such intellectual debris with so much creative power.

Though surely Dreiser's major achievement, *An American Tragedy* is not the work of a master who, at the approach of old age, decides upon a revolutionary break from the premises and patterns of his earlier writing. For that order of boldness Dreiser lacked a sufficient self-awareness and sophistication as an artist; he was cut off from too much of the tradition of Western, even American, culture to do anything but continue with his version of naturalism. He was the kind of writer who must keep circling about the point of his beginnings, forever stirred by memories of his early struggles and preoccupations. All such a writer can hope for—a very great deal—is to mine his talent to its very depth; and that Dreiser did in *An American Tragedy*. Still, there are some changes from the earlier novels, and most of them to the good.

The prose, while quite as clotted and ungainly as in the past, is now more consistent in tone and less adorned with "literary" paste gems. Solecisms, pretentiousness and gaucherie remain, but the prose has at least the negative virtue of calling less attention to itself than in some of the earlier books. And there are long sections packed with the kind of specification that in Dreiser makes for a happy self-forgetfulness, thereby justifying Philip Rahv's remark that one finds here "a prosiness so primary in texture that if taken in bulk it affects us as a kind of poetry of the commonplace and ill-favored."

For the first and last time Dreiser is wholly in the grip of his vision of things, so that he feels little need for the buttress of comment or the decoration of philosophizing. Dreiser is hardly the writer whose name would immediately occur to one in connection with T. S. Eliot's famous epigram that Henry James had a mind so fine it could not be violated by ideas; yet if there is one Dreiser novel concerning which something like Eliot's remark might apply, it is *An American Tragedy*. What Eliot said has sometimes been taken, quite absurdly, as if it were a recommendation for writers to keep themselves innocent of ideas; actually he was trying to suggest the way a novelist can be affected by ideas yet must not allow his work to become a mere illustration for them. And of all Dreiser's novels *An American Tragedy* is the one that seems least cluttered with unassimilated formulas and preconceptions.

Where the earlier novels dealt with somewhat limited aspects of American life, *An American Tragedy,* enormous in scope and ambition, requires to be judged not merely as an extended study of the American lower-middle-class during the first years of the 20th Century but also as a kind of parable of our national experience. Strip the story to its bare outline, and see how much of American desire it involves: An obscure youth, amiable but weak, is lifted by chance from poverty to the possibility of winning pleasure and wealth. To gain these ends he must abandon the pieties of his fundamentalist upbringing and sacrifice the tender young woman who has given him a taste of pure affection. All of society conspires to persuade him that his goals are admirable, perhaps even sacred; he notices that others, no better endowed than himself, enjoy the privileges of money as if it were in the very nature of things that they should; but the entanglements of his past now form a barrier to realizing his desires, and to break through this barrier he must resort to criminal means. As it happens, he does not commit the murder he had planned, but he might as well have, for he is trapped in the machinery of social punishment and destroyed. "So well defined is the sphere of social activity that he who departs from it is doomed."

Now this story depends upon one of the most deeply-grounded

fables in our culture. Clyde Griffiths, the figure in Dreiser's novel who acts it out, is not in any traditional sense either heroic or tragic. He has almost no assertive will, he lacks any large compelling idea, he reveals no special gift for the endurance of pain. In his puny self he is little more than a clouded reflection of the puny world about him. His significance lies in the fact that he represents not our potential greatness but our collective smallness, the common denominator of our foolish tastes and tawdry ambitions. He is that part of ourselves in which we take no pride, but know to be a settled resident. And we cannot dismiss him as a special case or an extreme instance, for his weakness is the essential shoddiness of mortality. By a twist of circumstance he could be a junior executive, a country-club favorite; he almost does manage to remake himself to the cut of his fantasy; and he finds in his rich and arrogant cousin Gilbert an exasperating double, the young man he too might be. Clyde embodies the nothingness at the heart of our scheme of things, the nothingness of our social aspirations. If Flaubert could say, *Emma Bovary, c'est moi,* Dreiser could echo, *Clyde Griffiths, he is us.*

We have then in Clyde a powerful representation of our unacknowledged values, powerful especially since Dreiser keeps a majestic balance between sympathy and criticism. He sees Clyde as a characteristic reflex of "the vast skepticism and apathy of life," as a characteristic instance of the futility of misplaced desire in a society that offers little ennobling sense of human potentiality. Yet he nevertheless manages to make the consequences of Clyde's mediocrity, if not the mediocrity itself, seem tragic. For in this youth there is concentrated the tragedy of human waste: energies, talents, affections all unused—and at least in our time the idea of human waste comprises an essential meaning of tragedy. It is an idea to which Dreiser kept returning both in his fiction and his essays:

> "When one was dead one was dead for all time. Hence the reason for the heartbreak over failure here and now; the awful tragedy of a love lost, a youth never properly enjoyed. Think of living and yet not living in so thrashing a world as this, the best of one's hours passing unused or not properly used. Think of seeing this tinkling phatasmagoria of pain and pleasure, beauty and all its sweets, go by, and yet being compelled to be a bystander, a mere onlooker, enhungered and never satisfied."

The first half of *An American Tragedy* is given to the difficult yet, for Dreiser's purpose, essential task of persuading us that Clyde

Griffiths, through his very lack of distinction, represents a major possibility in American experience. Toward this end Dreiser must accumulate a large sum of substantiating detail. He must show Clyde growing up in a family both materially and spiritually impoverished. He must show Clyde reaching out for the small pleasures, the trifles of desire, and learning from his environment how splendid are these induced wants. He must show Clyde, step by step, making his initiation into the world of sanctioned America, first through shabby and then luxury hotels, where he picks up the signals of status. He must show Clyde as the very image and prisoner of our culture, hungering with its hungers, empty with its emptiness.

Yet all the while Dreiser is also preparing to lift Clyde's story from this mere typicality, for he wishes to go beyond the mania for the average which is a bane of naturalism. Everything in this story is ordinary, not least of all the hope of prosperity through marriage—everything but the fact that Clyde begins to act out, or is treated as if he had acted out, the commonplace fantasy of violently disposing of a used-up lover. This is the sole important departure from ordinary verisimilitude in the entire novel, and Dreiser must surely have known that it was. In the particular case upon which he drew for *An American Tragedy,* the young man did kill his pregnant girl; but Dreiser must nevertheless have realized that in the vast majority of such crises the young man dreams of killing and ends by marrying. Dreiser understood, however, that in fiction the effort to represent common experience requires, at one or two crucial points, an effect of heightening, an intense exaggeration. Clyde's situation may be representative, but his conduct must be extreme. And is that not one way of establishing the dramatic: to drive a representative situation to its limits of possibility?

In *An American Tragedy* Dreiser solved the problem which vexes all naturalistic novelists: how to relate harmoniously a large panorama of realism with a sharply-contoured form. Dreiser is endlessly faithful to common experience. No one, not even the critics who have most harshly attacked the novel, would care to deny the credibility of Clyde and Roberta Alden, the girl he betrays; most of the attacks on Dreiser contain a mute testimony to his achievement, for in order to complain about his view of life they begin by taking for granted the "reality" of his imagined world. Yet for all its packed detail, the novel is economically structured—though one must understand that the criterion of economy for this kind of novel is radically different from that for a James or Conrad novel. In saying all this I do not mean anything so improbable as the claim that whatever is in the book belongs because it is there; certain sections, especially those which prepare for Clyde's trial, could be cut to advantage; but the over-all architecture has a rough and impressive craftsmanship.

The action of the novel moves like a series of waves, each surging forward to a peak of tension and then receding into quietness, and each, after the first one reenacting in a more complex and perilous fashion the material of its predecessor. Clyde in Kansas City, Clyde in Chicago, Clyde alone with Roberta in Lycurgus, Clyde on the edge of the wealthy set in Lycurgus—these divisions form the novel until the point where Roberta is drowned, and each of them acts as a reflector on the other, so that there is a mounting series of anticipations and variations upon the central theme. Clyde's early flirtation with a Kansas City shopgirl anticipates, in its chill manipulativeness, the later and more important relationship with Sondra Finchley, the rich girl who seems to him the very emblem of his fantasy. Clyde's childhood of city poverty is paralleled by the fine section presenting the poverty of Roberta's farm family. The seduction and desertion of Clyde's unmarried sister anticipates Clyde's seduction and desertion of Roberta. Clyde receives his preliminary education in the hotels where he works as bell-boy, and each of these serves as a microcosm of the social world he will later break into. Clyde's first tenderness with Roberta occurs as they float on a rowboat; the near-murder, equally passive, also on a rowboat. The grasping Clyde is reflected through a series of minor hotel figures and then through the antipathetic but complementary figures of his cousin Gilbert and Sondra; while the part of him that retains some spontaneous feeling is doubled by Roberta, thereby strengthening one's impression that Clyde and Roberta are halves of an uncompleted self, briefly coming together in a poignant unity but lacking the emotional education that would enable them to keep the happiness they have touched. There are more such balancings and modulations, which in their sum endow the novel with a rhythm of necessity.

Reinforcing this narrative rhythm is Dreiser's frequent shifting of the distance he keeps from his characters. At some points he establishes an almost intolerable closeness to Clyde, so that we feel locked into the circle of the boy's moods, while at other points he pulls back to convey the sense that Clyde is but another helpless creature among thousands of helpless creatures struggling to get through their time. In the chapters dealing with Clyde upon his arrival at Lycurgus, Dreiser virtually *becomes* his character, narrowing to a hairline the distance between Clyde and himself, in order to make utterly vivid Clyde's pleasure at finding a girl as yielding as Roberta. By contrast, there are sections in which Dreiser looks upon his story from a great height, especially in the chapters after Roberta's death, where his intent is to suggest how impersonal is the working of legal doom and how insignificant Clyde's fate in the larger motions of society. Through these shifts in perspective Dreiser can show Clyde in his double aspect, both as solitary figure and symbolic agent.

In the first half of the novel Dreiser prepares us to believe that Clyde *could* commit the crime: which is to say, he prepares us to believe that a part of ourselves could commit the crime. At each point in the boy's development there occurs a meeting between his ill-formed self and the surrounding society. The impoverishment of his family life and the instinctual deprivation of his youth leave him a prey to the values of the streets and the hotels; yet it is a fine stroke on Dreiser's part that only through these tawdry values does Clyde really become aware of his impoverishment and deprivation. Yearning gives way to cheap desire and false gratification, and these in turn create new and still more incoherent yearnings. It is a vicious circle and the result is not, in any precise sense, a self at all, but rather the beginning of that poisonous fabrication which in America we call a "personality." The hotels are his college, and there he learns to be "insanely eager for all the pleasures which he saw swirling around him." The sterile moralism of his parents cannot provide him with the strength to resist his environment or a principle by which to overcome it. The first tips he receives at the Green-Davidson hotel seem to him "fantastic, Aladdinish really." When he tries to be romantic with his first girl, the images that spring to his mind are of the ornate furnishings in the hotel. Later, as he contemplates killing Roberta, the very idea for the central act in his life comes from casual reading of a newspaper. It would be hard to find in American literature another instance where the passivity, rootlessness and self-alienation of urban man is so authoritatively presented. For in one sense Clyde does not exist, but is merely a creature of his milieu. And just as in Dreiser's work the problem of human freedom becomes critically acute through a representation of its decline, so the problem of awareness is brought to the forefront through a portrait of its negation.

Even sexuality, which often moves through Dreiser's world like a thick fog, is here diminished and suppressed through the power of social will. Clyde discovers sex as a drugstore clerk, "never weary of observing the beauty, the daring, the self-sufficiency and the sweetness" of the girls who come to his counter. "The wonder of them!" All of these fantasies he then focusses on the commonplace figure of Sondra Finchley, Heloise as a spoiled American girl. Apart from an interval with Roberta, in which he yields to her maternal solicitude, Clyde's sexuality never breaks out as an irresistible force; it is always at the service of his fears, his petty snobbism, his calculations.

Now all of this is strongly imagined, yet what seems still more notable is Dreiser's related intuition that even in a crippled psyche there remain, eager and available, the capacities we associate with a life of awareness. False values stunt and deform these capacities, but in some pitiful way also express and release them. Clyde and Roberta are from the beginning locked in mutual delusion, yet the chapters in which they discover one another are also extremely tender as an unfolding of youthful experience. That this can happen at all suggests how indestructible the life-force is; that Dreiser can portray it in his novels is the reward of his compassion. He is rarely sentimental, he reckons human waste to the bitter end; but at the same time he hovers over these lonely figures, granting them every ounce of true feeling he possibly can, insisting that they too —clerk and shopgirl, quite like intellectual and princess—can know "a kind of ecstasy all out of proportion to the fragile, gimcrack scene" of the Starlight Amusement Park.

Dreiser surrenders himself to the emotional life of his figures, not by passing over their delusions or failures but by casting all his energy into evoking the fullness of their experience. And how large, finally, is the sense of the human that smolders in this book! How unwavering the feeling for "the sensitive and seeking individual in his pitiful struggle with nature—with his enormous urges and his pathetic equipment!" Dreiser's passion for detail is a passion for his subject; his passion for his subject, a passion for the suffering of men. As we are touched by Clyde's early affection for Roberta, so later we participate vicariously in his desperation to be rid of her. We share this desire with some shame, but unless we count ourselves among the hopelessly pure, we share it.

Other naturalists, when they show a character being destroyed by overwhelming forces, frequently leave us with a sense of littleness and helplessness, as if the world were collapsed. Of Dreiser that is not, in my own experience, true. For he is always on the watch for a glimmer of transcendence, always concerned with the possibility of magnitude. Clyde is pitiable, his life and fate are pitiable; yet at the end we feel a somber exaltation, for we know that *An American Tragedy* does not seek to persuade us that human existence need be without value or beauty.

No, for Dreiser life is something very different. What makes him so absorbing a novelist, despite grave faults, is that he remains end-

lessly open to experience. This is something one cannot say easily
about most modern writers, including those more subtle and gifted
than Dreiser. The trend of modern literature has often been toward a recoil from experience, a nausea before its flow, a denial of
its worth. Dreiser, to be sure, is unable to make the finer discrimina-
tions among varieties of experience; and there is no reason to expect these from him. But he is marvelous in his devotion to whatever portion of life a man can have; marvelous in his conviction
that something sacred resides even in the transience of our days;
marvelous in his feeling that the grimmest of lives retain the possibility of "a mystic something of beauty that perennially transfigures the world." Transfigures—that is the key word, and not
the catch-phrases of mechanistic determinism he furnished his detractors.

Santayana, in his lecture on Spinoza, speaks of "one of the most
important and radical of religious perceptions":

> "It has perceived that though it is living, it is powerless to live; that
> though it may die, it is powerless to die; and that altogether, at every
> instant and in every particular, it is in the hands of some alien and
> inscrutable power.
>
> Of this felt power I profess to know nothing further. To me, as
> yet, it is merely the counterpart of my impotence. I should not ven-
> ture, for instance, to call this power almighty, since I have no means
> of knowing how much it can do: but I should not hesitate, if I may
> coin a word, to call it *omnificent:* it is to me, by definition, the doer
> of everything that is done. I am not asserting the physical validity of
> this sense of agency or cause: I am merely feeling the force, the
> friendliness, the hostility, the unfathomableness of the world."

Dreiser, I think, would have accepted these words, for the power
of which Santayana speaks is the power that flows, in all its feverish
vibration, through *An American Tragedy*.

The Finesse of Dreiser

by Ellen Moers

We are reading Dreiser again. Without benefit of editorial fanfare or critical hoopla, a revival is upon us, solidified by that blessed invention of the fifties, the quality paperback book, with its attraction for the young, the poor, the serious, the curious, the follower of fashion—for, in short, the reader. There are seventeen Dreiser volumes now in paper, including seven different imprints of *Sister Carrie*. (For the record, which has its interest as a signpost to taste, there are also seven Ambassadors, fourteen Red Badges of Courage, ten Moby Dicks, fifteen Scarlet Letters, twelve Huckleberry Finns.)

Young people have good reason to be reading Dreiser, as they obviously are, beyond the fact of his quality. He forms a bridge between the self-consciously inarticulate poets and novelists of their generation (the devotees of what Robert Brustein has called the Cult of Unthink) and the humanitarians of the last century, for whom the inability to articulate was in itself tragic, even disgusting. It is as the novelist of the inarticulate hero that Dreiser comes again upon the literary scene.

"One thing that you are to be praised for is that you have always been low," Edgar Lee Masters wrote Dreiser; "you have always loved low company, as Hawthorne and Emerson did and Whitman and before them as Goethe did. This passion conduces to honesty." But how is Dreiser in fact *low*? What is the social milieu of his novels? It is not low, certainly, in the Marxist sense, which seems relevant only because Dreiser's final political stand was with the Communist Party. Dreiser never wrote a proletarian novel: his favorite characters are an actress, a saloonkeeper, a traveling salesman, an art-collecting financial manipulator, a street preacher, a painter, a mistress, a bellboy. The fringe figures, wasters and spoilers and enjoyers, were for Dreiser, as for his master Balzac, the irresistible subject.

"The Finesse of Dreiser" by Ellen Moers. From *The American Scholar*, 33 (Winter 1963): 109–14. Copyright © 1963 by Ellen Moers. Reprinted by permission of the author and Curtis Brown, Ltd.

Dreiser's characters are low in the sense of being stupid. Carrie and Jennie and Clyde would probably rank well below the norm in any verbal intelligence test. Neither sentimentality nor disgust mars Dreiser's handling of inarticulate people—although both these patronizing attitudes repeatedly disfigured the "naturalist" tradition to which he is supposed to belong. That Dreiser loved his helpless, unconscious people has often been said, but he did so with the very special love of a sibling, carrying with it acceptance, identification, shame, detachment and an honesty related to the contempt that is bred by familiarity. In the most literal sense, as his letters and autobiographical writings show clearly, Dreiser wrote as a brother. This is the central fact about his work, far more important than the clichés thrown at him in the 1930's and '40's: that he was a peasant, a linguistic immigrant, a naturalist, a People's realist, an American and so on.

One of Dreiser's sisters ran off with a married saloon-manager who stole money to keep her (Carrie); one bore a rich man's illegitimate child (Jennie Gerhardt); one brother hung around hotel lobbies looking for easy money, got into trouble and ran off to peddle candy on trains (Clyde). His beloved brother Paul, the song writer "Dresser," ran away from the seminary where he was training to be a priest, spent some time in jail and lived off the bounty of a "madam" on his easy-going way to success. Without much in the line of theory, using only family materials, Dreiser could easily work out a view of life somewhat at variance with the conventional homilies of his day. More important, from the contrast between day-by-day life as it was lived by his brothers and sisters, and life as it was played out in popular melodrama, he devised a literary style that gave form, and even heroism, to the inarticulate.

Dreiser's triumph in this enterprise is Clyde Griffiths in *An American Tragedy,* the last novel published in his lifetime and the sum of his experience as man and artist. But from his first novel, *Sister Carrie,* he addressed himself to the problem of expressing the inexpressibles and, what is more, carried it off with virtuosity and delicacy. These two books are Dreiser's masterpieces. The *Tragedy* is in every way more profound, more complex in structure, more rich in suggestions. That is where we are to look for the tragic sense, the compassion and the sociological subtlety that have won Dreiser the respect, if not the affection of his readers. But Dreiser would never have been able to manage the complex architectonics of *An American Tragedy* without his abundant natural, literary gifts as a novelist, which *Sister Carrie* most patently displays. Like *The Scarlet Letter,* which appeared exactly fifty years earlier, *Sister Carrie* is one of those first novels that show off the almost shameless virtuosity of the novice.

Dreiser wrote *Sister Carrie* somewhat by accident, at the insistence of a friend. He was already, in 1900 (like Hawthorne in 1850), a mature man and an experienced writer; he was the author of so many competent magazine articles (many of them showing a verbal smoothness lacking in *Sister Carrie*) that he had been listed by *Who's Who*. He had also written a few short stories, also at the urging of his friend, but what he really wanted to write was plays, not fiction. "Had I been let alone," he told Mencken, "I would have worked out in that form." *Sister Carrie* shows it. It is, as no later Dreiser book would be, a novel of *scenes*, some of them so "gorgeous" that they remain in the mind like things in *Madame Bovary* or *Anna Karenina*.

There is, for example, the Hurstwood-Carrie love scene, acted out in a slow-moving horse-drawn carriage pacing along the flat, new, empty stretches of Washington Boulevard; the opening scene, Carrie's meeting with Drouet in the railroad car; Carrie's night of triumph on the stage, before an audience of "stout figures, large white bosoms, and shining pins" that includes her two blazing lovers; and the final stunningly illuminated scenes of Hurstwood in degeneration, one bum among many on a snowy night in the Bowery:

> In the drive of the wind and sleet they pushed in on one another. There were wrists, unprotected by coat or pocket, which were red with cold. There were ears, half covered by every conceivable semblance of a hat, which still looked stiff and bitten. In the snow they shifted, now one foot, now another, almost rocking in unison.

Rhythmic effects of every variety (the train, the streetcar, the carriage horse, the shuffling feet of the bums, the rocking chair) are scattered through the novel so profusely that its lyrical quality becomes at times almost too rich. There are effects of light and color that point to Dreiser's early and lasting passion for painting and architectural decoration, which has hardly been taken seriously by his critics. There are contrapuntal effects with speech—urban and rural; common, middling and "cultivated"; slang and theatrical bombast—that very few other novelists (James Joyce is one) have ever attempted. To say that the best scenes in *Sister Carrie* are cinematic rather than theatrical is another way of saying that Dreiser was a born, virtuoso novelist, for the movies learned more from the novelist than from the playwright. But it is often helpful, as Robert Penn Warren has shown in an essay on *An American*

Tragedy, to write of Dreiser's effects in terms of the "sweep of the lens," the "shift of focus," the "movie in our heads."

If there is a crucial scene in *Sister Carrie,* on which the success of the book hangs, it is the early episode in the downtown restaurant, where Carrie is "seduced" by Drouet. This is hardly one of the memorable showpieces of the novel, yet it goes far to set the tone of the whole. For here Dreiser must take a stupid, commonplace girl, whose only charm is her youthful prettiness (and a certain something else that must here be established finally for the reader) and turn her into a heroine—without letting her think or feel or behave in the heroic style. She must take the first decisive step of her life—down a path that she, her family, her world know to be morally wrong—without seeming to understand what she is about and without incurring the reader's exasperation or provoking his blame. For Dreiser has set himself the task of making Carrie sufficiently null to skirt moral criticism, but vital enough to personify the creative force itself—to be, in effect, his Emma Bovary.

The writing in the seduction scene is careful to the point of finesse—a word I would like to bring forward in connection with Dreiser, if only because it challenges the old and worn-out complaints against his style. In one of the recent favorable statements about Dreiser (they are still relatively rare) Saul Bellow asked a useful question about the nature of "bad writing" by a powerful novelist, but moved away from the answer with the lamest recommendation: that "Dreiser's novels are best read quickly." The reverse is true. "Fine" writing (some of James's or Virginia Woolf's, for instance) often fails on slow and close examination, while the coarse, dense, uneven language of the more subtle novelists (like Dickens) yields surprising rewards—and explanations of the art of fiction—to the careful reader.

Dreiser has brought the farm girl, Carrie Meeber, to Chicago, introduced her to the drab home of her married sister, sent her about the city looking for poorly paid, tedious work, and then had her fall ill and lose her job at the outset of her first winter in the big city. Now he sets the stage for temptation. Carrie is spending her fourth weary day of job-hunting wandering the downtown streets of the city with a borrowed ten cents in her pocket for lunch, when Dreiser confronts her with that delectable specimen of brainless virility, Drouet, the traveling salesman Carrie had met on the train but had not seen again since her arrival in Chicago. Four pages later Carrie has taken money from Drouet, and the loss of her virtue is in plain view. But the scene ends as Dreiser has it begin: unstrained, calm, inevitable in a comfortable, flat sort of way, even cosy. Here is the beginning, several pages into Chapter VI:

> . . . Suddenly a hand pulled her arm and turned her about.
> "Well, well!" said a voice. In the first glance she beheld Drouet. He was not only rosy-cheeked, but radiant. He was the essence of sunshine and good-humour. "Why, how are you, Carrie?" he said. "You're a daisy. Where have you been?"
> Carrie smiled under his irresistible flood of geniality.
> "I've been out home," she said.
> "Well," he said, "I saw you across the street there. I thought it was you. I was just coming out to your place. How are you, anyhow?"
> "I'm all right," said Carrie, smiling.
> Drouet looked her over and saw something different.
> "Well," he said, "I want to talk to you. You're not going anywhere in particular, are you?"
> "Not just now," said Carrie.
> "Let's go up here and have something to eat. George! but I'm glad to see you again."
> She felt so relieved in his radiant presence, so much looked after and cared for, that she assented gladly, though with the slightest air of holding back.
> "Well," he said, as he took her arm—and there was an exuberance of good fellowship in the word which fairly warmed the cockles of her heart.

The literary clichés in this last sentence are ugly, but they have a purpose: to throw into relief Drouet's final *"Well"*—which is positively elegant. In this short passage Drouet speaks that homely Americanism five times; more than "Say!" and "George!" his other expletives, it is his trademark. Dreiser was a master of the use of senseless speech to establish character—and those who believe that mastery does not enter here need only examine the hundred different cries of inarticulate passion expressed by Clyde Griffiths' "Gee!" or compare Drouet's speech with Carrie's. In this passage, as throughout the novel, Carrie says almost nothing. Her short, primer sentences carry the flat farm twang without Dreiser's insisting on it: "I've been out home," "I'm all right," and "Not just now."

It is relatively easy for Dreiser to show why Carrie succumbs to Drouet, but much trickier to establish that this timid farm girl—naïve, compliant, decently conventional and without a notion of the seductive arts—can tie Drouet to the most permanent relationship of which he is capable, move on to a more complex lover, prompt Hurstwood to a crime of Balzacian dimensions and then move on again to solitary theatrical triumphs. Carrie hardly talks or thinks, but the warmth of her presence must be at the center of every scene in which she appears. To the men around her she must, without words, respond; here as everywhere, she smiles.

In this scene Dreiser first sets forth the idea that Carrie's fall is to be a triumph, that her sexual adventures stimulate the unfolding of her temperament, much as the sun's heat brings the plant to flower. The pervading atmosphere, the underlying sensual image of this scene is, in fact, physical warmth. It emanates from Drouet, who (in the passage I have quoted) is "rosy-cheeked," "the essence of sunshine" to whom Carrie is the "daisy" of the farm. His *geniality* and *exuberance* are the sun that *warms her heart*. Dreiser uses the word *radiant* twice at the opening of the scene to characterize Drouet, and the shining, gleaming, warming quality of the man is reinforced in the restaurant episode that immediately follows. Drouet summons the "full-chested, round-faced" Negro waiter with a hissing "Sst!" and his ordering of the meal, punctuated with the waiter's repeated "Yassah," turns into a little duet full of sizzling *ss* sounds. (It does not include the silent Carrie; but its last line is "Carrie smiled and smiled.") Drouet's apotheosis as a warming, radiating presence comes, again with intricate sound effects, as the waiter returns, bearing on his "immense" tray the "hot savoury dishes."

> Drouet fairly shone in the matter of serving. He appeared to great advantage behind the white napery and silver platters of the table and displaying his arms with a knife and fork. As he cut the meat his rings almost spoke. His new suit creaked as he stretched to reach the plates, break the bread, and pour the coffee. He helped Carrie to a rousing plateful and contributed the warmth of his spirit to her body until she was a new girl. He was a splendid fellow. . . .

Now Dreiser has been careful, in the opening chapters of the novel, to show that Carrie, although momentarily unfortunate, is *not* in the grip of a massively malign fate. She is *not* starving; she is far from destitution; she has two decent homes to go back to. What is at stake is not Carrie's survival but her growth. Dreiser has therefore established the sense of spreading cold that grips Carrie, a cold which is seasonal and physical but also emotional, and to which this scene, full of Drouet's "radiant presence," provides a warm alternative. The whole cold-warmth pattern has been cued to the reader with a sentence about the difficulty of *transplantation* "in the matter of flowers or maidens," which focuses our attention on Carrie as an organism, significantly a plant rather than an animal, whose response to temptation will be less conscious than instinctive.

About a page before Carrie meets Drouet Dreiser announces the arrival of cold weather with a few carefully composed sentences (the penciled manuscript, ordinarily clean, shows erasures and excisions):

> There came a day when the first premonitory blast of winter swept over the city. It scudded the fleecy clouds in the heavens, trailed long, thin streamers of smoke from the tall stacks, and raced about the streets and corners in sharp and sudden puffs. Carrie now felt the problem of winter clothes.

Carrie falls ill. "It blew up cold after a rain one afternoon. . . . She came out of the warm shop at six and shivered as the wind struck her." A "chattering chill" follows; "she hung about the stove." She recovers, goes out again to look for work, but hates to return to her sister's home at night: "Hanson [her brother-in-law] was so cold." This sort of preparation throws into relief the sunny radiance of Drouet and the answering, smiling warmth of Carrie. It also clarifies, in the most prosaic way, her acceptance of Drouet's money, which Carrie takes to buy the warm clothing she needs for the winter. But the whole cold-warmth pattern, and the accompanying suggestions of sun, heat and soft, young greenness, are there to be drawn on when, at the close of the scene, Dreiser makes the transfer of money a climactic act.

When *Sister Carrie* was new it was regularly denounced, even by the firm that published it, as an immoral and indecent book. Inevitably, later critics, even those so well disposed as F. O. Matthiessen, have reproached Dreiser for his timidity in avoiding sexual contact between his characters. It is true that Dreiser never removes Carrie's clothes or shows her in the act of love. (When, much later, he came to handle sex openly, as in *The Stoic,* the effect is breathless and not quite sane—directing our attention more to Dreiser's temperament than to that of his characters.) What I have called the seduction scene in *Sister Carrie* culminates in nothing more physical than a pressing of hands. Yet Carrie's acceptance of Drouet's money points clearly and richly to her acceptance of Drouet as a lover, not merely because we know that this is the way the world (and the novel) goes, but because Dreiser's language drenches the transfer of money itself with sexual excitement.

Here is how he does it. The food is served. The man and the girl sit across the table from each other, talking banalities. A sexual current arises, for the first time, between them, and is phrased by Dreiser with deliberation: a matter-of-fact, businesslike sentence, then a colloquialism Carrie herself would use, then a literary sentence, suggestively metaphorical:

She felt his admiration. It was powerfully backed by his liberality
and good-humour. She felt that she liked him—that she could continue
to like him ever so much. There was something even richer than that,
running as a hidden strain, in her mind. . . .

It is important here that our attention be focused on Carrie, and
her wordless, actually thoughtless reaction to Drouet's masculinity.
(Dreiser cut from the beginning of the scene a sentence about
Drouet's liking for Carrie's "mould of flesh" that might have
spoiled the tone of the scene.) Drouet looks, admires, and then
acts; in two sentences rich with suggestion, he begins to fondle—
his cash.

> There were some loose bills in his vest pocket—greenbacks. They
> were soft and noiseless, and he got his fingers about them and crum-
> pled them up in his hand.

The first physical contact then takes place, in words that seem to
do nothing but state a gesture, but the key suggestion of warmth
is there:

> She had her hand out on the table before her. They were quite alone
> in their corner, and he put his larger, warmer hand over it.

Drouet "pressed her hand gently . . . he held it fast . . .
he slipped the greenbacks he had into her palm. . . ." Carrie
takes the money, agrees to meet Drouet again, goes out onto the
street. The last sentences of the chapter resolve the play of hands
of the climax, and refer back to the gesture ("Suddenly a hand
pulled her arm and turned her about") with which the scene
opened. They also resolve the underlying imagery of the whole:
the exchange of warmth, the soft greenness of the farm warmed
by the heat of the sun.

> Carrie left him, feeling as though a great arm had slipped out before
> her to draw off trouble. The money she had accepted was two soft,
> green, handsome ten-dollar bills.*

---

* Dreiser thought at one point of using another transfer of money to prefigure
Carrie's capitulation to Hurstwood, her second lover. For very good reasons he
penciled the passage out of the manuscript, probably as soon as it was written.
(The more subtle love affair between Carrie and Hurstwood would not have been
glorified by such a transaction; and the climactic scene, Carrie's stage debut before
both her lovers, would have lost some of its effectiveness, for Hurstwood was
offering Carrie money to pay for the clothes she would wear on stage.) But
Dreiser's choice of words for the discarded "money" scene is interesting. Hurstwood pulls out, not the loose, soft, noiseless, crumpled greenbacks of Drouet, but
"a thin clean roll" of new hundred dollar bills. Taking off one bill. he "put it in
her little green leather purse and closed it up."

What did Dreiser *avoid* doing with this scene? There is no sentiment, no moralizing, no foreshadowing of conclusions. Carrie's charm for Drouet has been established without destroying her simplicity of temperament; and Drouet's masculine heat has pervaded the scene without the element of lust. Drouet remains vulgar and coarse, but not disgusting. The natural forces of growth and change, the mysteriously casual interactions of creature with environment that always roused in Dreiser the emotions of wonder and awe, have been suggested by a metaphorical (but essentially novelistic) language which in turn gives a surprising eloquence to this tawdry encounter between trivial personalities. The people, Carrie and Drouet, are neither glorified nor idealized.

Two chapters and several days, perhaps weeks, later, Carrie becomes Drouet's mistress. Dreiser puts off the denouement, and indeed avoids presenting the event directly to the reader, not from mere prudery but from a conscious desire to destroy the significance of the act as action, to minimize the element of free will (in which he was a strenuous nonbeliever) and to make credible the lack of reflection in such a girl as Carrie. So we are given much detail about Carrie's shopping and pleasure in her new clothes; about Drouet's pleasure in her appearance and care for her material comfort; and about all the practical problems arising from Carrie's move out of her sister's home and into an apartment Drouet takes for her.

Dreiser's commentary insists, too heavily but never stupidly, on the importance of money, the force of instinct, the significance of habits—abstract topics that drain from Carrie's action the last vestige of moral or sentimental tone. He is particularly careful to keep Carrie's mind blank, her speech halting. A thought of home brings a gesture of despair and a query from Drouet: "What's the matter?" Carrie answers with a line that is at once accurate American slang and literal truth: "Oh, I don't know." Carrie recognizes in a crowd of poorly-dressed factory girls a face she had known at work, and for the first time senses some of the consequences of her move from decent poverty to comfortable disgrace. Her reaction is again a gesture, a start, and Drouet's comment pulls us up with its irony: " 'You must be thinking,' he said."

Dreiser cut from the manuscript a long paragraph making clear how aware he was of the literary significance of what he was doing. The paragraph comes near the beginning of Chapter VIII, after Carrie has gone to Drouet's apartment but before she takes him as her lover. The book as it stands retains nearly all of Dreiser's original reflections on the moral implications (or lack of them) of

Carrie's actions; but this excluded paragraph probes—in language
so clumsy as to justify the excision—the stylistic problems of inarticulate fiction.

> We are inclined sometimes to wring our hands much more profusely
> over the situation of another than the mental attitude of that other,
> towards his own condition, would seem to warrant. People do not
> grieve so much sometimes over their own state as we imagine. They
> suffer, but they bear it manfully. They are distressed, but it is about
> other things as a rule than their actual state at the moment. We
> see, as we grieve for them, the whole detail of their blighted career,
> a vast confused imagery of mishaps, covering years, much as we read
> a double decade of tragedy in a ten hour [?] novel. The victim mean-
> while for the single day or morrow is not actually anguished. He
> meets his unfolding fate by the minute and the hour as it comes.

So spoke the novelist who was, in every sense, the brother of Sister
Carrie.

Mr. Trilling, Mr. Warren
and *An American Tragedy*

by *Charles Thomas Samuels*

For a moment in *The Liberal Imagination* Lionel Trilling
adopts the inspirational mode:

> . . . with us it is always a little too late for mind, yet never too late
> for honest stupidity; always a little too late for understanding, never
> too late for righteous, bewildered wrath; always too late for thought,
> never too late for naive moralizing. We seem to like to condemn our
> finest but not our worst qualities by pitting them against the ex-
> igency of time.

Aux barricades! In behalf of intellect and art, Trilling issued a challenge to admirers of Theodore Dreiser.

We know the famous case which Trilling made against him.
Dreiser is not to be cherished for being true to life at the cost of art
since he is "literary" in the worst sense; he is not to be forgiven for
his intellectual vulgarity since his "anti-semitism was not merely a
social prejudice but an idea, a way of dealing with difficulties": his
was a failure of mind as well as art.

One would have thought the ghost exorcised. Trilling's case was
sound—a writer's beliefs are neither separable from his art nor more
valid than his means of expression. The very critics whom Trilling
had to fight prove his point. Alfred Kazin valued Dreiser's fiction
since "it hurts because it is all too much like reality to be 'art.' "
Eliseo Vivas condoned Dreiser's prose because "the prose is the
man."

Before Trilling, Dreiser criticism had begun to sound like a character reference or the introduction to an after-dinner speaker. Dreiser
serving up great gobs of bleeding reality salted with his tears and
garnished with prosy sincerity to a hall full of people who were already salivating. What difference does it make whether Dreiser is

"Mr. Trilling, Mr. Warren and *An American Tragedy*" by Charles Thomas
Samuels. From *The Yale Review*, 53 (Summer 1964): 624–40. Copyright © 1964
by Yale University. Reprinted by permission of the author and *The Yale
Review*.

speaker or writer, waiter or cook if what you want is life in the raw?

The fight over Dreiser has always involved presumed relationships between "reality" and "art." Critics friendly to him define "reality" as a complex of anti-proletarian forces which Dreiser, fine human being that he was, hated, as good men ought. He was for *us* and against *them:* that conspiracy of wealth and power which oppresses and deprives us and then outrageously demands that we describe oppression and deprivation in fancy prose. Dreiser's friends always defend him as if he were Walter Reuther and you were a Rotarian. If you deride his mechanistic philosophy, you embrace the morality of the ruling class; if you detest his illiterate style, you admire the bloodless chic of *The New Yorker*; if you deplore his mindless devotion to detail, you probably hate life itself.

That line of defense is its own refutation.

In 1950, after Kazin's eulogies and Trilling's attack, the American Men of Letters series published posthumously the appreciation which was to do Dreiser justice. In it, F. O. Matthiessen shows how very temperate a responsible critic must be in Dreiser's behalf. Beginning with the usual references to Dreiser's person and his contemporary pertinence, Matthiessen proceeds to say everything that can be said about *An American Tragedy* as a work of art. He points to the structural parallels, the faithful depiction of milieu in the Green-Davidson Hotel, the tenderness and compassion which Dreiser has for his characters. Yet his chapter is full of poignant doubts and shame-faced disclaimers:

> For some readers interest breaks down under the sheer weight of details, for others the exhaustiveness of Dreiser's treatment is what builds up to an effect of final authority.

> A crucial element in our final estimate of this novel is how far [Dreiser] can enable us to participate in his compassion.

> Some of these details may seem stock in themselves, but . . .

> . . . what Clyde finds in his "baby-talking girl" is what Dreiser never manages to convey to us concretely.

In conclusion, Matthiessen recalls Krutch's insistence that *An American Tragedy* was "the great American novel of our generation," but he continues with a more modest claim that comes nearer the truth:

> Clyde's whole experience was too undifferentiated, too unilluminated to compel the attention of some readers already habituated to the masterpieces of the modern psychological novel. But for young men growing up in the 'twenties and 'thirties here was a basic account of the world to which they were exposed.

Matthiessen's conclusion seemed the authentic farewell to that veteran warrior against Victorian morality and Social Darwinism. The late nineteenth century had asked what social classes owed one another, William Graham Sumner had answered "nothing," the Captains of Industry had agreed, and up went the breadlines, the apple-sellers, the strikes—the whole world over which Dreiser shed so many tears and such a quantity of typescript. It was a bloody and a good fight; but the old soldier was gone, and his book would live as a mute witness to the awful past.

Trilling riddled the body, but Matthiessen, turning it into a period piece, neatly interred it. But, in its Autumn 1962 number, *The Yale Review* staged an exhumation, by, of all people, Robert Penn Warren. As Mr. Trilling might have said, here is a "cultural episode."

After the battles and the insults, after Trilling's brilliant attack and Matthiessen's more damning defense, the former Southern Agraian, New Critical fabulist of innate depravity pays homage to the Populist, illiterate poet of exculpation. Mr. Warren finds in *An American Tragedy* all Dreiser's well-known selling points. And because Mr. Warren *can* write, they now appear more palatable than anyone had thought them.

The relic is restored with a few cosmetic touches of the critic's art. An image here: "the image of the boy Clyde looking up at the 'tall walls' of the world is the key image of the novel." A touch of point of view there: at the close of Book II, "Dreiser jerks back his camera from [the] lonely figure and begins Book III by withdrawing into magisterial distance for a panoramic sweep of the lens. . . ." If the writing is bad, let's forget words. Behold "the language of the unfolding scenes, the language of the imagery of enactment, with all its primitive massiveness—the movie in our heads, with all the entailed questions of psychological veracity and subtlety, of symbolic densities and rhythmic complexities." Add a little "search for identity." And the "basic account" of a dead world lives again in its symbolically dense and rhythmically complex reenactment of the ritual search for identity.

But Mr. Warren has rewritten the book. Not the movie which George Stevens found in its pages: a film that *is* ritualistic (the love scenes), that does make Sondra desirable (Elizabeth Taylor) and Clyde a character (Montgomery Clift with his tubercular chest and hungry eyes). Not the troubling insight into a society which defiled sex by dirtying its face and laying it out for money. The words which are the book. The words which tell the story, which set the scene, which force you to believe in Dreiser's people and what they mean.

What are Dreiser's words like? First, as F. R. Leavis has said, they are like the work of a man who lacked a native language. Not only because of Trilling's "paste gems"—the "scene more distingué than this," the man *"soi-distant* and not particularly eager to stay at home." Dreiser's words travesty not only themselves but the hero they are meant to create. Clyde is introduced as a "tall and as yet slight figure, surmounted by an interesting head." Explaining the pained response to his family's sidewalk church which must convince us of Clyde's fine-grained soul and which must excuse his later repudiation of religion, Dreiser asserts: "all that could be truly said of [Clyde] now was that there was no definite appeal in all this for him."

Dreiser cannot make us see his characters (his only detailed descriptions are of clothes); he cannot create their responses; nor, despite his vaunted compassion, can he take us into his characters' hearts so that we may join him in his empathy. After a long and stormy scene in which Clyde feels the stirrings of healthy young libido, we get this:

> And suddenly now, as he felt this yielding of her warm body so close to him, and the pressure of her lips in response to his own, he realized that he had let himself in for a relationship which might not be so very easy to modify or escape. Also that it would be a very difficult thing for him to resist, since he now liked her and obviously she liked him.

The words fail to make us feel the heat of sex, the heat of life, which cannot be denied and which Lycurgus is evil for denying in order that business may be more efficient. When Dreiser talks of sex and man's destiny, "What man, short of saint or sage," Warren asks, could fail to respond "in some secret way however different from Clyde's way. . . ." Yet Dreiser speaks of sex as a "chemism," as the "sex lure or appeal," and Dreiser illustrates destiny merely by creating a character full of "mental and material weakness before pleasure," by presenting that character with pleasure and an impediment, and by drearily establishing the preconceived certainty that the character, since he lacks "mental and material" strength, will remove the impediment by whatever means. Sex becomes a behavioristic tic and destiny a charade.

The book's admired structural parallels reveal a want of invention. If Hortense is like Rita and Sondra, couldn't Dreiser have done without one of them? Must we have every bit of evidence, every "objection sustained," every hackneyed bit of journalese in the trial scene?

The novel is held together by its big scenes, but these invariably fall flat. This, for example, is Dreiser's description of the first meeting between Clyde and Roberta at Crum Lake:

> Almost before he had decided, he was quite beside her, some twenty feet from the shore, and was looking up at her, his face lit by the radiance of one who had suddenly, and beyond his belief, realized a dream. And as though he were a pleasant apparition suddenly evoked out of nothing and nowhere, a poetic effort taking form out of smoke or vibrant energy, she in turn stood staring down at him, her lips unable to resist the wavy line of beauty that a happy mood always brought to them.

All is seen through smoke and poetry (perhaps that accounts for "the wavy line"; Leslie Fiedler reminds us that Dreiser comes from "the kind of people who copulate in the dark and live out their lives without ever seeing their sexual partners nude . . ."). Then the apparition speaks:

> "My, Miss Alden! It is you, isn't it? . . . I was wondering whether it was. I couldn't be sure from out there."
>
> "Why, yes it is. . . ."

Thud.

But doesn't this dialogue faithfully reflect Dreiser's inarticulate characters? Some such argument has been the classic defense of Dreiser's unspeakable dialogue. Notice, however, how Dreiser expresses Roberta's thoughts:

> . . . in spite of her obvious pleasure at seeing him again, only thinly repressed for the first moment or two, she was on the instant beginning to be troubled by her thoughts in regard to him—the difficulties that contact with him seemed to prognosticate.

When Dreiser is faced with the task of describing Roberta's first, pathetic overtures to Clyde, this is what he comes up with:

> She wavered between loyalty to Clyde as a superintendent, loyalty to her old conventions as opposed to her new and dominating desire and her repressed wish to have Clyde speak to her—then went over with the bundle and laid it on his desk. But her hands, as she did so, trembled. Her face was white—her throat taut. [She speaks] "There's been a distake" (she meant to say 'mistake'). . . . In a weak, frightened, and yet love-driven way, she was courting him. . . .

Equally slight is Dreiser's equipment for creating the emotional expression of his characters. When they are happy they are always in Paradise, or the scene before them is Alladinish; when they are impressed they say "Gee!"; when they are entranced they say "Thrill-

ing!"; when sad, they say "God!" The exclamation point is to
Dreiser what the drum is to Eugene O'Neill.

In *An American Tragedy*, Dreiser is no more able to create scenes
and characters than he is to write a sentence that is both moving
and grammatical. Some of what I have said has been acknowledged.
More crucial and less well-known is the book's confusion and dis-
honesty.

An American Tragedy is a thesis novel. Its thesis, moreover, is
meant to be tragic, to appall and harrow. There but for the grace
of God, we are meant to say. If you had been Clyde Griffiths. If
you had been susceptible and poor. If you had wanted Roberta
and had been denied her in the interest of more and better collars.
If she wanted you but denied you in the interest of a mean little
morality. If you loved her and she became pregnant and you had,
by this time, fallen in love with another, more desirable woman who
could give you all that your world valued. If narrow religious training had made you ignorant, and poverty had made you helpless, and
hypocrisy denied you the only expedient that could have solved
your dilemma. If you lacked convictions and strength, and had
lately read a newspaper account of a tragedy suffered by a man in
your situation. . . . Then, you should have come to murder. It
was all circumstance and chemism. You could not help it. Weep for
you.

Yet Dreiser seems to have doubted whether his readers would
weep for stupid, weak Clyde when Roberta was equally pathetic and
appealingly feminine. Dreiser was not certain that our love would
flow to the unlovely. His was a compassion without courage. It
could not hold Clyde up before us and say: "He is abject and guilty,
but he is human. That is enough." Instead, at the very moment
when Clyde is performing the murder, Dreiser undertakes his re-
habilitation.

In the scene to which the whole novel has been moving, Dreiser's
mechanism becomes psychomachia:

> . . . there had now suddenly appeared, as the genii at the accidental
> rubbing of Aladdin's lamp—as the efrit emerging as smoke from
> the mystic jar in the net of the fisherman—the very substance of some
> leering and diabolic wish or wisdom concealed in his own nature,
> and that now abhorrent and yet compelling, leering and yet intrigu-
> ing, friendly and yet cruel, offered him a choice between an evil
> which threatened to destroy him (and against his deepest opposition)
> and a second evil which, however it might disgust or sear and terrify,
> still provided for freedom and success and love.

Suddenly, amoral, unreflective Clyde undergoes an inner moral
struggle. If he acts without moral qualm, we might regard him as

a tool of circumstance and so deny him our sympathy. We are not likely to approve of a monster without shame, who moves toward crime like a sleepwalker. So, at the last crucial moment, Dreiser gives Clyde a hitherto undemonstrated moral sense which recoils at a hitherto undemonstrated principle of internal evil.

But there is another problem. If Clyde consciously chooses what he knows to be wrong, he is more than the hand that held the weapon through which the whole weight of the world came down on poor Roberta. If Clyde wills the crime, we may understand it, because of his past, but we cannot excuse him for it. More important, we may deny him our love.

Dreiser is caught between a mechanism that denies responsibility and thereby a fully human response and a humanistic ethic which can only convince us of Clyde's profound guilt. He solves his problem metaphorically, by making the indwelling evil inaccessible to Clyde's will. The rational will is sealed off from the rest of its owner's psyche so that Clyde can be both morally repelled and actually helpless to reverse the course upon which he had been determined:

> Indeed the center or mentating section of [Clyde's] brain at this time might well have been compared to a sealed and silent hall in which alone and undisturbed, and that in spite of himself, he now sat thinking on the mystic or evil and terrifying desires or advice of some darker or primordial and unregenerate nature of his own, and without the power to drive the same forth or himself to decamp, and yet also without the courage to act upon anything.

Circumstance drove Clyde to Big Bittern; when he arrives, the devil takes over. Society brought him to the lake; invincible depravity makes him a murderer. He had no more control over one than the other. What matter if this be faulty thinking; it is masterly emoting.

In the celebrated scenes which lead up to the crime, Dreiser finds still other sources of responsibility. The genii conquers Clyde and begins insinuating its orders:

> Go to the lake which you visited with Sondra! . . . Go to the south end of it and from there walk south, afterwards.

When the hapless couple arrive at the lake the genii is assisted by the landscape: the very trees suggest death—there is even a Poesque weir-bird. The crime itself is covered by a veil of unreality: Roberta, "an almost nebulous figure . . . now . . . [steps] down into an insubstantial rowboat upon a purely ideational lake." Finally, when Clyde hits her with his camera, he does not intend to kill her, and she tumbles out of the boat by accident.

Lest the exculpation be incomplete, after the murder, Dreiser begins suggesting that other people are worse than Clyde. The prosecuting attorney uses the case for political gain while claiming righteous indignation. One of Clyde's lawyers had a Roberta in his youth, but, being rich, escaped the need to kill her. The coroner falsifies evidence, and people gape at Clyde out of some obscene prurience. Then, when Clyde is finally convicted, Dreiser submits us to a detailed account of his torments in the death house. And if all this were not enough—Clyde's essential innocence, his comparative virtue, his extreme suffering—Dreiser makes Clyde finally accept an essentially Christian view of his guilt from the Reverend McMillan: this despite the novel's theme and the repeatedly anticlerical and anti-religious comments made both by Clyde and by his author.

Yet the novel's final confusion is the result of Dreiser's inability to recognize the form most appropriate to his insights. There is nothing wrong, as Mr. Trilling recognizes, with Dreiser's view of life as a struggle between inner drives and outer environment. But in a dramatization of such a viewpoint the antagonists must be individual men and the world which thwarts them. Yet Dreiser fails utterly to particularize the social and economic worlds of *An American Tragedy*. Clyde peering at the "tall walls" of the city is more than a key image; it is almost all we ever get of his confrontation with socio-economic reality. Outside of the Green-Davidson (which Dreiser, almost hysterically, asserts but does not dramatize as Sodom and Gomorrah) and the row of houses on Wykeagy Avenue, there is no outer world in Dreiser's book. The cream of the jest is that Dreiser fails to give us reality, fails to pile on the right details. Only in the melodramatic trial, which captures his imagination in much the same way that trials fascinated Mark Twain, do we get anything like the minute verisimilitude for which Dreiser has been admired. If you think of Flaubert, or Zola, or that underrated American naturalist Dos Passos, you will see how deficient Dreiser is exactly where you would expect him to be strong.

Dreiser's genuis is for feeling, feeling uncontrolled by, unaided by thought. It is characteristic of his peculiar confusion that when he wished to tell a tale of American youth destroyed by the inequalities of a corrupt, money-mad class system he should have declined to do anything more than sketch the system so that he could devote all his effort to recreating a banal and wordless triangle between a weakly, good-looking, utterly uninteresting man, and two women—one of whom is merely pathetic and the other of whom is capable not of conveying "the pain of wanting and not having" but only pain.

Dreiser lacked more than art; he lacked a sense of what he lacked.

If I am right about the book, if it is worse than one gathers from Mr. Trilling's attack, why should a critic like Robert Penn Warren (who is also a better novelist than Dreiser) attempt at this late date to eulogize the giant from Terre Haute? Warren demonstrates a sense of his anomalous position. In his earlier essay, Trilling had articulated a conception of literary art which Warren himself had helped to create. In 1946, Trilling reminded his readers, with a fine note of exasperation, that in literature "from the earth of the novelist's prose spring his characters, his ideas, and even his story. . . ." Yet Warren now complains of the "tendency to freeze the question of Dreiser as an artist at the question of prose style."

We have a pertinent parallel for this strange debate. Some years ago, Trilling was involved in a position as uncharacteristic as Warren's eulogy of Dreiser's book. In 1948, he was asked to write the introduction to a new edition of *Huckleberry Finn.* (Warren's essay is likewise the introduction to a paperback reprint.) Though Twain's masterpiece has never been thought faulty on anything like the scale I have found relevant to Dreiser's book, the ending of *Huck Finn* is often roundly attacked. Trilling's introduction undertakes to defend the last fifth of the novel on formal grounds: Huck's abdication to Tom Sawyer aptly permits Huck "to return to his anonymity, to give up the role of hero. . . ." Coincidentally, T. S. Eliot published, two years later, an introduction to another edition of Twain's book, making an even more elaborate defense of the novel on formal grounds.

Three years after that, Leo Marx published a significant article in *The American Scholar* entitled "Mr. Eliot, Mr. Trilling, and *Huckleberry Finn.*" After showing in convincing detail why the ending is objectionable, Mr. Marx makes some charges against the Eliot-Trilling effort at revaluation which are even more important than his critical remarks about the novel. Since he had demonstrated that the ending is a cruel travesty of the book's humane, unillusioned attack on hypocrisy and discrimination, Marx neatly proves that Trilling and Eliot had stressed form and ignored morality. He then shrewdly speculates that so egregious a blunder in critics so eminent could only result from an indifference to the book's moral point. Marx suggests that Trilling and Eliot could stomach the gratuitous brutality which Tom displays toward Jim in the "Evasion" and which Huck uncharacteristically approves because of their exclusive interest in personal development and related uninterest in morals operating in the social or political realms. They rejoice at the anonymity which will protect Huck's selfhood while they ignore its cost: Huck's immoral assent to the debasement of Jim. Huck's story is neatly rounded off, but the novel is about larger issues.

Mr. Marx's justly famous essay implies the intimate connection between form and content. The irony of the debate is that such a point had to be made against Mr. Trilling when Mr. Trilling had years earlier made the same point against the partisan admirers of Theodore Dreiser. How could Trilling acknowledge the connection between form and content when attacking Dreiser and ignore it when defending Twain?

This is to ask the same question about Robert Penn Warren. How could Warren admire Dreiser despite his formal incompetence when Warren's entire critical career has assumed the identity of theme and mode of expression? The answer to this question must be cautionary.

Trilling's essay on *Huck Finn* and Warren's essay on *An American Tragedy* share a common flaw which accounts for their surprising advocacy of shoddy materials. Both of them conceive the novel in terms of consistency of form and feeling; neither of them questions the consistency of form and idea. Thus Trilling can admire the formal excellence of language and structure in *Huck Finn,* noting that they cooperate to create a mood of nostalgia for the honest, untainted youth both of Huck and of America. In the same way, Warren can admire the formal excellence of plotting and pacing that produce a feeling of *"entrapment"* (his term and italics) in the heavy fate of Clyde Griffiths. Both critics ignore the assertions and insights which these moods and emotion are meant to sustain. The notorious unself-consciousness of Twain and Dreiser abet a critical disposition to regard the novel as a personal reverie which cannot and should not be tested by any public canons of truth or logic. When Warren displaces Dreiser's mechanism from the center, finding "the real drama" in "the individual story," when Trilling ignores the social crime, finding the real meaning in Huck's individual development, they are subscribing to more than a radical shrinkage of the novels which they so admire: they are diminishing the novelist's role. Neither critic is interested in those large social or moral propositions subsumed within the structure of *Huckleberry Finn* or *An American Tragedy*. And by ignoring these propositions, each critic can impose, with fatal ease, a private intellectual bias on the reverie he appreciates. So Trilling reads *Huck Finn* as nostalgia, while Warren reads *An American Tragedy* as a search for the self. No admirer of either critic needs to be told the marked affinity of each for the interpretation he advances.

Everyone sees himself in what he reads. But that is not the only error that needs guarding against. Too easy identification of critic and book could never have overcome the acknowledged convictions of Trilling and Warren, could not have produced contradictions as blatant as those which Marx pointed out in one and which I am attempting to show in the other. Both critics made their identifications and ignored their novels' fault because neither was thinking of what the writer meant to "say." Trilling implicitly, Warren explicitly voices indifference to theme. But what Marx asserts about *Huck Finn* and what I have asserted about *An American Tragedy* is that both novels suffer from faults which are conceptual or thematic. Moreover, the contradictory ending of *Huck Finn* and the pervasive confusion of *An American Tragedy* are, at the same time, formal flaws. The conclusion of *Huck Finn* is dull and unpleasant, and the whole of *An American Tragedy* is ponderous and vague. In short, the intellectual failing is first perceived as an artistic lapse. Conversely, to deny the artistic lapse is to ignore the intellectual failing. This Trilling and Warren both do, I suspect, because neither of them, when they wrote these essays at least, felt bound to regard the serious novel as essentially cognitive. If it is not that, what is it? If it is not making a statement about life, how can we call it "serious"? Why do we study it? Why do we teach it in the University? The neglect of the novelist's mind must not be authorized now. Those French theoreticians (Mme. Sarraute & Cie.) are even now outside the house of fiction waiting to sweep out people as well as ideas and leave only the furniture.

At the end of his essay, Marx called for "a criticism alert to lapses of moral vision." He could not have failed to be aware that Lionel Trilling is a critic of the deepest moral concern. If I call for a criticism alert to the cognitive content of fiction, I am also aware that Robert Penn Warren is our only distinguished novelist of ideas. Yet if Trilling can advocate a lapse in morality and Warren can advocate a lapse in mind, how much more must the rest of us be vigilant.

We have heard rather too much lately of the irrelevance of a writer's ideas. If we mean by that that a writer's ideas need not be agreeable, what honorable critic would disapprove? But it does not follow that a writer need not have ideas or that he may be more irresponsible in treating them than in treating characters or fashioning prose. Art may begin in reverie and solitude, but it performs in the rational daylight of the public world. The critic departs from that world to his cost. The artist departs from it to our deep impoverishment.

Chronology of Important Dates

1871	Born in Terre Haute, Indiana. Father a Roman Catholic and German immigrant, mother a Mennonite. Eighth of ten children.
1887	Leaves High School in Warsaw, Indiana, to seek work in Chicago.
1890	Mother dies in Chicago.
1892	Starts newspaper work: Chicago *Globe,* then St. Louis *Globe-Democrat.*
1894	Leaves St. Louis, for Toledo, Pittsburgh, New York. Marries Sara White.
1898	Hack newspaper work during this period.
1900	*Sister Carrie.*
1902	Psychological distress, nervous breakdown.
1904	Editing dime novels for Street & Smith.
1907	Editor of Butterick publications, circulation near a million.
1908	Begins friendship with Mencken.
1910	Fired from Butterick because of amorous adventures.
1911	*Jennie Gerhardt.* Visit to Europe.
1912	*The Financier.*
1913	*A Traveler at Forty,* based on European visit.
1914	*The Titan.* Separates finally from Sara White Dreiser.
1915	*The "Genius."*
1916	*A Hoosier Holiday* (autobiography). *Plays of the Natural and Supernatural.* Virtual suppression of *The "Genius"* for "immorality."
1918	*Free and Other Stories. The Hand of the Potter.*

1919   *Twelve Men.* Starts living with Helen Richardson.

1920   *Hey, Rub-a-Dub-Dub.*

1922   *A Book About Myself* (autobiography).

1923   *The Color of a Great City.*

1925   *An American Tragedy.*

1927   Visit to U.S.S.R., on invitation.

1928   *Dreiser Looks at Russia.*

1929   *A Gallery of Women.*

1931   *Dawn,* autobiography.

1939   Edits *The Living Thoughts of Thoreau.*

1941   *America is Worth Saving.*

1944   Marries Helen Richardson.

1945   Finishes *The Bulwark.* Tries to finish *The Stoic.* Joins Communist Party. Dies 28 December, buried in Forest Lawn.

1946   *The Bulwark* published.

1947   *The Stoic* published.

Notes on the Editor and Contributors

JOHN LYDENBERG, editor of this volume, has written essays on various aspects of American literature, among them pieces on Emerson, Henry James, Cozzens, and Faulkner. He is Professor of English and of American Studies at Hobart and William Smith Colleges.

RANDOLPH BOURNE died in 1918 at the age of thirty-two. A precocious critic, he was a major figure in the movement that led to the renaissance of American literature in the 1920s, an editor of *The Seven Lively Arts*, and an outspoken opponent of American involvement in World War I.

MALCOLM COWLEY, author and editor of more books and articles than one can possibly recall, has been known since the 1920s as one of the most penetrating interpreters of American literature.

LESLIE FIEDLER is an ever provocative, controversial, and seminal critic. *An End to Innocence* is one of his many books. He is Professor of English at the State University of New York at Buffalo.

IRVING HOWE, author of books on Faulkner, Sherwood Anderson, Thomas Hardy, editor of *Dissent*, is Professor of English at Hunter College.

ALFRED KAZIN, one of the foremost critics and historians of American literature, is author of *On Native Grounds* and many other books, and editor with Charles Shapiro of *The Stature of Theodore Dreiser*, the first collection of critical essays on Dreiser. He is Professor of English at Hunter College.

KENNETH LYNN, author of *The Dream of Success* and *Mark Twain and Southwest Humor*, is Professor of History at The Johns Hopkins University.

H. L. MENCKEN, one of our greatest journalists and polemicists, was the gad-fly of the "booboisie" during the 1920s and a leading defender of all that was new and offensive in American literature.

ELLEN MOERS, author of *The Dandy: Brummell to Beerbohm* and *Two Dreisers*, teaches at Barnard College.

CHARLES THOMAS SAMUELS, Associate Professor of English at Williams College, has written on John Updike, Bernard Malamud, and Bonnie and Clyde.

STUART SHERMAN, a "humanist" and conservative critic, well-known in his day, came to take a somewhat broader view of the new trends in literature, and even of Dreiser, than he shows in this famous article.

LIONEL TRILLING, one of America's outstanding teachers and academic critics, author of many searching interpretive essays on English as well as American literature, is George Edward Woodberry Professor of Literature and Criticism at Columbia University.

CHARLES CHILD WALCUTT, author of *American Literary Naturalism: A Divided Stream,* and many articles on pedagogy and reading, is Professor of English at Queens College (CUNY).

ROBERT PENN WARREN, poet, novelist, and critic, one of America's most distinguished and respected men of letters, is Professor of English at Yale University.

GERALD WILLEN is an artist—a painter—as well as a critic, and is Associate Professor of English at Hunter College.

Selected Bibliography

Indispensable and excellent is the chapter on Theodore Dreiser by Robert H. Elias in *Fifteen Modern American Authors: A Survey of Research and Criticism,* ed. Jackson R. Bryer, Durham, North Carolina: Duke University Press, 1969. Thanks to it, the following bibliography can safely be very short. I omitted from the bibliography anything included in the body of this TCV.

Books on Dreiser

Dreiser, Helen. *My Life with Dreiser.* Cleveland: The World Publishing Company, 1951. A personal memoir by Dreiser's second wife, who remained with him till his death. Gives clear impression of Dreiser's "varietism" and also of his personal magnetism.

Dudley, Dorothy. *Forgotten Frontiers: Dreiser and the Land of the Free.* New York: Harrison Smith & Robert Haas, 1932. The first biography of Dreiser. Thoroughly partisan and often inaccurate, but insisting properly on Dreiser's relation to the social developments of his time.

Elias, Robert H. *Theodore Dreiser: Apostle of Nature.* Philadelphia: University of Pennsylvania Press, 1949. The first "academic" study of Dreiser, and the only one by a scholar who knew Dreiser. Despite the refinements of subsequent scholarship, this still remains one of the best and most interesting.

Gerber, Philip L. *Theodore Dreiser.* New York: Twayne Publishers, Inc., 1964. Balanced, and reasonably objective.

Lehan, Richard. *Theodore Dreiser: His World and His Novels.* Carbondale, Illinois: University of Southern Illinois Press, 1969.

McAleer, John J. *Theodore Dreiser: An Introduction and Interpretation.* New York: Holt, Rinehart and Winston, 1968.

Matthiessen, F. O. *Theodore Dreiser.* New York: William Sloane Associates, 1951. Primarily literary criticism, by one of the great critics of American literature, left in still somewhat rough form at the time of his tragic suicide.

Moers, Ellen. *Two Dreisers.* New York: Viking Press, 1969. The most exciting new work on Dreiser, concentrating on *Sister Carrie* and *An American Tragedy,* but seeing them in marvelously broad perspective.

Rascoe, Burton. *Theodore Dreiser.* New York: Robert M. McBride Company, Inc., 1926. An early, lively, passionate defense.

Shapiro, Charles. *Theodore Dreiser: Our Bitter Patriot.* Carbondale, Illinois: Southern Illinois University Press, 1962.

Swanberg, William A. *Dreiser.* New York: Charles Scribner's Sons, 1965. An enormous, detailed biography, filled with information about the many unpleasant aspects of Dreiser's life. From it, one would scarcely know that Dreiser was a novelist, to say nothing of a great one. Valuable for what it does, however.

Tjader, Marguerite. *Theodore Dreiser: A New Dimension.* Norwalk, Connecticut: Silvermine Publishers, 1965. Interesting memoir by a friend and secretary of his during the last two decades of his life.

A few of the books containing chapters on Dreiser

Brooks, Van Wyck. *The Confident Years: 1885–1915.* New York: E. P. Dutton and Company, 1952. Excellent summary in Brooks' ripest manner.

Farrell, James T. *The League of Frightened Philistines.* New York: The Vanguard Press, 1945. Farrell recognizes his kinship to Dreiser and writes with close sympathy.

Farrell, James T. *Literature and Morality.* New York: The Vanguard Press, 1947.

Geismar, Maxwell. *Rebels and Ancestors: The American Novel, 1890–1915.* Boston: Houghton Mifflin Company, 1953. Long, penetrating analysis.

Gelfant, Blanche H. *The American City Novel.* Norman, Oklahoma: University of Oklahoma Press, 1954.

Hicks, Granville. *The Great Tradition.* New York: Crowell-Collier and MacMillan, Inc., 1933. Marxist interpretation.

Kazin, Alfred. *On Native Grounds.* New York: Reynal & Hitchcock, Inc., 1942.

Lewisohn, Ludwig. *Expression in America.* New York: Harper & Row Publishers, 1932.

Mencken, H. L. *A Book of Prefaces.* New York: Alfred A. Knopf, Inc., 1917. Because Mencken was Dreiser's closest literary friend, everything he wrote on Dreiser is of the greatest intrst.

Mencken, H. L. *Prejudices: Fourth Series.* New York: Alfred A. Knopf, Inc., 1924.

Pizer, Donald. *Realism and Naturalism in Nineteenth-Century American Literature.* Carbondale, Illinois: University of Southern Illinois Press, 1966.

Rideout, Walter B. *The Radical Novel in the United States, 1900–1954.* Cambridge, Mass.: Harvard University Press, 1956.

Weimer, David R. *The City as Metaphor.* New York: Random House, 1966.

Whipple, T. K. *Spokesmen: Modern Writers and American Life.* New York: D. Appleton and Company, 1928.

A highly selected list of critical articles

The Stature of Theodore Dreiser, ed. Alfred Kazin and Charles Shapiro. Bloomington, Ind.: Indiana University Press, 1955. The first, and only other, collection of Dreiser criticism, including much that is not in this TCV volume.

Bellow, Saul. "Dreiser and the Triumph of Art," *Commentary* (May 1951): 502–503.

Freedman, William A. "A Look at Dreiser as Artist: The Motif of Circularity in *Sister Carrie,*" *Modern Fiction Studies,* 8 (Winter, 1962): 384–92.

Grebstein, Sheldon N. "Dreiser's Victorian Vamp," *Midcontinent American Studies Journal,* 4 (Spring 1963): 3–11.

Hakutani, Yoshinobu. "Dreiser and French Realism," *Texas Studies in Literature and Language,* 6 (Summer 1964), 200–212.

Handy, William J. "*Sister Carrie* Reexamined," *Texas Studies in Literature and Language,* 1 (Autumn 1959): 380–93.

Hoffman, Frederick. "The Scene of Violence: Dostoievsky and Dreiser," *Modern Fiction Studies,* 6 (Summer 1960): 91–105.

Kern, Alexander. "Dreiser's Difficult Beauty," *Western Review* (Winter 1952): 129–36.

Krim, Seymour. "Theodore Dreiser," *Hudson Review,* 4 (Autumn 1951): 474–77.

Krim, Seymour. "Dreiser and His Critics," *Commonweal* (June 1, 1956), 229–31.

Kwiat, Joseph J. "Dreiser and the Graphic Artist," *American Quarterly,* 3 (Summer 1951): 127–41.

Kwiat, Joseph J. "Dreiser's *The 'Genius'* and Everett Shinn the 'Ash Can' Painter," *PMLA,* 67 (March 1952): 15–31.

Lane, Lauriat, Jr. "The Double in *An American Tragedy,*" *Modern Fiction Studies,* 12 (Summer 1966): 213–20.

Markels, Julian. "Dreiser and the Plotting of Inarticulate Experience," *Massachusetts Review,* 2 (Spring 1961): 1–48.

Phillips, William L. "The Chapter Titles of *Sister Carrie,*" *American Literature,* 36 (November 1964): 359–65.

Phillips, William L. "The Imagery of Dreiser's Novels," *PMLA,* 78 (December 1963): 572–85.

Salzman, Jack. "The Publication of *Sister Carrie:* Fact and Fiction," *Library Chronicle* (University of Pennsylvania), Spring 1967. A cor-

rection of some of the myths grown up around the event. But it does
not alter the basic interpretation as given by Cowley.

Simpson, Claude. *"Sister Carrie* Reconsidered," *Southwest Review,* 44
(Winter 1959): 44–53.